EVOLUTION TOWARD DIVINITY

EVOLUTION TOWARD DIVINITY

Teilhard de Chardin and the Hindu Traditions

by

BEATRICE BRUTEAU

THE THEOSOPHICAL PUBLISHING HOUSE
Wheaton, Ill. U.S.A.
Madras/India London/England

Bruteau, Beatrice, 1930-
Evolution toward divinity.

Bibliography: p.
1. Teilhard de Chardin, Pierre. 2. God. 3. Evolution.
4. Philosophy, Hindu. I. Title.
B2430.T374B78 194 73-16198
ISBN 0-8356-0216-8

Printed in the United States of America

ACKNOWLEDGMENTS

The author and publisher gratefully acknowledge permission to quote as noted from the following:

Cambridge University Press, New York, from S. Dasgupta, *A History of Indian Philosophy.*

Ganesh & Company, Madras, from Sir John Woodroffe, *The World as Power;* from Woodroffe and Mukhyopadhyaya, *Mahamaya;* from M. P. Pandit, *Studies in the Tantras and the Veda* and *Gems from the Tantras;* from Pandit Siva Chandra Vidyarnava, *Principles of Tantra,* Majumdar's Introduction.

George Allen & Unwin, Ltd., London, from S. Radhakrishnan, *The Principal Upanishads.*

Harper & Row, New York, from works by Pierre Teilhard de Chardin as follows: *Writings in Time of War,* tr. René Hague; *Hymn of the Universe,* tr. Simon Bartholomew; *Science and Christ,* tr. René Hague; *The Divine Milieu,* tr. ed., Bernard Wall; *The Appearance of Man,* tr. J. M. Cohen; *The Future of Man,* tr. Norman Denny; *The Phenomenon of Man,* tr. Bernard Wall; *The Vision of the Past,* tr. J. M. Cohen; *Man's Place in Nature,* tr. René Hague; and *The Making of a Mind,* tr. René Hague.

Ohio University Press, Athens, from Troy Wilson Organ, *The Hindu Quest for the Perfection of Man.*

Oxford University Press, 1969, and by permission of the Clarendon Press, Oxford, R. C. Zaehner translation, *The Bhagavad-Gita.*

Sri Aurobindo Ashram Press, Pondicherry, from Sri Aurobindo, *The Life Divine,* Vol. III, Sri Aurobindo Center of Education Collection.

CONTENTS

INTRODUCTION 1

1 GOD AND THE WORLD

The Problem of Two Loves 10

Creation, Divine Incarnation, and the Sacramental Universe 16

The One and the Many 28

2 COSMIC DIVINITY

The Vedic Vision 43

The Cosmic Christ 52

The "Pervader" and His Avatars 58

Pantheism and the Personal God 78

3 THE EVOLUTION OF CONSCIOUSNESS

Complexity/Consciousness and Sāmkhya 106

Śakti: Evolving Psychic Energy 122

Collective Consciousness 156

4 EVOLUTION TOWARD DIVINITY

Man's Responsibility to Act 181

The Problem of Death and the Taste for Life 203

Christogenesis and the Yoga of Transformation 221

EPILOGUE 243

BIBLIOGRAPHY 257

INDEX 261

INTRODUCTION

It may be fairly said that Teilhard de Chardin's intellectual odyssey centered around his lifelong struggle to reconcile in his thought and in his career two attractions which he seems to have experienced equally strongly and which he initially felt to be divergent: the love of God, on the one hand, and, on the other, the love of the earth together with knowledge of the earth, which is science. Devotion to science caused him a particular problem because science showed him earth-life in evolution, a view which his religious culture denied, avoided, or at best viewed with misgiving. The notion of evolution was especially significant vis-à-vis a religious context because it gave ground for expecting, in the face of the obvious evils of finite existence, that the world might become better, might indeed have some value of its own. To a religious culture which largely based its value-system on a future life in *another* world, this view could very well seem a threat. The achievement of Teilhard is that he succeeded in developing the inner thoughts of both his traditional religious culture and the contemporary scientific structures in such a way that, instead of conflicting, they converged. Life in the light of the Divine remained the goal, but it was to be achieved through evolution. Earthly evolution became evolution toward divinity.

Teilhard's own struggle was within the context of Christianity, and specifically of Roman Catholicism. Nevertheless, much of his thought can be received with sympathy by adherents of other traditions, and the synthesis he conceived can alert us to new aspects under which we may continue the work of integrating the diverse consciousness of Earth. In this book I propose to discuss some of the links which we can see between Teilhard's ideas and certain

Hindu traditions. Of course, there is a tremendous variety within Hindu thought, and only a fraction of it will be touched on here. But those traditions selected are of interest because they are especially consonant with Teilhard's pronouncements and exemplify the contribution which these classical thought-forms can make to an emerging Noosphere.

Having said this, we must note with sadness that it is one of the ironies of his brilliant career that Teilhard, whose doctrines of cosmic divinity and evolving consciousness so resemble certain strains of Hindu thought, had a very slight knowledge of this tradition and even less respect for it. There is no indication that he ever made a scholarly study of Hindu religious literature. He may have picked up part of his feeling toward the East from Kipling,[1] and he was undoubtedly influenced by the opinions of his friend and colleague, the orientalist René Grousset.[2] His only visit to India, in 1935, lasted three months[3]; aside from being annoyed by the inconvenient presence of cows,[4] he reacted to the experience in terms of finding individuals "gentle" and "charming" and the upper classes "highly civilized," but the country as a whole "incapable of self-government."[5] He regarded it as unfortunate that Indians should desire their independence and judged that the English were quite right to refuse to grant it.[6] The Hindus were lacking in creative power, he reported: "You have to go to India to realise the numbing and deadening effect of religion obsessed by material forms and ritualism."[7]

But more often Teilhard made just the opposite complaint against the Hindu way of life, accusing it of denying materiality and multiplicity. Maryse Choisy, in *Teilhard et l'Inde,* gives an account of a conversation with Teilhard in which the latter characterized Vedānta as a simplistic monism in which all multiplicity disappeared without leaving a trace. This evaluation is repeated in *The Divine Milieu,* in which pantheism is spoken of as "seducing" us with a "vista of universal union" which really means "unconsciousness."[8] And in the short paper, "The Spiritual Share of the Far East," Teilhard contends that all of the Indian systems have in common a *"very particular conception of Unity,"* gained by the simple expedient of denying or suppressing the multiple. The typical exercise would be one in which the seeker after Unity eliminates from his consciousness "all iridescent or painful nuances in which Being pulverises itself to form the appearance of the world around us. . . . *Below all conceivable determinations,* a universal essence is there, *underlying* all, which only awaits your return to it to absorb you and *identify* you with itself."[9] When Choisy pointed out to Teilhard that this position was not embraced by every Hindu thinker, Teilhard replied only that in that case there must have been some Western influence.[10]

A similar dismissal of evidence contrary to his thesis appears in Teilhard's assessment of Hindu theism. Hinduism is a religion very "faintly marked by the love of God," he says in a passage in which he avers that without Christianity no one would know of a loving God and the world would be "dark and cold."[11] The metaphysics of Vedānta makes real love impossible, he argues, for *identification is not union.* He takes note of the obvious counter-example to this charge, Bhakti-yoga, but calls it "an 'occidental' type . . . irreducible to the . . . authentic tendencies of Vedānta."[12]

The root of Teilhard's rejection of oriental philosophical and religious thought can be found in his judgment that these systems would not justify and inspire work for the progress of the world. Pierre Leroy tells us that Teilhard had a great intolerance for anything that suggested "disgust with life, contempt for the works of man, fear of the human effort."[13] Following the oriental path, Teilhard believed, we could be lulled to sleep in "the cradle of nirvana,"[14] having obtained "a sort of abstraction of God . . . by loosening the effort of differentiation whereby we engage the cosmic phenomenon."[15]

The ancient religions, he held, with their dark view of the world and their orientation to escapism, cannot, out of their own resources, adjust to the immense perspectives of space-time revealed by modern science.[16] But they can join themselves to the mainstream of the West, the present axis of advancing evolution. In "The Spiritual Share of the Far East" Teilhard points to accommodations which

India is even now making to Western technology and Western humanistic attitudes and cites these as symptoms that the East is gradually being drawn into the mystical current of the West. The West, he believes, is opening the way for "a new drive of human consciousness," and all the traditions of the world, like so many streams, are turning to flow into the breach which the West has made. The oriental traditions will each bring their own privileged insights to the confluence and make their "spiritual contribution" to the new planetary culture.[17]

This is as far as Teilhard goes in according value to the Hindu tradition. In *The Phenomenon of Man* he acknowledges mankind's debt to India for its contribution to mystical wisdom and recognizes that there is a place reserved for it in the general convergence of cultures which he foresees,[18] but he still feels that it has taken a wrong turn. "India allowed itself to be drawn into metaphysics, only to become lost there. . . . Phenomena regarded as an illusion (Maya) and their connections as a chain (Karma), what was left in these doctrines to animate and direct human evolution? A simple mistake was made—but it was enough—in the definition of the spirit and in the appreciation of the bonds which attach it to the sublimations of matter."[19]

Of course, it was not Teilhard's business to be an expert on Indian philosophy and spirituality; the superficial contact he made with them, plus his absorption in his own vision of reality, could understandably have led him to the simplistic and negative opinions which he formed. Nevertheless, it is unfortunate that he should have written off this great culture as easily as he did. How much more constructive it would have been if, with the help of more profound scholarship and especially with an appreciation of the work of the leaders of the Indian Renaissance, he had at least elaborated on the strengths of that Hindu spiritual contribution which he reluctantly admits. He might have been led to modify or reassess his views and to discover many things which would have pleased him. However, Teilhard never had the opportunity to test any of his general, philosophical, or religious ideas in the open forum of the academic world—he was forbidden by his religious superiors to teach or to publish on these subjects—and both he and we have been the losers.

In any case, what we shall do here, as an introduction to the work Teilhard could not do, is to investigate a whole constellation of themes in the variegated Hindu tradition which can be seen as highly congenial to Teilhard's own vision of the world. Far from being so "narrowly bound to untenable myths" and "steeped in a pessimistic and passive mysticism"[20] that it cannot adjust to the modern space-time outlook, Hinduism, as represented in these themes, may well be seen as quite capable of accommodating the world picture projected by contemporary science. The current expansion of its spirituality in the West would also seem to corroborate the contention that its "myths and mysticism"—and the metaphysics on which they are based—are perhaps not so unsuited to the mid-twentieth century as Teilhard thought. In fact, they may offer in some instances just the perspective which is needed to balance and make sense of contemporary experience.

The topics of the four chapters of this book are all themes of this type, on which Teilhard is in general, and sometimes profound, agreement with some current in the Hindu mainstream. The discussion intertwines an exposition of Teilhard's thought and the corresponding Hindu doctrines. As the similarities and affinities between the two are documented, it also becomes apparent that these doctrines are large enough, flexible and imaginative enough, to remain viable in our time.

We will begin with Teilhard's peculiar problem of the reconciliation of God and the world, his solution through the working out of the implications of the notions of creation as evolution, of divine incarnation, and of a sacramental universe, and his position on the root problem of the one and the many. The vision of cosmic divinity which emerges will be found also in the Vedic literature (Chapter II), especially in the powerful hymns of the Rig Veda. For Teilhard, the vision focuses and concretizes itself in his conception of the cosmic Christ. A very parallel structure is to be found in the Hindu image of the All-Pervading God, especially Viṣṇu and His avatars. Lord Kṛiṣṇa, as portrayed in the Bhagavad Gītā, is the plenary version of this image. However, some aspects of these classical traditions have often been judged to be pantheistic, and Teilhard also was so accused. This point in our discussion might therefore be an appropriate place at which to analyze this whole difficulty and try to lay it to rest.

There is divinity in the world, then, in some sense, and the world is evolving. The important thing about it, from Teilhard's point of view, is that it is an evolution of consciousness (Chapter III). His general theory of evolution is unified under the Law of Complexity/Consciousness and includes a set of thresholds at which the different major strata of being appear, each time revealing a higher degree of the consciousness which was somehow dimly present even from the beginning. The ancient involution/evolution theories of the Sāmkhya system show some surprising agreements with him. But the sense of God active and moving in the world is perhaps most vividly set forth in the Śakti tradition, in which the Mother Goddess is represented not only as transcendent but as immanent in a world of evolving psychic energy. The Śakti-vāda gives strong support to Teilhard's thesis of the unicity of energy in its psychic form and complements him in a number of details.

Another way in which Teilhard presents the evolution of consciousness is in terms of "amorization," or the development of love-energy to form a "world" of persons in which collective as well as individual values are attained. This is a central concern of Teilhard's and might have had little correspondence in the Hindu line if it had not been for the contemporary yogin and philosopher, Aurobindo Ghose. Śrī Aurobindo's scheme of divine evolution, more similar to Teilhard's than is that of any other thinker, Eastern or Western, is developed within a Hindu context, as Teilhard's grew up within a Christian one. The comparison of these two, unfortunately brief though it must be here, is therefore of special interest.

A world of evolving consciousness is necessarily one in which the free actions of human beings are crucial. Teilhard consequently devotes a good deal of space to the discussion of the justification of worldly action and the responsibility of man to work (Chapter IV). Here the supporting Hindu voices rise from all sides: from the Rig Veda, the great epics, the Tantras, and especially from the Bhagavad Gītā. But how can the motivation to act be maintained in the face of death? It is a delicate problem for Teilhard, and his proposed solution, although brilliant, has some difficulties for which the Hindu traditions can offer some help. They are also full of encouragement when Teilhard urges the importance of developing a "taste for life."

The ultimate solution to all of Teilhard's problems is found with the passing of natural evolutionary "cosmogenesis" into the supremely mystical "Christogenesis." Scientific history reveals itself as a cosmic yoga of transformation. The world is an evolution toward divinity, and the Cosmic Christ is its Evolver. Evolution was aimed at divinity from the beginning, and the Christified universe was always its goal. In parallel fashion, the whole art of yoga, the sādhana to which the soul of Hindu India has devoted itself so persistently, is focused on the growth and unfolding which achieves freedom and immortality and culminates in union with the Divine.

Nevertheless, evolution and man's work do not proceed unimpeded toward higher consciousness and consummating divinity. All along the way there is evil. Teilhard was very conscious of this fact and it is in the background of all his thought. Evil must be accounted for—if that is possible—and it must be dealt with. The complexity of evolution itself offers some possibility of an account, but even better, it provides a guide for making use of unavoidable suffering. Hindu thinkers had faced the same problem, and some of them had reached the same basic conclusions as those of Teilhard. The one thing on which they are all emphatic is that evil is not the last word, that the reality of the universe is bliss, and that the destiny of man is to share in that bliss.

These parallels, complements, and comparisons between a Western thinker who attempted to synthesize the two most extreme poles of his own culture, and the seers and philosophers of an Eastern civilization who also strove to integrate all aspects of their human experience, may serve as a small contribution to the growing unification of world thought in which we may each inherit all the traditions and all the sciences.

Teilhard has captured or stimulated the minds and souls of many in the years since his death. He has awakened faith by outlining a religious response to the modern experience of the world which makes sense of both secular and sacred values. He has renewed hope by projecting a vision of the future in which our dreams of unity, peace, and full development come true through an almost inevitable evolution. He has not, of course, delivered us from all insecurity, because the evolution is not absolutely inevitable, but depends upon our own actions. Man's freedom constitutes the very path along which the forces of evolution now must pass—or in which they can be blocked. Teilhard admits that the issue may fall either way.[18] And, apart from describing the loving relations of persons that must be developed in the converging Noosphere fast closing in upon us, and urging science and religion to cooperate in a concentrated research upon the subject of man,[19] Teilhard himself does not set forth in any detail the concrete steps we must take to assure a favorable outcome.

This is where the long-treasured wisdom of the Hindu tradition has something useful to say. Yoga is, and has been, a concentrated scientific and religious research upon the subject of man, and the long yogic tradition already has answers to offer to many of the questions we pose. Centuries of meditation on the nature of human selfhood have disclosed the complexities and subtleties of the psychological world and uncovered the roots of freedom. Disciplines have been designed, tested, modified, and adapted in the effort to attain, control, and direct this freedom. Personal development and, especially of late, community development, have been intensively studied. A serious review of these psycho-ontological propositions would well reward the effort invested.

Teilhard has pointed out the Promised Land, but we have still to enter into it. For this a convergence of the talents, energies, and loves of all peoples is required. Not least in this collaborative endeavor could be the Hindu contribution. It not only shares doctrinal frameworks hospitable to modern scientific and religious views, but it may be able to point the way toward solution of the pragmatic problem of concretely achieving the desired future world.

REFERENCES

[1] Pierre Teilhard de Chardin, *The Making of a Mind:* Letters from a Soldier-Priest 1914-1919, tr. René Hague (New York: Harper & Row, 1965), p. 279.

[2] Pierre Teilhard de Chardin, *Letters from a Traveller* (New York: Harper & Row, 1962), p. 333 n. 1.

[3] *Ibid.,* pp. 21-17.

[4] *Ibid.,* p. 219.

[5] *Ibid.*

[6] *Ibid.,* p. 220.

[7] *Ibid.,* p. 216.

[8] Pierre Teilhard de Chardin, *The Divine Milieu,* rev. ed. (New York: Harper & Row, 1965), p. 116. Cf. Teilhard's *The Phenomenon of Man* (New York: Harper Torchbook, 1961), p. 262, where he speaks of the error of losing the individual in the whole under the image of "a drop in the ocean" or "a dissolving grain of salt."

[9] "The Spiritual Share [*Portion*] of the Far East," 1947, unpublished manuscript, unofficial translation, italics Teilhard's.

[10] Maryse Choisy, *Teilhard et l'Inde,* Carnets Teilhard 11 (Paris: Editions Universitaires, 1963), pp. 12-14. Choisy comments that this was not the usual style of Teilhard: in his scientific work "he was more honest."

[11] *Letters from a Traveller,* p. 302 n. 3. In this same vein Teilhard claims that although many times in the past mankind had groped its way toward the idea that God, who is Spirit, can be reached only by the spirit, "it is only in Christianity that the movement is definitively realised." *Ibid.,* p. 231, a note quoting "I'Energie humaine."

[12] "The Spiritual Share of the Far East."

[13] Introduction to *Letters from a Traveller,* p. 46.

[14] *The Making of a Mind,* p. 60.

[15] "The Spiritual Share of the Far East."

[16] *The Phenomenon of Man,* p. 296.

[17] "The Spiritual Share of the Far East."

[18] *The Phenomenon of Man,* p. 210.

[19] *Ibid.,* pp. 208-9.

[20] *Ibid.,* p. 296.

1

GOD AND THE WORLD

The Problem of Two Loves

From his earliest childhood Pierre Teilhard de Chardin had felt the appeal of two Gods: the Lord Jesus, whom his mother taught him to love, and Matter, for which he had a mysterious spontaneous adoration. Both devotions were for him expressions of a more fundamental passion for "some 'One Thing Sufficient and Necessary.' "[1] At the age of six, he records, although he piously loved "the little lord Jesus," he also secretly worshiped a "God of Iron," feeling its "full personality, sharply individualised,"[2] in its hardness and durability. His idols were such homely objects as a plough-key, a staple head, and a set of shell splinters, but contemplating them, even his infant spirit strove to commune with "something that 'shone' at the heart of Matter."[3] Several years later the child was thrown into consternation by the discovery that iron can be scratched and that it can rust.[4] It was not, then, the absolute, basic, indestructible being which he sought! Its place was taken by stone,[5] and the course of the future geologist was set.

Much later still, Teilhard found, of course, that the true Absolute is to be sought in the realm of spirit, in the world of persons.[6] But looking back, at the age of sixty-nine, he recognized in his youthful devotion "a strong sense of self-giving and a whole train of obligations,"[7] of which his mature spiritual life had been merely the development. How true this is may be seen when we come to his arguments for the reality of Omega and his insistence that a center, focus, or goal of evolution is useless if someday, even in the far distant future, it finally disintegrates. He cannot risk that the fruit of all his labors and the ideal in which he has set his heart should rust away as did the early God of Iron. In his cosmic mysticism, Teilhard is especially sensitive to the fact that material beings are liable to be reduced to dust. His soul reaches out instinctively for "the stable, the unfailing, the absolute. . . ."[8]

This "passion for some tangible absolute"[9] was in one way or another the driving power of Teilhard's whole life, and he easily recognized it in anyone else who was attracted by "the other God"—"the great universe."[10] He identified himself as a "son of earth"[11] and even remarked that his taste for the earth might initially seem anti-Christian.[12] But he was also a "child of heaven"[13] and insisted that in him the passion for the world and the passion for God were "to some degree united."[14]

The union did not come easily. The suggestions of conflict rose up from every side. Those who loved the world labored for it and strove to achieve lasting results in the secular order, while those who loved God practiced the religious virtues and looked for the life of the world to come. The children of earth cultivated their own lives and sought to bring their personal potentialities to full bloom. The pious Christian practiced self-denial and preferred to sacrifice his personal fulfillment to manifest his love of Christ. The world itself was the source of knowledge to the secular sage. The Catholic received his knowledge of the principles and destiny of his life from divine revelation through scripture, tradition, and especially the teaching authority of the Church.

The Church taught that the salvation of the world had been wrought once for all by the death and resurrection of Christ. But men and women were still giving their lives to the search for a way to save this world by technology and social cooperation. If the former were true, what could be the use of the latter? "How can the man who believes in heaven and the Cross continue to believe seriously in the value of worldly occupations?"[15] In heaven, our true home, we will have a life utterly different from this present existence. So how retain our interest in this life and its passing forms? Yet some instinct binds us strongly to the only world we surely know and to our present drives to understand and to create. Is not this a lack of loyalty to the Lord who has revealed His intention to bestow such great favors and who has commanded us to renounce the world and seek our happiness only in Him?[16] It seems that entrance into the Kingdom of God requires a rupture with our world, and this is profoundly shattering, says Teilhard.[17] How can we consent to be wrenched from our beloved material environment in which we sense "a beatifying presence" in order to answer the summons even of the personal God, whom we also vitally need?[18]

It is true, Teilhard grants, that even a deeply religious experience of unity with the Cosmos cannot satisfy us, because it makes no provision for our personal immortality. But a supernatural religion which promises personal immortality to each private soul, isolated from the enveloping and pervading Universe, also fills us with a deep distrust.[19] We are torn between those who say that we need only await the return of Christ and those who instead labor at building the earth.[20] Where does our salvation lie? *ahead,* in time, on the earth? or *above,* in eternity, in heaven? This is the great question, Teilhard feels, and not answering it is the root of all our religious troubles.[21]

There was something wrong in his day in the way God was being represented to people, Teilhard charged.[22] The images conceived in the consciousness of an earlier age were still being offered to modern minds whose whole social and technological experience constituted a new and totally different milieu. How could the Christ imagined in the medieval world—a world of fixed forms of being and living, situated in the center of a small universe of crystalline spheres—possibly be capable of being the center of the expanding universe of the twentieth century?[23] Contemporary man must do his own homework. He must integrate *his* world and the ever-living Christ in *his* consciousness.[24]

This can be done, Teilhard insists, within the bounds of the most orthodox Christian tradition.[25] But he must also admit that his own way of seeing that tradition is not exactly the usual Christian perspective.[26] Perhaps the fundamental difference is that Teilhard's way of seeing accepts *change*. Change, growth, expansion, convergence, above all, evolution —these are holy words in Teilhard's vocabulary; they describe his God's living world. Consequently, they describe also what happens to the holy people's consciousness. Our understanding of revelation must be constantly enlarged[27]; our conception of God must be steadily expanded to match the expanding dimensions of the world.[28] The more we can realize the immensity, the complexity, the unity, and the movement of this marvelous world, the more will our religious consciousness be enriched.[29] In fact, the future of our religious life, Teilhard feels, necessarily lies very close to our understanding and response to our universe.[30]

The enriched spirit of the future religion may well include a sense of adventure and discovery that we have learned from science.[31] Knowledge of the world has magnified our spirit and strengthened our vitality. We now are "drawn to science as a source of life," Teilhard says; "to fulfill ourselves we must *know*."[32] Confidence in revelation is good, but we, children of the scientific age, need something more in our integral religion. We need *research*.[33] Teilhard does not even hesitate to call research "the highest form of adoration."[34] Without knowledge and research, he declares, there is for us no mystical life.[35] The "mystical vibration" is inseparable from the "scientific vibration."[36]

The converse is also true. Science cannot go it alone, either. Natural philosophy, freed from the Church, gloried briefly in its command of the world, but once the deeper questions began to come, it discovered the void at the center of its structure.[37] If science tries to replace religion or to create its own religion of the earth, then it assumes the responsibility for giving an ultimate meaning to all being and all experience—or of trying to convince us that ultimate answers are impossible and unnecessary.[38] And it is not properly fitted for this task. Its business is to analyze and correlate processes and develop theoretical syntheses, not to give ultimate philosophical explanations.[39]

Nevertheless, if its analysis of the process is faithfully and *thoroughly* carried out, says Teilhard, science will lead the modern consciousness precisely into the arms of an appropriately modern religion.[40] Far from rendering religion obsolete, the advance of science emphasizes the need for faith, because it reveals that the world-process can no longer go forward except as it is motivated by hope and confidence.[41]

The line of reasoning is this: Cosmic evolution tends to construct more and more complex entities, binding into more and more highly organized unities the diversity of lower order beings. On the physical level this means atoms, molecules, and crystals. On the biological level it means cells, organisms, and the whole range of plant and animal life. On the human level it means the uniting of people in society, which involves (at least) morality. And, if such union is to be lasting, productive, and progressive, it implies the presence of ideal motivation, or inspiration, i.e. religion.[42]

Science has identified many forms of energy; Teilhard proposes that his analysis of the pattern of evolution uncovers still another, which may even be regarded as underlying all the others: the will to go further. Evolution, which has culminated (temporarily) in the human being, can now proceed with the construction of its unities only as people are sincerely drawn to form these unions. But they must be convinced that the ideal which draws them is not foredoomed to failure, or to a final barrier at some point. It must be absolutely secure and it must represent a supreme achievement beyond any finite limit. But if this is true, then evolution is "not supported by its base but suspended from the future."[43]

Finally, Teilhard argues, if the supreme achievement of unification is the union of persons, then it must be a process of deep and intense personalization, consolidated around a Supreme Person.[44] And thus, he concludes, shining, as it were, out of the scientific analysis of the processes of the world—and we are reminded of young Teilhard's instinctive reverence before "something that shone at the heart of Matter"—"not violating but preserving the integrity of science, the face of God reappears."[45]

The only true science, in Teilhard's view, is that which discloses the growth of the universe,[46] and such science inevitably becomes tinged with mysticism, both in its own impetus, or need for inspiration, and in its construction, which studies the process we have outlined above, culminating in a union of persons around a Supreme Person.[47] Science cannot always analyze and catalog; it must also synthesize its data. But when it comes to synthesis, then it comes by generalization to projections into the future. Projections into the future involve options, and options imply a concern for ultimates and for the All.[48] There is a longing today, says Teilhard, for a philosophy which would cover this whole range of experience: "a theoretical system, a rule of action, a religion, and a presentiment [a feeling for the future]."[49] But it could not be "philosophy" as usually understood, for while that discipline brings light to the mind, it does not beget life as religion does.[50] In the end it is mysticism itself which is "the great science and the great art, the only power capable of synthesising the riches accumulated by other forms of human activity."[51]

Teilhard himself was a unique type of mystic, driven as he was by a simultaneous love for God and for the world. One of his friends described it as a love for God through the world, and for the world as a function of God.[52] Teilhard himself said that he could not tell which is "the more radiant bliss," to have found God as Creator of the World and so to have been able to master matter, or to have mastered matter and so to have been able to reach "the light of God."[53] His sense of his vocation was entirely built around this unique mysticism. He felt he was called to "disclose God in the world" and to "personalise the world in God."[54] And he was faithful to the call. After his death Julian Huxley (who was nevertheless not converted by him) could testify of him that "he has forced theologians to view their ideas in the new perspective of evolution, and scientists to see the spiritual implications of their knowledge."[55] Teilhard himself felt that he had found the Lord seated "in the heart of the universe of matter . . . amidst the splendor of a universal transparency aglow with fire."[56] By bringing together, like the two rods of a brilliant carbon arc lamp, the two poles of experience, the tangible and the intangible, everything had suddenly burst into flame and been set free.[57]

Creation, Divine Incarnation, and the Sacramental Universe

We have seen that Teilhard affirms the righteousness of adhering both to a faith in God and to a faith in the world, and he justifies this by claiming somehow to find God in the world and the final satisfaction of the world-process in God. Perhaps in the end he even came to feel that the whole thing was a false problem generated by the mistaken, though well-intentioned, teaching of spiritual leaders.[58] After all, only what is at odds requires reconciling. One who sees far enough ahead sees the unity.[59] The reconciliation, if any were needed, has already taken place on the plane of action, Teilhard protests, in the lives of all Christians who have found a "harmonious collaboration of nature and grace." All that remains is to find a way of expressing it rationally.[60]

The most general line of rational expression which Teilhard attempts is his conception of creation as evolution. Already implied in this are the ideas of Christ, the Incarnate God, as the Center and Goal of the evolving creation, and of the Universe as filled with His mystic presence, but for convenience we shall discuss them successively.

Teilhard was a geologist who became a paleontologist, and evolution was the basic principle of his scientific life. But in the Church there was an enormous amount of opposition to the idea of evolution—or to what people feared evolution implied. Teilhard had constantly to reassure believers that this scientific perspective was not a threat to their religion.[61] Evolution is not contrary to the Christian doctrine of creation,[62] and it does not undermine the spiritual view of man[63]—in fact, it supports it, as we shall see. As a scientific framework, evolution proves nothing either for or against God, Teilhard insists. But it is, or should be, especially congenial with Christianity, which holds that man is the pinnacle of creation and that Christ is not only the supernatural but the physical consummation of humanity.[64] Striving to hold both sides together, Teilhard, as a scientist and as a religious thinker, tried to present creation, the work of God, as taking place in an evolving universe. The Creator-God is one who brings things to birth by successive stages, according to a pattern. This should not make people feel that He is somehow less essential to the process, or that creation is less universal, or even less intimate.[65]

The trouble is caused by the classical Christian notion that Nature is static. Each kind of thing is fixed in its being and cannot change. And this is understandable. A common sense, or layman's, view of the world makes it appear so. Nature's exceedingly slow motion deceives us into thinking that she does not move at all.[66] One of the consequences of this belief is that human nature, among others, is also fixed. No *natural* improvement in it is to be expected; therefore the perfect world of freedom and justice which we all long for must be sought outside, in another world.[67] The reality of motion and growth as a principle characterizing all being is inevitably upsetting to this world-picture, but it has to be faced and the adjustment in thought made.

Evolution, Teilhard says over and over, is to be understood as a general principle for the whole of Nature before it is considered as a set of specific hypotheses in biology. Fundamentally, it is only a dynamic sense of "universe." All of Nature forms one whole through interconnecting *processes.* All natural phenomena are either processes or parts of processes, as Julian Huxley says.[68] There is an overall pattern of physical dependence and continuity among organized forms.[69] Everything is part of a sequence,[70] and the unity of the universe requires any new being to enter in context.[71] That is, it must be connected to something previous.[72] Each being has its place and could not have come at a different time than it did.[73]

The most general proof for this view is the very structure of the world as an organization of organized being.[74] If we first of all classify beings according to their order of complexity, we find that we have also put them in their order of appearance in the world.[75] Again, if we plot the complexity of beings, their degree of organization, against time, we see clearly that the organizational pattern repeats itself, smaller units being incorporated into larger according to the same scheme, so that the complexity always increases with time. The conclusion is that the whole system took shape progressively.[76]

So understood, evolution is not a hypothesis but the law which conditions all our knowledge of the universe.[77] It is the framework of thought without which no scientific explanation is possible.[78] It is, says Teilhard, "a general condition to which all theories, all hypotheses, all systems must bow and which they must satisfy henceforward if they are to be thinkable and true. Evolution is a light illumining all facts, a curve that all lines must follow."[79]

When we look at the universe, Teilhard says, we see that everything is born out of the past, from some predecessor, and it grows by passing through successive phases.[80] Matter reveals itself to us, even in its most distant formulations on the atomic and molecular levels, as *genesis*.[81] *Genesis* is quite different from mere *becoming*.[82] Becoming implies only change. It can be random, disordered, repetitive, meaningless. Genesis is directed change, organized becoming, patterned process, cumulative order. Because life is a genesis, it adds to itself, like a memory; some whole thing is growing through the sequence of living beings.[83] Evolutionary genesis is a cosmic phenomenon; it is what binds the whole universe together. The universe is all one great organized process. And therefore Teilhard calls it *cosmogenesis*.[84]

When Teilhard speaks of a *directed* evolution, we should note, he distinguishes himself from the majority of biologists. Successively more improbable arrangements of matter have appeared, the latter admit, but "direction" implies a goal, or at least a standard of judgment according to which one can determine whether a given being has advanced in that "direction" farther than another. Science is in no position to acknowledge any such standard, many scientists hold.[85] Teilhard, however, believes that he can discern an orientation and what he calls "a privileged axis" along which the cosmos is progressing.[86] He finds it in the development of nervous systems,[87] and specifically in the apparent concentration of Nature on the head—"cephalization"—and on making bigger and better brains.[88]

Here another correlation enters the argument, for Teilhard points out that parallel to the advancing quantity and complexity of cerebral matter is the advancing interior quality of consciousness, as displayed in range, spontaneity, and freedom or inventiveness of behavior.[89] He formulates this correlation in his Law of Complexity/Consciousness.[90] This, then, will constitute the privileged axis of cosmic development[91]: it has taken the direction of more and more brain with the result—or was it the intention?—of achieving more and more consciousness.[92] Teilhard himself, perhaps now exceeding the bounds of "science" set by his colleagues, unhesitatingly affirms that the fundamental line of growth in Nature—even its "absolute direction of progress"—is toward "the values of growing consciousness."[93]

This line of growth shows most plainly in the primates and has culminated finally in man.[94] From the end of the Tertiary Period on, it is in man that all the evolutionary energy of the earth seems to have been concentrated. No other great development in evolution has appeared in the last two million years.[95] Man is a summary and synthesis of all the preceding levels of organization. Many factors which had been prepared during the long ages coincided in Man, and "a critical transformation" took place[96]: consciousness became reflexive, conscious of itself. This is the birth of Thought, and while it is in continuity with the general advance of consciousness, it also represents a discontinuity and a leap to a totally new kind of being.[97] The new consciousness, aware of the world, aware of itself, aware of itself *in* the world, immediately organizes the world *around* itself.[98] The new being consolidates the whole universe in himself at the same time that he establishes himself as an individual and as a person, rather than as a member of a species.[99] Most important of all, evolution itself now depends upon him. All the developments from here on will be developments of his consciousness, a consciousness which is free.[100]

Evolution reaches a critical point in man, after which it becomes psychosocial.[101] It is consciousness itself, or spirit, which is now evolving.[102] Material heredity is replaced by spiritual heredity, the transmission by education of the "acquired characteristics" of culture.[103] Progress from now on will be through our own deliberate moral organization rather than through physiological organization.[104] "Since man and in man, simple evolution tends gradually to mutate into auto- (or self-) evolution."[105] We, the evolved, now become the evolvers.

The argument takes a remarkable turn at this point. If evolution is now evolution of reflexive consciousness, then consciousness is also consciousness of evolution. That is to say, the consciousness itself in its dynamic reality *is* evolution, and therefore what *it* is conscious of we may say *evolution* is conscious of. This is why Teilhard says that evolution can best be known through man: *we* can know the springs of evolution *from the inside*.[106] How does this progression of forms, the sequence of increasingly complex organizations, appear from the inside? What is the "drive" of Nature toward greater cerebralization when it is experienced subjectively?[107] It appears interiorly as motive, as desire, specifically the desire to be more, to be more conscious.[108]

So *that* is the key to the whole pattern which we have heretofore known only from the outside! All of life has been struggling toward more and more consciousness[109]; evolution is "primarily psychical transformation."[110] Moreover, it has not been a totally blind struggle. If we admit that humanity is an extension of the general evolution of life, in a world which operates by universal law, and if we observe that humanity's own evolution of consciousness and culture is *"planned from within,"* then, concludes Teilhard, we must grant that evolution as a whole is in some sense "planned from within." The "external forces of chance" do not completely account for it; "certain internal forces of preference" also play a role.[111]

Teilhard now feels completely confident in declaring that "spirit is the goal toward which nature's age-long labors are directed." Everything that participates in the process of evolution is driven by the same (unconscious or conscious) urge for greater freedom, greater power, and greater truth.[112] In this perspective the world appears as a potency for novelty, a response to a call from somewhere up ahead, rather than as a set of fixed natures, or even as the unfolding of some pregiven character through a series of fated steps. The stability of the whole process, it now appears, is not at the "bottom" in the elements of matter, but at the "top" in the synthesis of spirit.[113] It is as though the ultimate mover of the entire cosmogenesis is something that is simultaneously *within* the sequence of beings as tendency, desire, and purpose, and *in front of* the advancing wave of development, beckoning it, as its ideal culmination. This Mover Teilhard identifies with God. The evolutionary pressure is the presence of God at every stage, helping, driving, drawing.[114] We had always assumed that God could be located "above," but now we realize that He can also be situated "ahead"—and "within," as well.[115]

This is Teilhard's picture of creation in the language of evolution. Turning it around now, evolution in creationist language means that "when the primal cause operates, it does not insert itself among the elements of this world but acts directly on their natures, so that God . . . does not so much 'make' things as 'make them make themselves.' "[116] The old "interventionist" image of creation, Teilhard holds, is not only "monstrous," but it adds nothing to the power being attributed to God as Creator. Divine action does not have to have a registrable temporal beginning, nor does it have to be observed here rather than there in order to be noticeable. On the contrary, it is present in all, always, and by its power the forms of Nature carry out their characteristic activities.[117] The creative act is immanent and continuous. In "The Mass on the World," Teilhard prays to the "blazing Power, you who mould the manifold so as to breathe your life into it" and speaks of God's Hands "which do not (like our human hands) touch now here, now there, but which plunge into the depths and the totality, present and past, of things so as to reach us simultaneously through all that is most immense and most inward within us and around us."[118]

Many believers feel that if humanity has arisen gradually from a process of evolution—even if one imagines God to be somehow immanent in it—there is no way to give proper value to the human soul or to establish spirit as a reality independent of and superior to matter. Teilhard replies to this that the growth of a single human being (ontogenesis) represents the same structural problem as the growth of mankind (phylogenesis). We accept it as quite natural that the ability to think and to grasp oneself as a person appears only gradually in the growing child, in perfect continuity with its biological growth. Why not admit, then, Teilhard asks, that "the absolutely free and special action by which the Creator decided that humanity should crown His work so influenced and preorganized the course of the world before man, that he now appears to us (as a result of the Creator's choice) to be the fruit naturally expected by the developments of life?"[119] In fact, Teilhard urges, the evolutionary view gives even higher significance to the human soul than does the idea of special creation. It is not a case of God's suddenly injecting a soul into a world separately prepared for it. The world itself, from the very beginning, has been integrally oriented to this production of conscious reflexivity and personality. The entire process of cosmogenesis is the birth of human spirituality—*that* is what the whole thing is all about![120] The universe *is* consciousness, born of and clothed in flesh and blood.[121]

Consequently, another fear can be laid to rest. Regarding the world as an evolutionary process and ourselves as its products will not cause us to grow lax morally ("after all, we're only animals") but will on the contrary inspire us with a more profound respect for ourselves and a more urgent sense of responsibility. The reorientation in the imagination which Teilhard is trying to communicate is a shift from identification with the past to identification with the future. We do not judge the oak tree, saying it is nothing but an acorn. Similarly, to know the true nobility of humanity we must look to what we are destined to become.[122] If so great an enterprise as the whole cosmogenesis has focused its best energies on the birth of our being with its transcendent consciousness, with what awe we must rightly regard ourselves! If the further advance of this mighty movement now lies in the realm of these our conscious beings, with what grave responsibility we must consider our every action, our every thought—the movement of the precious consciousness! With what devotion we must dedicate ourselves to the furtherance of the universal purpose![123]

I do not wish to anticipate here by entering into a detailed discussion of what Teilhard conceives that holy purpose of the universe to be. That will be treated at some length in Chapter III and again in Chapter IV. But something must be said about it, and also about his concept of Omega, to clarify how his understanding of Christ contributes to his synthesis of the two faiths, in God and in the world.

Evolution, we have seen, is regarded in Teilhard's scheme as a parallel and coordinated development of successively higher degrees of complexity and consciousness. At the level of man, the full energy of evolution appears to shift from attempts to improve the physical vehicle to efforts to elevate the consciousness in its own proper terms. This means, Teilhard will explain at length (see Chapter III), that our life as *persons* is to be intensified. *Personalization* becomes the intention of cosmogenesis, and it takes place primarily by means of what Teilhard calls *amorization,* or the focusing of love-energy. More and more we may expect our lives to be centered around collectivities, or unions of persons, in which not only the physical organization of life will be shared, but the characteristically *conscious* aspects of life. "Culture," of course, has always meant this, but the present expanding population, the finitude of Earth's space and resources, the rapid development of our means of transportation and communication are now forcing us into one another's arms and one another's minds at accelerating speeds. The pressures of advancing life—and the threat of universal destruction—will oblige us to live together in a far more intimate way than has been known in the history of the world. If we are to survive we must love one another in some genuine, thoroughgoing. and spontaneous way.

It is very similar, Teilhard points out, to what happens when any new order of being is formed by the union of elements from a lower order—as a molecule from atoms or a cell from molecules. The pressure on the elements builds up until there is a break to the new level, a "change of state," and a new *center (or principle) of organization* appears, structuring the components into the new entity. Since the general evolutionary pattern always repeats itself, the "survival-union," if we may so call it, of humanity must also be gathered together in terms of a new center or principle of organization: a principle of personalization, of course, and a principle of love. But since this Center is now visualized as the life-principle of the "adult" state of humanity, and all of cosmogenesis is to be regarded as the embryonic or infant states of humanity, the Center must be the life-principle of the entire cosmogenesis. Just as the principle of organization which finally produces the adult human being is the same principle of organization which governs the first divisions of the fertilized egg, so the Center of the world of consciousness is the guiding growth-principle of the whole evolution.

This Center of ideal personalization and Principle of pure love Teilhard identifies with Christ. As He stands at the goal of the evolutionary journey as Omega, so He was present in the first subatomic particles as Alpha. He is "the First and the Last,"[124] "all things were created through him and for him . . . and in him all things hold together"[125] as in their single organizing principle.[126] The latter passage, from the Epistle to the Colossians, was one of Teilhard's favorites, for by it he could justify that cosmic sense of the reality of Christ which was essential to his purpose.

But how did he tie this view to the ordinary understanding of Christ as God incarnate in Jesus of Nazareth? We must observe that the final state of the world, as Teilhard envisions it, is a social union, a new entity composed of elements which are themselves persons. Each person is already a center of organization of all the energies which compose him. Christ, therefore, is a Center of centers.[127] The transforming consciousness which will characterize the union of all persons in Christ-Omega must therefore be a consciousness which is actually the consciousness of each person in the union. But this transforming consciousness must appear for the first time in some one person. In Teilhard's Christian view it did: the person was Jesus.[128] Relative to the new life of consciousness which He for the first time embodied, a lower level would be lacking in vitality. Jesus may therefore be called "the beginning, the first-born from the dead."[129] And as He loved other persons, taught them by word and example to love in turn, and united them about Himself, the new social union began to grow as an organic body.

He Himself—remember evolution's accent on cephalization—"is the head of the body."[130]

This is not merely an event in human moral history; it is a cosmic event. "The Incarnation," Teilhard declares, "is a making new . . . of *all* the universe's forces and powers; Christ is the Instrument, the Centre, the End, of the *whole* of animate and material creation; through Him, *everything* is created, sanctified, and vivified."[131] The Incarnation is prolonged throughout the universe; Christ has extended His body and soul to all creation.[132] The Galilean ministry was not the whole of the Incarnation. Everything has continued to move, ever since that tremendous event, because Christ has not yet attained His fullness.

> He has not gathered about Him the last folds of the garment of flesh and love woven for Him by His faithful. *The mystical Christ has not reached the peak of His growth —nor, therefore, has the cosmic Christ.* . . . It is in the continuation of this engendering that there lies the ultimate driving force behind all created activity.[133]

The establishment of the Kingdom of God may thus be considered as "a prodigious biological operation."[134]

It is the physical relation of Christ—through humanity—to the entire cosmos which constitutes the reconciliation of the two spheres of value—the material world and the Kingdom of God.[135] Since "immanent progress is the natural Soul of the cosmos," and "since the cosmos is centred on Christ," cooperation with the progress of the universe is a religious duty and pertinent to salvation.[136] Hence participation in worldly actions and the service of Christ, far from being incompatible, even coincide. The building up of the earth is the preparation of the Kingdom.[137] Cultivation of our own being and that of our world is not in competition with God; the more people come to control their own potentials and to fulfill them, the more beautiful, unified and centered creation becomes and the more Christ gathers to Himself a living body.[138] In fact, in order that Christ *can* enter into His Kingdom, we *must* achieve the world.[139]

Christ entering into and fully possessing His Kingdom, Christ coming in glory, Christ handing over to His Father the perfectly united world—these are all images of Christ-Omega. But the same Christ is also active *on the way,* steadily drawing the evolutionary currents to His perfect end. He is "not only the Centre of all final repose" but "also the bond that holds together all fruitful effort."[140] In Christ one may consistently love both *Him Who is* and *Him Who is becoming.*[141]

The implication is that nothing on earth is profane. Life itself is God in each of us, pursuing the endless task of the Incarnation.[142] We do not know all that the Incarnation will eventually call forth from the earth's potentialities, but even now it embraces all the works of man that constitute the civilized world.[143]

The whole universe has become, in Teilhard's eyes, the temple of the living God.[144] Everything that exists is sacred, and everything that happens is adorable.[145] The rhythms of Nature are the movement of the Lord; the idea of Christ evolving has divinized the world.[146] The innate perfectibility of a world in progress has been identified, for Teilhard, with the transcendent action of a personal God.[147] The cosmic sense and the Christic sense have coincided,[148] and both ways of expressing our faith, our commitment, and our joy have been justified.[149]

Teilhard aims to develop in himself a type of mysticism based on this vision, one which causes us to seek God in the core of every substance and every action.[150] To be pure of heart, he says, means to love God *above* all things and at the same time to see Him everywhere *within* all things.[151] We ourselves must understand that we have God within us at the beginning and the end of every action.[152] And when we simultaneously realize how deeply rooted we are in the earth, then we will have some perception of the sacred value of life. Those who already have faith in the world must follow it to the limit and thereby come to see that it implies continuous transcendence of any attained stage of growth, that it implies sacrifice and self-abandonment for the sake of something greater beyond; thus their very secular commitment will acquire an element of worship.[153] Yes, the universe *is* capable of fulfilling our highest mystical aspirations.[154]

The universe is, in fact, a sacrament—in Teilhard's religious language, a visible means by which God's own life is transmitted to us. The Lord comes to us through the becoming of things, and it is through insight into the world in movement that we attain the vision of God.[155] It is not the relative exteriority of an *epiphany* that so arouses Teilhard's enthusiasm; it is not as though God artificially appeared in a borrowed form so that men might see Him. At the heart of the universe Teilhard has discovered a *diaphany* of the Divine: God Himself shining through the transparency of created beings because He *is* in the midst of them—and this is perfectly *natural,* both to them and to Him.[156]

In Christianity, as in Hinduism, contact with God may be conceived under the aspect of the sacrifice in which God is offered to God, closing and completing the mystic movement from the Infinite to the Infinite. Now Teilhard is able to include the world in this sacred action, for since our whole environment is suffused with the Divinity, everything has become for us "the self-giving, transforming God,"[157] and we may righteously offer the whole universe to God as the holy sacrifice. In his famous "Mass on the World" Teilhard prays:

> All the things in the world to which this day will bring increase; all those that will diminish; all those too that will die; all of them, Lord, I . . . hold . . . out to you in offering. . . . The offering you really want . . . is nothing less than the growth of the world borne ever onwards in the stream of universal becoming.
>
> Receive, O Lord, this all-embracing host. . . .
>
> Do you now . . . pronounce over this earthly travail your . . . efficacious word: the word without which all that our wisdom and our experience have built up must totter and crumble—the word through which all our most far-reaching speculations and our encounter with the universe are come together into a unity. Over every living thing which is to spring up, to grow, to flower, to ripen during this day say again the words: This is my Body.[158]

The One and the Many

The poetic images in which Father Teilhard has clothed his revolutionary thought may give the impression that, in his eagerness to reconcile them, he has uncritically merged God and the world. This, however, is not the case, and he is at pains in many passages to clarify this. God and the world are not to be separated, Teilhard stresses, but neither are they to be confused.[159] These two foci of man's love must be seen as invoking one another in mutual complementarity: God makes use of the world to reach us, and the world depends on God to escape contingency.[160] Earth reaches up to God, and God bends down to earth.[161] God must not be conceived as in any way "blending" with the creation which He sustains, animates and unifies; He is rather the principle and goal of the final consummation.[162] The Incarnate God does "take shape" in the midst of creatures, but His central reality is clearly of a "higher order" than those substances which His presence gathers into unity.[163] God may be said to be the "heart" of all, but all could disappear and He would remain, His "rays . . . drawn back into their Source."[164]

The need to establish this balance between God's intimate presence in the world and His inviolable transcendence of the world is the aspect under which Teilhard confronts the perennial problem of the one and the many. The basis for his solution is found, as we have already seen to some extent, in his doctrine of creation as evolution. It may help us to appreciate the elegance of this doctrine if we again compare it with some other popular theories of creation, which we have touched on earlier. The most familiar in the West is the doctrine of creation, once for all, at the beginning of time, out of nothing. Sometimes joined to this doctrine is a notion of continual, or intervening, creation, according to which each being—especially each human soul—is specially created when its time comes. The doctrines of Providence and of the occurrence of miracles can also be construed as a kind of interventionist creationism in which each condition, or some special condition, of the subject is directly created by God.

Such views, according to Teilhard's criticism, do not provide any foundation for God's immanence in the world. They leave God "*structurally* detached" from creation, acting only as an external "efficient cause."[165] And from this imagery of God's relation to the world all of the painful dilemmas which we described earlier have arisen. Teilhard proposes instead that God must be somehow dynamically interior to creation, more as a "formal cause," bringing all things to their full being as His image by gradual steps which constitute a single creative act spanning all time. The coming into being of the world proceeds by successive and additive stages of unification of the relatively lower orders and is not complete until the final and total unification has taken place. "Creation," therefore, is more accurately to be located, not at the "beginning" of the world but at its "end"!

Teilhard calls this doctrine *creative union,* because it represents the act of creation as an act of immanent unification, and he proposes to show by means of it how the one and the many can be most intimately and harmoniously joined, without blurring or invalid reduction of one to the other. It is not exactly a metaphysical doctrine, he says, but an attempted synthesis of the established conclusions of empirical science with the felt need to discover the Divine *in* the world rather than *apart* from it.[166]

The doctrine says simply that the world is in process of being created by the gradual unification of multiplicity.[167] When we regard the homogeneous diffusion of fundamental particles at the structural base of the universe, says Teilhard, when we see them being bound into nuclei and atoms, the atoms again united in chemical compounds, the molecules intricately organized in the amazing union of the living cell, and so on through the advancing complexities of living matter concentrating itself into the intense unities of the conscious animals, crowned by the self-conscious human being, we are forced to conceive of our world as a vast unorganized multitude passing into a compressed, highly organized and centered unity to form a single *cosmos.*[168] We are overwhelmed by the sense of the organic, the intrinsically related links among all the beings, the extraordinarily felicitous unions that develop out of what might be mere collections of elements or successions of accidents.[169] As we remember food chains, the "balance of Nature," everything that "ecology" means to us today, the spectacle of life presents itself to us as a single development, a pattern of unity underlying the tremendous variety of its forms.[170] The zoological groups are organic parts of some unique natural entity.[171] An organization of organizations, the world of life —the biosphere—appears to us as one whole, a kind of "super-organism" composed of all living things.[172]

Looking closer now, we can discern several principles: To begin with, *fuller being consists in closer union;* and *union differentiates.*[173] The higher and more conscious beings have the tighter and more intimate relations of dependence among their constitutive parts. As whole areas of natural development expand, the relations among the individuals also display the same intensifying union. But every advance in unity has a corresponding effect in sharpening the differentiation among the constituents. Division of function among cells, among organs, among individuals have characterized the rising steps of the unification process. Furthermore, there has been a *recurrence of pattern*—lower level entities become constituents of higher level entities—together with a persistent *emergence of novelty*: each such unification has resulted not merely in a sum of the parts but in a totally new type of being.[174] The new being has *recapitulated* in its own structures the essential gains of all the unifications preceding it, and has added one more.[175]

Teilhard visualizes evolution as a cone, resting on a base of the least organized, most multiple, fundamental particles, and ascending through successive levels and stages toward an apex of perfect unity. Each level unifies that on which it rests, of which it is composed, incorporating all the organization there present and superorganizing it into a new form. No stage can be said to be complete, and none can exist in isolation from the others. Each entity in the complex is constructed out of a series of its predecessors, which in turn support one another, and so the whole pyramid advances toward a Supreme Point at which the organization will attain an all-encompassing unity.[176]

> Everything happens as though the One were formed by successive unifications of the Multiple—and as though the One were more perfect, the more perfectly it centralized under itself a larger Multiple.[177]

But Unity and Multiplicity are not perfect reciprocals of one another. Multiplicity is dependent on Unity as Unity is not dependent on Multiplicity. The Multiple cannot unify itself. The Multiple as such is simply dispersion—the opposite of any kind of structure or form of being. It therefore requires a principle of Unity beyond and above itself if it is to achieve any type of synthetic consistency.[178] And since this will be true successively at each level of increasing unity, we see that the whole process is ultimately dependent on some Final Unity which does not need any principle beyond itself to unify it. It is the "already One," and attracted and synthesized by It, all the rest of the multiple world rises toward its culmination.[179]

Here we experience again a reversal of gravity in the Teilhardian image. We had just spoken of a cone "resting on its base." Now we are obliged to realize that actually the cone "hangs from its apex." Everything holds together—both physically and intelligibly—from on high, that is, as a result of synthesis, or Unity.[180] The synthesis can be broken down, but with each successive analysis (of animal into organs, of cell into molecules, etc.) a constructive principle of unity will escape—and *intelligibility will decline*.[181] This is a startling and important thing that Teilhard says. We had so unthinkingly assumed that the way to understand a thing is to take it apart and find out what it is made of. The whole was to be explained in terms of its parts. But even everyday observation teaches us that the organic whole is something far different from the sum of its parts and that the qualities of the elements can never account for the characteristics of the composed entity. Why then did we believe that explanation and understanding were to be gained in this way? Intelligibility—insight into the nature of the reality—is to be had in each instance on the level of the synthesis, at the point where unity is finally achieved.[182] And expressed in terms of evolution, intelligibility is not in beginnings, but in the end, in the future.[183]

An interesting corollary of this principle is Teilhard's remark that the universal may sometimes come to be understood through the exceptional. The example he gives is radioactivity. If radium had simply been regarded as aberrant and its qualities not sought in other elements, the whole of modern physics might have escaped our notice. He uses the example to support his contention that interiority—obvious in man as self-consciousness—is not an exceptional feature but a universal characteristic of all being.[184] Consciousness, of course, appears so extraordinary compared with the rest of reality that by common sense we refuse to attribute it to any but ourselves. But, Teilhard argues, if it is present in man it must have predecessors, in attenuated form, all the way back down the line of evolution. Its final surfacing in humankind only served to confront us with the reality in an inescapable way. Consciousness is—from humanity on, at least—the principle of synthesis which has been drawing the whole evolution forward.

Intelligibility, or meaning, is found, then, primarily and essentially in the synthesis, or the apparently exceptional, and derivatively, or by attenuation, in the analyzed components or evolutionary precursors of the given synthetic unity. How shall we identify the highest such unity? It is the "already One," the "goal in the future." These are images of Omega, the Teilhardian Christ. It is Christ, Teilhard affirms, who is the principle of Unity which holds the whole universe together. He is the Shepherd who brings together sheep from many folds.[185] He is the physical, or ontological, center of the universe,[186] and He is, in a way, the "soul" of the evolutionary movement, i.e. He is what ultimately animates it.[187]

A further thought occurs here, which would seem to be implied by what Teilhard has already said, although he himself did not develop it exactly this way. If the exceptional can be the clue to the universal, why should we not also interpret Christ in this way? Teilhard says that "Christ is . . . the supremely perfect individuality that has passed through our human society."[188] His perfection is vested most simply and essentially in His union with the Divine

Source, His Father. And here we may extend our reading of one of Teilhard's favorite texts, "that they all may be one"[189] to continue "even as thou, Father, art in me, and I in Thee, that they also may be in us."[190] This source of perfection, then, the union with Divinity which appears so exceptional when seen incarnate in human society, should, by our principle, actually be the universal characteristic (in graduated degrees) of all being. As such it would be the most powerful synthetic principle possible—the immanent unity which both sustains and draws forward to higher participations in itself. In this view the cosmos is immediately revealed as an evolution toward Divinity.

This is, of course, Teilhard's ultimate conclusion. "In every creature there exists physically . . . *besides* the individual material and spiritual characteristics we recognize in it, . . . *something of Christ* . . . that is born and develops, and gives the whole individual . . . its . . . final ontological value."[191] Cosmogenesis will finally be revealed as Christogenesis, the transformation of the body of the cosmos—from brute matter through living matter to self-conscious matter —into the Body of Christ.[192]

The identification of the Christ of revelation with the Omega of evolution gives Teilhard the over-all synthesis of his system. He will "Christify" evolution in order to "bring out the universal nature of the historic Christ"[193] and to display "a universe on the road to Christification."[194] He will try to establish the fundamental role in the world of what he calls "Christic energy"[195] penetrating all matter,[196] and show that the world carries within it the reserves of being to bring about its total Christification.[197] Evolution is a tremendous undertaking of the incorporation of physical matter into humanity and of humanity into Christ and therefore into God.[198] It is Christ who is the "organic form of the universe thus divinized" and who "gradually gathers into himself all the unitive energy scattered through his creation."[199] And one who allows himself to be so gathered up into the organism of Christ, who "is filled with an impassioned love of Jesus hidden in the forces which bring increase to the earth, him the earth will lift up . . . and . . .

enable . . . to contemplate the face of God."[200]

For the one who sees the world so, objects lose their surface aspect of raw multiplicity. The latent divinity can be seen in each, and the seer lives in a realm of "immense unity."[201] He recognizes that "all consistence comes from Spirit"[202] and that God is the animating force behind every event.[203]

Teilhard is now in a position to generalize his views on the relation of the one and the many. They can be reduced to a few simple and exceedingly fundamental principles. First, it is better to be than not to be. Consequently, it is better to be more than to be less. Being more means being more complex and more conscious. And both mean being more unified. Greater complexity implies that a greater variety of elements are unified, and greater consciousness implies that the degree, or intensity, of unification is greater. But complexity may be said to be on the side of multiplicity and consciousness to be on the side of unity. Better being for the multiple, then, means that it should *be united* with more, and better being for the one means that it should *unite* more.[204] And *creation,* which is the summary of the entire process of evolution, thus consists precisely in the graduated but continuous act of uniting. *To create is to unite.*[205]

But the activity of uniting is completely internal to the entity in the process of unification. It is that which makes it to be "an entity" at all, to be itself. Unification is clearly therefore not an "efficient cause," something which acts on an object from a separated position outside. If he has to liken it to one of the four Aristotelian causes, Teilhard would say it is most like the "formal cause" in that it is an intrinsic determining principle.[206] Just as it is important to him to show that God is not *separate* from the world, so it is important to him to show that God's motive in creating the world is not *arbitrary.* While God is in no way identical with the world, He must nevertheless be, Teilhard feels, intrinsically *involved* in it, both ontologically and morally.[207]

Guided by the perspective just outlined, we should be able, Teilhard suggests, from our position in the midst of the evolutionary movement of creation, to look both backward and forward in time. Behind us, it seems that the natural world fans out into greater and greater disorder and multiplicity, approaching, as it were, a lower limit of "complete diversity" which would equal "complete exteriority or total 'transience'" and would be "synonymous with nothingness." However, Teilhard says, "that absolute multiplicity . . . never existed."[208] If we adhere to what we can actually observe, we are always in the presence of something which exists; some degree of unification is always present. And as we climb the scale of evolution, the story of creation becomes "the story of the struggle in the universe between the unified *multiple* and the unorganized *multitude*."[209] The "creative influence" of the unifying principle is gradually felt more and more insistently. Initially the power is vague and general, as in gravitational and magnetic fields; then the stronger pull of life appears, at first seeming still very mechanical, but steadily acquiring more and more subjective substantiality until the universal force of affinity blossoms in the human experience of love and we have our first direct and immediate look at the springs of "Being as being united."[210]

Possessing ourselves of this key to the pattern of reality, we can now turn our faces to the future and speculate on the even greater affinities and unions that must lie before us. Some kind of superconsciousness is to be expected, we say; something like a community of individual reflections uniting themselves in "a single unanimous reflection."[211] Multiplicity will, of course, be preserved in this final unity[212]; as each person "loses himself" in the great One, he will actually find in it all the perfections of his own individuality.[213] The ultimate state of the world must be "a system whose unity coincides with a paroxysm [or extreme intensity] of harmonised complexity."[214]

Such is Teilhard's adjustment of the claims of the One and the Multiple, his way of reconciling God and the world. It was a many-faceted problem for him, and this general formulation will find repeated applications in the chapters to follow. Spirit and matter, good and evil, the community and the individual are all ordered and balanced under the governance of the principle of creative union. Reviewing also the problems with which we began this chapter, we can see how the doctrine of God making creatures "make themselves" by acting as the principle of unification within them, is a most credible way of resolving the apparently competing loyalties to the transcendent God and the advancing world. Knowledge of God is gained through knowledge of the moving universe, and worship of God is offered through wholehearted cooperation with the as yet incomplete creative enterprise. The phenomena observed by science and the always partially frustrated efforts of the secular laborers find a synthesis and a comfort in the promise given, *by* God, Teilhard would say, but *through* the world's own recurrent and cumulative patterns, that there is a cosmos with a meaning and there is a goal in which all our works shall be fulfilled.

Christ, as the creative, unifying "form" of the world, dominates the world as "a power that assimilates" it. But because His particular mode of "assimilation" is love, His "domination" results in each element's achieving its own unique completion and fulfillment. Or, taking it from the other side, the more we strive to advance ourselves toward our personal ends, the more we are obliged—because of the transfinite nature of our desires—to submit to the unifying action of the transcendent principle which alone can accomplish them. The effort to build our world leads to the necessity of renouncing any egocentric attachment to it in favor of surrender to the universal Divinity who is being formed in it; and on the other hand, the aspiration to be lost in God leads to the necessity of sharing in His work of building the world. If the world is essentially Christ, then it already exists, secure beyond contingency. But if Christ is the world, still growing and maturing, then it awaits completion and we have a vital role to play in it. Through Christ, therefore, as "the Principle in whom the world develops," these apparent paradoxes are reconciled and harmonized. In Him "the apparently most incompatible attitudes of . . . (moral) pragmatism and self-surrender—of contempt for the world and the cult of the earth—are effortlessly combined." In a word, through Him "it becomes possible to use *all life's forces to produce one and the same real thing.*"[215]

Teilhard's vision is an integral one,[216] factual and realistic, yet strengthening and inspiring. It robs neither God nor Nature of an account given in their own proper terms. And perhaps most importantly, it does not rob man of his opportunity to contribute, to create, to participate significantly in his own life in which both God and Nature are fully and intimately met.[217]

REFERENCES

[1] Nicolas Corte, *Pierre Teilhard de Chardin: His Life and Spirit,* tr. Martin Jarrett-Kerr (New York: Macmillan, 1960), pp. 3-4, quoting Teilhard's *The Heart of the Matter* (unpublished). Cf. Pierre Leroy, "Teilhard de Chardin: The Man," a prefatory essay appearing in both Teilhard de Chardin, *The Divine Milieu* (New York: Harper & Row 1960)—see page 18—and in Teilhard de Chardin, *Letters from a Traveller* (New York: Harper & Row, 1962)—see page 20.

[2] Leroy, *loc. cit.,* quoting Teilhard (without reference).

[3] Corte, p. 4, quoting Teilhard's *The Heart of the Matter.*

[4] Leroy, *loc. cit.*

[5] *Ibid.*

[6] Leroy, pp. 21-22 (in *The Divine Milieu*).

[7] Corte, p. 5.

[8] Pierre Teilhard de Chardin, *Hymn of the Universe* (New York: Harper & Row, 1965), p. 98.

[9] Pierre Teilhard de Chardin, *The Making of a Mind:* Letters from a Soldier-Priest 1914-1919, tr. René Hague (New York: Harper & Row, 1965), p. 291.

[10] *Ibid.*

[11] *Hymn of the Universe,* p. 21.

[12] *The Making of a Mind,* p. 165.

[13] *Hymn of the Universe,* p. 21.

[14] *The Making of a Mind,* p. 165.

[15] *The Divine Milieu* (see note 1 above), p. 51.

[16] Cf. *ibid.,* pp. 51-52.

[17] Pierre Teilhard de Chardin, *Writings in Time of War,* tr. René Hague (New York: Harper & Row, 1968), pp. 54-55.

[18] *The Making of a Mind,* p. 159.

[19] *Writing in Time of War,* pp. 45-47.

[20] Pierre Teilhard de Chardin, *The Future of Man,* tr. Norman Denny (New York: Harper & Row, 1964), p. 260.

[21] *Ibid.,* p. 263.

[22] *Ibid.,* p. 260.

[23] *The Divine Milieu,* p. 46.

[24] *Ibid.,* p. 41.

[25] *The Divine Milieu,* p. 11.

[26] *The Future of Man,* p. 22.

[27] *Writings in Time of War,* p. 140.

[28] Pierre Teilhard de Chardin, *Letters from a Traveller* (New York: Harper & Row, 1962), p. 168.

[29] *The Divine Milieu,* p. 45.

[30] *Letters from a Traveller,* p. 143.

[31] Lucile Swan, "Memories and Letters," in *Teilhard de Chardin: Pilgrim of the Future,* edited by Neville Braybrooke (New York: Seabury, 1964), p. 44, quoting Teilhard.

[32] *The Future of Man,* p. 19.

[33] *Writings in Time of War,* p. 83.

[34] Pierre Teilhard de Chardin, *Building the Earth* (Wilkes-Barre, Pa.: Dimension Books, 1965), p. 56.

[35] *Letters from a Traveller,* p. 119.

[36] *Ibid.,* pp. 152-53.

[37] *Writings in Time of War,* p. 85.

[38] Cf. Robert L. Faricy, *Teilhard de Chardin's Theology of the Christian in the World* (New York: Sheed & Ward, 1967), pp. 11-12. The entire first chapter is an excellent discussion of this very problem of "the two faiths."

[39] Pierre Teilhard de Chardin, *The Appearance of Man,* tr. J. M. Cohen (New York: Harper & Row, 1965), p. 130: science recognizes laws of process, philosophy discerns intent. Cf. Pierre Teilhard de Chardin, *The Vision of the Past,* tr. J. M. Cohen (New York: Harper & Row, 1966), p. 245.

[40] Cf. Pierre Teilhard de Chardin. *The Phenomenon of Man* (New York: Harper Torchbook, 1961), p. 29, where he says that he has marked the points in the phenomenal analysis from which philosophical and religious thought can proceed.

[41] Cf. *Building the Earth,* pp. 58 ff., and *The Vision of the Past,* p. 232. Teilhard, of course, stresses that Christianity is the religion par excellence which gives men the will to go forward with evolution.

[42] *The Vision of the Past,* p. 173.

[43] *Ibid.,* p. 231.

[44] Cf. *Building the Earth,* pp. 110-11: a common science is not enough to unite humanity; we need a common attraction to the same Person.

[45] *The Vision of the Past,* p. 231. Cf. Pierre Teilhard de Chardin, *Man's Place in Nature (The Human Zoological Group),* tr. René Hague (New York: Harper & Row. 1966), p. 121: Science shows the need for Omega (God as Center and as Goal of evolution) and its necessary character as Mover, Gatherer, and Consolidator of evolution. See also *Building the Earth,* p. 38: "Perhaps, impelled by the necessity to build the unity of the World, we shall end by perceiving that the great object unconsciously pursued by science is nothing else than the discovery of God."

[46] *Letters from a Traveller,* p. 102.

[47] *The Phenomenon of Man,* pp. 283-84.

[48] *Ibid.,* p. 285.

[49] *The Future of Man,* pp. 20-21.

[50] *The Phenomenon of Man,* p. 294.

[51] *Letters from a Traveller,* p. 87.

[52] Leroy, p. 37 *(The Divine Milieu).*

[53] *Hymn of the Universe,* p. 27.

[54] *Letters from a Traveller,* pp. 219, 222.

[55] Introduction to *The Phenomenon of Man,* p. 26.

[56] *Hymn of the Universe,* p. 150.

[57] *Ibid.*

[58] Cf. *The Divine Milieu,* p. 65.

[59] Braybrooke's Introduction to *Pilgrim of the Future,* p. 11.

[60] *Writings in Time of War,* p. 57.

[61] See, *e.g., The Vision of the Past,* p. 162 n. 1.

[62] *The Appearance of Man,* p. 270.
[63] *Ibid.,* pp. 67, 92.
[64] *The Vision of the Past,* p. 23.
[65] *Letters from a Traveller,* p. 360 n. 2.
[66] *The Making of a Mind,* pp. 61-62.
[67] Cf. Faricy, p. 20.
[68] Introduction to *The Phenomenon of Man,* p. 13.
[69] *The Vision of the Past,* p. 8.
[70] *Ibid.,* p. 25.
[71] *Ibid.,* p. 104.
[72] *Ibid.,* p. 101; cf. *ibid.,* p. 129.
[73] *Ibid.,* p. 22.
[74] *Ibid.,* pp. 116-17.
[75] *Man's Place in Nature,* p. 25.
[76] *The Vision of the Past,* pp. 152, 122.
[77] *Ibid.,* p. 25.
[78] *Ibid.,* p. 87.
[79] *The Phenomenon of Man,* p. 218.
[80] *The Vision of the Past,* pp. 245-46.
[81] *The Phenomenon of Man,* p. 49.
[82] *Ibid.,* p. 227.
[83] *The Future of Man,* p. 25.
[84] *The Vision of the Past,* p. 246.
[85] *The Phenomenon of Man,* p. 141.
[86] *Ibid.,* p. 142.
[87] *Ibid.,* p. 146.
[88] *The Appearance of Man,* pp. 220-22.
[89] Cf. *The Future of Man,* p. 292.
[90] *The Phenomenon of Man,* pp. 57, 60-61. See also *Man's Place in Nature,* pp. 90-91.
[91] *The Appearance of Man,* p. 215.
[92] *The Vision of the Past,* p. 21.
[93] *Ibid.,* p. 246; cf. *ibid.,* p. 165.
[94] *The Phenomenon of Man,* pp. 168, 180.
[95] *Man's Place in Nature,* p. 73.
[96] *The Phenomenon of Man,* p. 171.
[97] *Ibid.,* pp. 171, 182.
[98] *Ibid.,* p. 172.
[99] *Ibid.,* pp. 172-73, 180.
[100] *Ibid.,* p. 181.
[101] *Ibid.,* p. 27; cf. *Man's Place in Nature,* p. 91.
[102] *Writings in Time of War,* p. 78.
[103] *The Phenomenon of Man,* pp. 224-25.
[104] *The Making of a Mind,* p. 166.
[105] *The Vision of the Past,* p. 254.
[106] *Ibid.,* pp. 67-68.
[107] Cf. *The Phenomenon of Man,* p. 151: "To write the true natural history of the world, we should need to be able to follow it from *within.*"
[108] *The Vision of the Past,* p. 72.
[109] *The Appearance of Man,* p. 124.
[110] *The Phenomenon of Man,* p. 167.
[111] *The Vision of the Past,* p. 254.
[112] *Writings in Time of War,* p. 137.

[113] *The Phenomenon of Man,* p. 271.

[114] *Writings in Time of War,* p. 61.

[115] Cf. *Letters from a Traveller,* p. 324 n. 1.

[116] *The Vision of the Past,* p. 25; cf. *ibid.,* p. 154. See also *Christianity and Evolution* (New York: Harcourt Brace Jovanovich, 1971), p. 28.

[117] *Ibid.,* p. 134.

[118] *Hymn of the Universe,* p. 22.

[119] *The Vision of the Past,* p. 135.

[120] *Ibid.,* p. 136.

[121] *The Phenomenon of Man,* p. 151. Cf. *Hymn of the Universe,* p. 27; "Spirit whose vesture is the magnificence of the material universe."

[122] *The Appearance of Man,* pp. 67, 196.

[123] Cf. *The Vision of the Past,* pp. 136-37.

[124] Rev. 1:17.

[125] Col. 1:16-17.

[126] *Writings in Time of War,* p. 58.

[127] *The Phenomenon of Man,* p. 294.

[128] Those who do not share Teilhard's religious allegiance but who follow the general outline of his argument with sympathy may be tempted at this point to remark that there are other figures in human history who might also be claimants to the honor of making this breakthrough. These readers may prefer to think in terms of a larger span of time—perhaps 600-1000 years—during which many breakthroughs of this type were occurring in different parts of the world. Loren Eiseley, in *The Invisible Pyramid* (New York: Scribner's, 1970), speaks of "the period of the creators of transcendent values," an era of "intellectual transformation" in which there was "a rejection of purely material goals" and "a turning toward some inner light" expressed "in different ways by such divergent men as Christ, Buddha, Lao-tse, and Confucius." We are still living, he says, in the inspirational light" of this "time of the good shepherds" which "opened up the human soul." See pp. 146-49.

The dissenting reader might also be interested in applying to this latest leap in evolution Teilhard's own rule of the "suppression of the peduncles": the first appearances of any new stage in cosmogenesis are always hidden, lost to our view. See, *e.g., The Vision of the Past,* pp. 242 f, and *The Phenomenon of Man,* p. 120.

[129] Col. 1:18.

[130] Col. 1:18.

[131] *Writings in Time of War,* p. 58.

[132] *Hymn of the Universe,* pp. 24, 76.

[133] *Writings in Time of War,* p. 59. Substantially the same passage appears in *The Future of Man,* p. 305.

[134] *The Phenomenon of Man,* p. 293.

[135] Cf. Christopher F. Mooney, *Teilhard de Chardin and the Mystery of Christ* (London: Collins, 1966), p. 13.

[136] *Writings in Time of War,* p. 62.

[137] *Letters from a Traveller,* p. 38.

[138] *The Divine Milieu,* pp. 153-54.

[139] Swan, p. 45 n. 3, referring to a letter from Teilhard.

[140] *Writings in Time of War,* p. 52.

[141] Cf. Eph. 4:12-13: ". . . building up the body of Christ until we all attain to . . . the measure of the stature of the fulness of Christ," and the following verses 15-16: "we are to grow up in every way into him who is

the head, into Christ, from whom the whole body . . . when each part is working properly, makes bodily growth and upbuilds itself in love." RSV translation.

[142] *Writings in Time of War,* p. 61.

[143] *The Divine Milieu,* pp. 154, 67.

[144] Cf. Henri de Lubac, *Teilhard de Chardin: The Man and His Meaning,* tr. René Hague (New York: Hawthorn, 1965), p. 28.

[145] *Letters from a Traveller,* p. 288.

[146] Cf. *The Future of Man,* p. 77.

[147] *Ibid.,* p. 224.

[148] Cf. Mooney, pp. 22-23, quoting Teilhard's *The Heart of the Matter.*

[149] *Hymn of the Universe,* p. 36; cf. *The Making of a Mind,* p. 241.

[150] *The Making of a Mind,* p. 190.

[151] *Hymn of the Universe,* p. 124; cf. *Writings in Time of War,* p. 108.

[152] *The Making of a Mind,* p. 199.

[153] *The Future of Man,* p. 266.

[154] *Ibid.,* p. 92.

[155] *Letters from a Traveller,* pp. 255, 40.

[156] Cf. *ibid.,* p. 16 and *The Divine Milieu,* pp. 46 n and 128 ff, esp. p. 131.

[157] *The Making of a Mind,* p. 192.

[158] *Hymn of the Universe,* pp. 20, 23.

[159] Cf. *Writings in Time of War,* p. 87.

[160] Mooney, pp. 23-24, quoting Teilhard's "Mon Univers" of 1918.

[161] *The Future of Man,* p. 80. Henri de Lubac (*The Man and His Meaning,* p. 39 and n. 1) points out that Teilhard's notion of the accord between science and religion is not concordism but coherence. A distinction must be made between the "discovered" and the "taught." Nevertheless, each line leads, like a meridian on a globe, to the pole, where it meets all other meridians in the same identical point.

[162] *Hymn of the Universe,* p. 143.

[163] *Ibid.,* p. 68.

[164] *Ibid.,* pp. 54-55.

[165] "Le Dieu de l'evolution," 1953, unpublished manuscript, cited in Donald P. Gray, *The One and the Many* (New York: Herder, 1969), p. 120.

[166] Pierre Teilhard de Chardin. *Science and Christ,* tr. René Hague (New York: Harper & Row, 1968), p. 44.

[167] Gray, p. 28. For an excellent and thorough discussion of the problem of the one and the many in all its aspects in Teilhard, see the entire book.

[168] *The Making of a Mind,* p. 215.

[169] *The Phenomenon of Man,* p. 34.

[170] *The Vision of the Past,* p. 81.

[171] *Ibid.,* p. 85.

[172] *The Phenomenon of Man,* pp. 94, 112.

[173] *Ibid.,* pp. 31, 262.

[174] *Science and Christ,* p. 46; *The Phenomenon of Man,* p. 110.

[175] Cf. *The Vision of the Past,* p. 65.

[176] *Science and Christ,* pp. 52-53.

[177] *Ibid.,* p. 45.

[178] *Writings in Time of War,* pp. 159-60.

[179] *Building the Earth,* p. 62.

[180] *Science and Christ,* pp. 49-50.

[181] *Ibid.,* p. 50.

[182] *Ibid.,* p. 52; *The Phenomenon of Man,* p. 268.

[183] *The Appearance of Man,* pp. 56-57.
[184] *The Phenomenon of Man,* pp. 55-56.
[185] Cf. *The Future of Man,* p. 23, and John 10:16.
[186] *Writings in Time of War,* p. 252.
[187] *Ibid.,* pp. 220, 299.
[188] *The Making of a Mind,* p. 180.
[189] Teilhard felt that this text was the key to the whole Gospel. See *Writings in Time of War,* p. 113.
[190] John 17:21.
[191] *Writings in Time of War,* p. 297.
[192] *The Phenomenon of Man,* pp. 296-97; *The Divine Milieu,* p. 143.
[193] *Letters from a Traveller,* p. 347.
[194] *Ibid.,* p. 298.
[195] *Ibid.,* p. 294.
[196] Cf. *The Divine Milieu,* pp. 61-62.
[197] de Lubac, *The Man and His Meaning,* p. 122.
[198] *Hymn of the Universe,* p. 144.
[199] *Ibid.,* p. 119.
[200] *Ibid.,* p. 30.
[201] *Ibid.,* p. 124.
[202] *Science and Christ,* p. 49.
[203] *Letters from a Traveller,* p. 28.
[204] *Science and Christ,* p. 45; cf. Gray, p. 31. "Being united" corresponds to what Teilhard calls "tangential energy," which "links the element with all others of the same . . . complexity and the same centricity," while "uniting" corresponds to what he calls "radial energy," which "draws [the elements] toward ever greater complexity and centricity." See *The Phenomenon of Man,* pp. 64-65.
[205] "Comment je vois," unpublished manuscript of 1948, cited in Gray, p. 19. There is the suggestion in this manuscript that a certain theological image of the Trinity is the archetype for Teilhard's structure of reality. He speaks there of God "opposing Himself trinitarianly to Himself," and says that "God Himself exists, strictly speaking, only by uniting Himself to Himself." If this is so, then even beyond saying that "to create is to unite," we may say that "to be is to be united." Cf. Gray, pp. 16-17, 21, and Michael H. Murray, *The Thought of Teilhard de Chardin* (New York: Seabury, 1966), p. 86. In an earlier essay, "Creative Union" (1917), Teilhard had said that his doctrine of creative union was a generalization of the theological doctrine of the Mystical Body of Christ. See *Writings in Time of War,* p. 174.
[206] Cf. "Le Dieu de l'evolution," cited in Gray, p. 120; and *Writings in Time of War,* pp. 297, 299.
[207] Cf. Gray, pp. 126-27, and *Writings in Time of War,* p. 295.
[208] *Science and Christ,* pp. 46-47.
[209] *The Phenomenon of Man,* p. 61.
[210] Cf. *Science and Christ,* p. 48.
[211] *The Phenomenon of Man,* p. 251.
[212] *Writings in Time of War,* p. 113.
[213] *Hymn of the Universe,* p. 26.
[214] *The Phenomenon of Man,* p. 262.
[215] *Writings in Time of War,* pp. 299-302.
[216] Cf. *ibid.,* pp. 301-2.
[217] Cf. *Science and Christ,* p. 85.

2

COSMIC DIVINITY

The Vedic Vision

We have set as our task to show certain selected parallels to the Teilhardian world-picture in the Hindu traditions. But before we plunge into that, a few cautionary words may be in order. We tend to speak loosely—generally and vaguely—of "Hinduism." The word itself owes its origin to foreigners, especially to the ancient Persians, who, finding it difficult to pronounce the name of the River Sindhu, called it "Hindu," and those who dwelt beyond it, "Hindus."[1] "Hinduism," consequently, means the way of life and the ideas of the "Hindus."

However, the Hindus themselves, when designating the root concerns of their culture, speak of *sanātana dharma,* the eternal way of righteousness. "Dharma" does not really have an adequate English translation. It refers to the conduct of life in its totality, in its aspect of obligation or what is due and fitting, and in its aspect of what is right for a given individual in given circumstances. Thus it does not really correspond to "religion," with its explicit note of a "tie" to some suprahuman realm, and it is broader and richer in connotation than our "duty." *Conduct* of life, generated by a certain *outlook* on life, and concern for a certain class of values, are the common notes in the sanātana dharma. It is not intended to be a culturally limited life-style, such as that developed, for instance, by the Hebrews. This dharma is eternal, always in force for all men.

Therefore, dharma is a wide ground of unity for many particular views. This is why what we call "Hinduism" can include harmoniously such diverse doctrines, and why when we are referring to *idea*-systems, we are obliged to speak of

Hindu "traditions," in the plural. "Hinduism" does not hold together by explicit propositional doctrines, intellectually affirmed by all its adherents. It experiences its own kind of unity through the sharing of a certain orientation and constellation of activities. Troy Organ has called the common concern which is the bond of unity in Hinduism "the quest for the perfection of man," and has suggested that it includes acceptance of the idea that man's life should be one of "progressive development" since it is "capable of tremendous expansion" from the "present . . . state of [relative] ignorance" to conditions of greater "reality," ultimately escaping altogether, through the help of "universal powers," the bondage to time that is the root of all suffering.[2] Within the broad area thus roughly delimited, India has "furnished . . . examples of every conceivable type of attempt at the solution of the religious problem," says A. C. Bouquet.[3] Different schools have asked different questions and therefore have given different answers. But they have preserved the unity of their agreement on the modes of conduct, and, protected by that oneness, the many different ideas have been allowed to flourish.[4]

Diversity in religion is even explicitly accepted; the recognition of it is counted as a religious attitude. "The worship of different sects, which are like so many small streams, move together to meet God, who is like the Ocean," says the poet Rajjab.[5] An ancient scripture, the *Mahimna-Stotra,* proclaims, "All these paths, O Lord, *Veda, Sāmkhya, Yoga, Pasupata, Vaishnava,* lead but to Thee, like the winding river that at last merges into the sea."[6] And the Bhagavad Gītā represents the Lord, Kṛṣṇa, as saying, "In whatsoever way any come to Me, in that same way I grant them favor."[7] Or, in a more poetic translation, "Whatever path men travel is my path: no matter where they walk, it leads to me."[8] It cannot help leading to the Lord, for Kṛṣṇa Himself is the cosmic totality, as He reveals in the eleventh hymn of the Gītā. All worlds, all powers, all attitudes of men toward God—all are within the Lord Himself, supported by and manifesting His power.[9]

Here already we begin to glimpse the point of view from which Hinduism will attack Teilhard's troublesome problem of the one and the many. As Madeleine Biardeau says toward the end of her sensitive and perceptive book, *India,* "The Hindu, therefore, has the strongest sense of the unity of everything, of the relativity of differences, but at the same time he immerses himself with delight in cosmic abundance. There is peculiar joy in the plurality of forms, in diversity for diversity's sake, as there is an ecstatic aspiration to unity, to merge with everything. He sees a connection between the one and the multiple which allows him, at will, to enjoy to the full the pleasures of life or give himself up to complete asceticism."[10]

This reconciliation of diverse attitudes was, however, an achieved integration, not a native endowment. What we call the mainstream Hindu tradition is a confluence of many tributaries. The earliest distinction we must recognize is that between the immigrant Aryas, or Aryans,* and the indigenous cultures of the Indus Valley and the south. The ascetical ideal seems to have been the contribution of the latter, while delight in the world characterized the former.

The Aryans were an active people, admiring physical strength, courage, and intelligence. "Give to man the strength of man," they prayed[11]; "Indra! in each and every fight, give manly strength to our bodies and ever conquering valor."[12] They desired life and health: "May we live for a hundred autumns"[13]; "May there be . . . sight in my eyes, hearing in my ears, may my hair not turn grey . . . may all my limbs be uninjured and my soul remain unconquered."[14] And they valued the virtue of the mind: "Thou Agni, . . . bestow on me intellectual brilliance"[15]; "the adorable glory of . . . God we contemplate. May he arouse our intellect."[16]

When the Aryans first came into India they would have been horrified by renunciation, says K. M. Sen, but by 1000 B.C. they had compromised with the values of the indigenous cultures and a composite religious outlook appears in the Vedic literature.[17] From a goal limited to a life on earth as a successful householder who through performance of sacrifices and rituals attains to heaven, the wider ideal

*That branch of the Indo-European peoples which first migrated from east of the Caspian Sea into northern India at the beginning of the Vedic Age.

arises of nonviolent life in harmony with all Nature, ultimate renunciation of the forms of wealth, and liberation from phenomenal being.[18]

The composers of the hymns came to speak of Heaven, the realm of transcendent and formless Unity, as Father, and of Earth, the realm of the phenomenal and multiple forms, as Mother. Whereas Teilhard was still struggling in the twentieth century to reconcile his love for God and his love for the world, the rishis simply prayed: "O Godhead, guard for us the infinite and lavish the finite."[19]

In fact, the Infinite, or the One, was seen precisely *in* the finite: "God of gods, the One and only One. . . . Lord of creation! no one other than thee pervades all these that have come into being."[20] Again, the One was seen as beyond all and the goal of all: "A steady Light, swifter than thought, is stationed among the moving things to show the way; all the Devas, of one mind and like wisdom, proceed devoutly to that One Intelligence."[21] And finally, the One is realized as dwelling in the heart of each person: "My ears strain to hear, my eyes to see this all-spreading Light lodged within my spirit"[22]; "There is the nine-portalled lotus covered under three bands*, in which lives the Spirit with the Atman within, that the Veda-knowers know."[23]

There are many concepts of the Divine Nature in the Rig Veda. Dorothea Jane Stephen, in *Studies in Early Indian Thought,* has identified eight characterizations of the Divine: as source of moral law, physical law, life, and material prosperity, as priest and as sacrifice, as a pure abstraction, and especially as the One behind the many.[24] Troy Organ says that the greatest discovery of the Vedic Saṁhitas was That One Thing (*Ekam Sat*), the objective reality of which all partake.[25] Probably the most famous verse from this collection is that which contains the words: "The One Being sages call by many names."[26] The various names for the Supreme Reality are recognized to be interchangeable: "Man calls the one Deity by the other's name," says a text in the Atharva Veda.[27] This is the view—apparently unique with the Hindus—to which Max Müller gave

*i.e. man, whose body is composed of the three types of qualities (guṇas) and possesses nine orifices.

the name "henotheism." Some scholars believe that this was a transitional position of Vedic theology which finally culminated in genuine monotheism. However, even the contemporary Indian religious consciousness retains this perspective in its tolerance of diverse deities worshiped by their respective cults, yet each acknowledging that it represents only a particular point of view on the one infinite absolute Being. Satischandra Chatterjee and Dhirendra Mohan Datta, in their *Introduction to Indian Philosophy*,[28] claim that "Indian monotheism in its living forms, from the Vedic age till now, has believed *rather in the unity of the gods in God, than the denial of gods for God.*"

The same hymn of the Atharva Veda[29] which explicitly recognizes this principle goes even deeper to sing of a "Fundamental Principle" or "Support (*skambha*) of the whole universe[30] as "the One among many . . . towards whom all pathways turn",[31] in whom both immortality and death lie in concord",[32] "in whom exist the past and the future and all the worlds."[33] The "Support" is identified with the supreme Brahman, which may be interpreted as ground of being.[34] It is not a question now of the unity of the gods only but of the unity of all existence. This conception is strengthened by Rig Veda X. 90, the Puruṣa-sūkta, which attempts to describe the organic unity of all being by comparing it with that found in the human person. This cosmic Person is imaged as if constituting the entire world by his own being *and extending beyond it.* "Pervading the Earth on all sides, he exists beyond the ten directions. . . . Purusha, indeed, is all this . . . but Purusha is greater than this; all beings are a fourth of him, three-fourths—his immortality—lie in heaven."[35] It is, perhaps, the first statement of the union of transcendence and immanence. As transcendent, the Reality evades all attempts at conceptualization. The Nasadiya-sūkta (Rig Veda X. 129) celebrates the ground of being as an indeterminate absolute which precedes even the distinction between existence and nonexistence and whose precise relation to creation escapes the highest knowledge.[36] But it is nevertheless That One—and nothing else—which is "manifested"[37] as this world.

This thought is continued in the Upanishads where, for

instance, an initial statement made about Reality is "It was not existent, not non-existent, neither existent nor non-existent."[38] But immediately after this the speaker sets out to trace the origin of all that does exist from this transcendent being: "From that emerged darkness, from darkness the subtle elements . . . the egg . . . the earth . . . the sky . . . the divine person."[39] Another treatise distinguishes the infinite and finite. The infinite is indicated by saying, "Where one sees nothing else, hears nothing else, understands nothing else, that is the infinite."[40] The finite is "Where one sees something else, etc." If it is beyond comparison—there is nothing "else" beside it and it is not established on some other being[41]—it is clearly transcendent. Yet that same infinite is next said to be "below . . . above . . . behind . . . in front. . . . It is indeed all this [world]."[42]

Thus, so far we have seen that Teilhard's fundamental problems of the union of the One and the Many and of the coexistence of immanence and transcendence are dealt with in the Vedic tradition with simplicity and forthrightness. Apparently the necessity for holding these two together was recognized very early and an artificial separation of a transcendent One God from a multiple phenomenal world was not allowed to develop. Once such a separation does occur in religious imagery, it is extremely difficult to reunite the two portions of reality, as Teilhard experienced.

The Hindus had strongly felt, as Teilhard himself did, the urgency to find some one fundamental thing which would be both necessary and sufficient to account for all possible questions and all existence, something in itself indestructible. This is why they asked "through what being known . . . does all this become known?"[43] and spoke of the One as prior to both death and immortality,[44] as the "prop" even of "the Lord of life . . . while he upheld all the worlds"[45] and as the goal of "all the pathways,"[46] in whom the Eternal Law is established.[47] They believed, too, that they had a general solution to the cosmic riddle. In the Upanishad which distinguished the infinite and the finite, we find that the same characteristics awarded the infinite are also affirmed of the self-sense (*aham*) and of the Self (*ātman*). They too are "below . . . above . . . behind . . . in front . . .

all this [world]."[48] All the ultimates—Brahman, Ātman, Puruṣa, Skambha, etc.—are identified, just as all the gods had coalesced into one God.

> Those who know Brahman in Purusha
> know the Being who is supreme;
> he who knows the Supreme Being
> and he who knows the Lord of life—
> these know the loftiest Brahman,
> and thence they know fully the Support of the universe.[49]

Consequently, there was in the Vedic tradition no particular problem about interest in the material world detracting from devotion to the Deity, nor was there a conflict of secular and religious values. The world and its duties were conceived as a microcosmic image of the heavenly realm; both were ruled by one law of right order: *Ṛta.* Religious action therefore consisted not only of worship but of proper performance of secular tasks according to one's calling.[50] The religious ideal, the seer, and the secular ideal, the righteous king, were often in Vedic times united in one individual. Janaka, Yajnavalkya, Parvahana Jaivali, and others are examples.[51] This ancient aspiration to comprehensive union carried over from the Vedic hymns to the Upanishadic treatises and is reaffirmed in our recent past by Rabindranath Tagore, who writes in "The Philosophy of Our People":

> The Ishopanishad has strongly asserted that man must wish to live a hundred years and so go on doing his work; for, according to it, the complete truth is in the harmony of the infinite and the finite, the passive ideal of perfection and the active process of its revealment; according to it, he who pursues the knowledge of the infinite as an absolute truth sinks even into a deeper darkness than he who pursues the cult of the finite as complete in itself.[52]

R. R. Diwakar also claims that "the Indian mind . . . has . . . succeeded to a great extent in coordinating and synthesizing . . . the outer world [and] the inner world. . . . Within the perspective of the synthesis, it has given to each one its due and created a harmony and an integration which is unique in the history of human thought and action."[53]

In the Vedic vision nothing on earth is profane; all is

sacred. The various nature-powers and processes are each referred to their proper deity, but the ultimate Divine Being "is the One and One alone, and in him all devas become the One alone."[54] This same basic attitude prevails even today and is evident in Hindu cult attitudes in which a plethora of sacred places, sacred images, and sacred persons receive uncritical and enthusiastic devotion. The objective claims to worthiness of such cult objects is of less importance than their ability to evoke the desired religious fervor in the devotee. As Biardeau puts it, "The divine, being nowhere, is also everywhere. Everything is a manifestation of it and, above all, whatever explicitly brings it back to people's memory."[55]

Śrī Aurobindo explains this apparently paradoxical lumping together of the crudest polytheism with the highest and most refined monotheism and even monism by pointing out that the Indian religious mentality saw the multitude of divinities and other images of the supreme Reality not only as symbols but as manifestations of that Reality itself: "Between the highest spiritual being and material being it is aware of other psychological planes of consciousness and experience and these things are truths of those planes no less real than the outward truths of the material universe." Furthermore, this continuous history of the cult attitude in Hinduism implies that "not only through aspects of the universal spirit and all inner and outer Nature can the Divine be approached but each individual object and being is in its spiritual being intimately one with the one divine Existence."[56]

Another way of summarizing this experience of that divine unity in and through diversity is in the notion of the sacrifice. The original sacrificial object of ancient Vedic times was the horse, but the symbolic meaning of the ritual passed into more and more universal, abstract, and interior terms[57] until in the Bhagavad Gītā it is condensed into a verse which Teilhard might have related positively to his own insight into the Eucharist:

> Brahman is the ritual, Brahman is the offering;
> Brahman is he who offers in the fire that is Brahman.
> If a man sees Brahman in all things, he comes to Brahman.[58]

The saving sacrifice has focused precisely on the realization of the Transcendent One in everything. What answer does this view offer to Teilhard's question, then, as to whether the source of salvation is in our own efforts or only in God? It is in both, of course, for all our efforts *are* the action of God himself, and God acts in our respect only *in* us, never *on* us. In the Veda it is noted both that "Gods befriend none but him who has toiled"[59] and also that "no one by work attains Him who works and strengthens ever more."[60] The synthesis is in the Gītā, which teaches, of the yogin who practices disciplined action, that "his self becomes [one with] the self of all beings," considering that " 'I am . . . doing nothing at all!' " but "casting [all] actions upon Brahman," "to Brahman" he "goes in no long time."[61]

Brahman is the Support of the world, transcends the world, manifests as the world, is the goal of the world, is the ultimate agent of all activity in the world. Thus, the Hindus could have supported Teilhard in his glimpse that the stability of the world-process is not at the bottom but at the top. The Kaṭha Upanishad describes Brahman in its manifestation as an Aśvattha tree with its roots above and its branches below. It is "pure . . . immortal. In it all the worlds rest and no one ever goes beyond it." But at the same time, "That is Brahman" and "this, verily, is That."[62] The earliest version of the image is the Rig Vedic verse:

> In the baseless region, King Varuna,
> of hallowed power, holds erect the tree's stem:
> Its rays, whose root is high above, stream downward.
> May they sink within us, and be hidden.[63]

The Vedic tradition clearly refutes Teilhard's characterization of Hinduism as a simplistic monism and the quest for a union of unconsciousness.[64] We also see here, as we will see repeatedly, how erroneous it is to claim that all the Indian systems establish their principle of Unity by denying or suppressing the multiple.[65] Phenomena are obviously not regarded as illusions by the Vedic poets and thinkers; the latter are not "pessimistic and passive"[66] and they are very far from encouraging disgust with life or contempt for the works of man.

The Vedas celebrate the senses as portals of knowledge: "Give sight to our bodies that they may see. May we survey and discern this world."[67] They affirm life—"We will hear for a hundred years, and speak for a hundred years. And we will hold our heads high for a hundred years, yea, even more than a hundred years"[68]—and glorify perpetual youth as the condition of one in contact with the divine: "We will be ever youthful in Thy friendship"[69] and will know the Ātman, "serene, ageless, and youthful."[70] Life should be delightful: "Make us today enjoyers of wide room and happiness."[71] "May we be masters of felicity now."[72] Vigorous action, as well as the aid of God, is required for successful life: "Go forward and conquer, ye heroes! May God give you protection. Valiant be your arms, so that you may remain unwounded."[73] Life does not simply carry one; it is to be crossed with courage and new and better areas entered:

> Stand erect! and cross, O friends!
> This stony river flows on.
> Leave here those that are opposed to good;
> Let us cross over to powers that are beneficent
> and pleasant.[74]

These qualities in a religious and cultural tradition, it seems, should be most hospitable to the sense of evolving, diversifying, unifying life, a taste for which Teilhard felt it so important to cultivate. Let us take a closer look now at some of these themes that are most outstanding both in Teilhard and in Hindu religious imagery: the sense of God in the cosmos, the sense of God as energy, the problems of action and the conquest of evil.

The Cosmic Christ

Everything has continued to move, Teilhard had said, because Christ has not yet attained His fullness. "The mystical Christ has not reached the peak of His growth—nor, therefore, has the cosmic Christ. . . . It is in the continuation of this engendering that there lies the ultimate driving force behind all created activity."[75] What does Teilhard mean by "the cosmic Christ"? Henri de Lubac has been at some pains to show that it is only a figurative way of speaking, that Teilhard did not really mean that Christ had a "third nature," a cosmic one, in addition to His divine and human natures.[76] De Lubac claims that Teilhard teaches only a cosmic function, significance or presence of Christ, not a cosmic nature,[77] and that he is opposed to those who would give the universe divine attributes.[78]

Nevertheless, it seems clear that Teilhard saw and felt *something*—and that strongly—for which his traditional language could not offer him any adequate image. He drew heavily from the words of St. Paul when he spoke of "the Body of Christ" or of Christ's role with respect to the whole of creation or of His "energy" which still presses the world-process forward toward its goal:

> He is the image of the invisible God, the first-born of all creation; for in him all things were created, in heaven and on earth, visible and invisible . . . all things were created through him and for him. He is before all things, and in him all things hold together. He is the head of the body, the church. . . .[79]

> The Father of glory [has shown] the immeasurable greatness of his power . . . according to the working of his great might which he accomplished in Christ. . . . He has put all things under his feet and has made him the head over all things for the church, which is his body, the fullness of him who fills all in all.[80]

> . . . How great among the Gentiles are the riches of the glory of this mystery, which is Christ in you, the hope of glory. Him we proclaim . . . that we may present every man mature in Christ. For this I toil, striving with all energy which he mightily inspires within me.[81]

> We know that the whole creation has been groaning in travail together until now . . . as we wait for . . . the redemption of our bodies.[82]

But Teilhard felt that the full cosmic significance of this vision and its *physical* reality had been overlooked among his coreligionists.

> In spite of the repeated assertions of St. Paul and the Greek Fathers, Christ's universal power over Creation has

> hitherto been considered by theologians primarily in an extrinsic and juridical aspect. . . . The organic side of the Incarnation . . . its physical presuppositions or conditions, were relegated to the background . . . the . . . increased dimensions of our universe . . . seemed . . . to make physical control of the cosmic totality by the Person Christ, inconceivable.[83]

Indeed, the Reverend C. C. Martindale admits that theologians have regarded St. Paul's exuberance with a degree of reserve: "A certain timidity has been felt about this apparent equipping *all* creation with a sort of consciousness: even the late Monsignor Ronald Knox said that if Saint Paul was referring to the whole of creation, he must be speaking with 'something of a poetic outlook.' "[84]

When Teilhard tried to stress the cosmic aspect and bring it forward as a central motif in the Christian view of reality, his friends were embarrassed. Fr. Pierre Smulders hastened to apologize for Teilhard's "somewhat thoughtless" way of expressing his idea[85] and Fr. de Lubac agrees that Teilhard "gives insufficient thought (here as elsewhere) to the precision of his language and to the respect due to accepted formulas."[86] That Teilhard did not mean any harm—"there was no intention of attacking dogma"[87]—is clear, says de Lubac, from the fact that when Teilhard risked mentioning a cosmic third "nature" of Christ he put "nature" in quotes and limited the idea to "a true sense."[88] It was only a "sort of 'third Christic nature' . . . if I may express it so."[89] "Whatever meaning 'physical' [as in Christ's "physical control of the cosmic totality"] is to have," Fr. Christopher Mooney adds, "it will have to be situated in the realm of the human and the personal."[90]

I do not mean to imply here that these commentators have inaccurately represented Fr. Teilhard. Teilhard himself always intended to be a loyal son of the Church, and so no doubt in terms of strict theological constructions his Jesuit brothers are correct in so defending his orthodoxy on this point. But these citations do give some indication of the kind of pressures to which speculation is subject in a dogmatic milieu. Teilhard apparently had an instinctive grasp of something which he was not free to express under the terms of his tradition. Yet it was a vital feature of his own system, in fact, it was the bond which he so desperately sought between his God in heaven, taught by his religion, and his God in the earth, taught by science and experience in life. The story of his life is the story of his struggle to bring this darkly sensed Mediator into such a form that both sides of him could live with it. It was a terrible conflict, but it produced a great many beautiful fruits both in his writings and in his own character. Would the conception of this link between the extremes of his life have been easier for Teilhard if he had been developing his thoughts in a Hindu context? It is an intriguing if not an altogether fair question. However, let us first examine what Teilhard himself says about the cosmic Christ and then explore some Hindu parallels before we judge.

The central conception in Teilhard's notion of the cosmic Christ is that "the universe forms one natural whole, which finally can subsist only by dependence from our Lord. That's the main thing."[91] Teilhard sees himself as "the evangelist" of *"Christ in the universe,"*[92] one who preaches Christ as containing "all the unyielding immensity and grandeur of the world."[93] His "fundamental vision" as expressed in *The Divine Milieu* is of Christ as All-in-everything, in its reality and in its future. By this synthesis he overcomes "the temptations of too large a world, the seductions of too beautiful a world." Earth for him has become, "over and above herself, the body of him who is and of him who is coming. The *divine* milieu."[94]

"There exists in all beings," says Teilhard, "a common centre" through which "they meet together at a deeper level . . . and we may call this Centre equally well the *point* upon which they converge, or the *ambience* in which they float [milieu in which they are immersed (Mooney, p. 79)]." This bond of unity constitutes the "*axis* of all individual and collective life. It is in virtue of this axis that we see that Christ has not only a *mystical,* but a *cosmic body.* . . . And this Cosmic Body, to be found in all things . . . is eminently the *mystical Milieu;* whoever can enter into that milieu is conscious of having made his way to the very heart of everything, of having found what is most enduring in it."[95]

This is, in Teilhard's view, the cosmic meaning of the divine incarnation. "The totality of all perfections, even natural perfections, is the necessary basis for this mystical and ultimate organism . . . the plenitude of the incarnate Word. . . . The whole world is concentrated and uplifted in expectancy of union with the divine. . . . Christ is loved as a person; he compels recognition as a world."[96] Teilhard confesses that he is not charmed exclusively by Jesus' "human life in the past." If he wanted to "cherish only a man," he says, he would turn to his living friends. But he requires much more than such friendship; he cries out for "a God to adore."[97] Adoration means rapture in the presence of "the unfathomable, . . . the inexhaustible, . . . the incorruptible, . . . immensity."[98] And it is Jesus whom he sees expanding to these dimensions:

> Disperse, O Jesus, the clouds with your lightning! Show yourself to us as the Mighty, the Radiant, the Risen! Come to us . . . as the Pantocrator! . . . So that we should triumph over the world with you, come to us clothed in the glory of the world.[99]

It will be interesting presently to compare this with Arjuna's plea to Śrī Kṛṣṇa to cease His revelation of His cosmic dimensions and appear again as a man and a friend.

How can Christ be so universal? "Simply as a magnification, a transformation, realized in the humanity of [Jesus], of the *aura* that surrounds every human monad."[100] "The universe takes on the lineaments of Jesus."[101] But His aura is not merely, as it is with other men, a medium of communication with His equals, but is a magnetic power of domination. It is through Christ that God "animates the whole complex of exterior events and interior experiences. . . . Our Lord is at the heart of all that moves us."[102] "Christ is . . . the Shepherd (the Animator) of the Universe." As "from the depths of Matter to the highest peak of the Spirit there is only *one evolution*," so all beings and all works serve "physically to complete the Body of Christ, whose charity animates and recreates all things."[103] Teilhard is referring here, no doubt, to the scripture, which, likening Jesus to the Good Shepherd, affirms that there is only "one fold and one shepherd."[104]

It is to be observed that Christ fulfills this function without displacing the reality of the elements which He unifies. He "sur-animates" them.[105] Therefore His role is not to be a "quasi-matter" of the world, "an agent of absorption," but a "quasi-Soul, . . . a determining force."[106] "The life of the Lord Jesus circulates in all things." He is "the true Soul of the world."[107] It is the immensity of God, the divine omnipresence, which permits us to touch Him everywhere, says Teilhard, but it becomes manifest and relevant to us only in "the Word incarnate, our Lord Jesus Christ."[108] He is the "organising soul of the Pleroma," that consummation of the world "in which the substantial *one* and the created *many* fuse without confusion in a *whole* which, without adding anything essential to God, will nevertheless be a sort of triumph and generalisation of being."[109] What the unitary evolutionary energy is striving to form is the superhominized human collectivity converging on Christ as Personal Center, and therefore while it is true (Teilhard acknowledges the usual Christian view) that Christ came exclusively for souls, He was obliged—because those souls were involved with life and matter—to enter the whole universe as its directive principle.[110] Teilhard summarizes his position and his faith this way:

> I believe that the universe is an evolution.
> I believe that evolution proceeds towards spirit.
> I believe that in man spirit is fully realized in person.
> I believe that the supremely personal is the Universal Christ.[111]

We begin to see how far-reaching is the mediatory operation of Christ, in Teilhard's mind. He is the "great Christ,"[112] the "centre of radiation for the energies which lead the universe back to God through his humanity."[113] He is the "ever greater Christ,"[114] who has no meaning or value except as an expansion of the Christ born of Mary,[115] and yet who, when risen, is realized to be "unimaginably great," the God beyond knowing.[116] Christ "invests Himself with the whole reality of the Universe" and the Universe "is illumined with . . . the immortality of Christ."[117]

> Christ of glory, hidden power stirring in the heart of matter, glowing centre in which the unnumbered strands of the manifold are knit together; strength inexorable as the world and warm as life; you whose brow is of snow, whose eyes are of fire, whose feet are more dazzling than gold poured from the furnace; you whose hands hold captive the stars; you, the first and the last, the living, the dead, the re-born; you, who gather up in your superabundant oneness every delight, every taste, every energy, every phase of existence, to you my being cries out with a longing as vast as the universe: for you indeed are my Lord and my God.[118]

The "Pervader" and His Avatars

One of the compelling reasons behind Teilhard's development of the cosmic aspect of Christ is his desire to avoid arbitrary interventionism in the natural world on the part of the Deity. The divine creative act, he felt, must be immanent and continuous, harmonious with universal principles of form and growth. This is where he had his greatest difficulty with his tradition, which was essentially a Judaic heritage. This tradition, in its eagerness to avoid polytheism and idolatry, had so severely separated God and the world of Nature that it was almost impossible to reunite them in any way. The Jews, indeed, would allow no union whatever, and therefore rejected the divine nature of Christ, central doctrine of the Christians. And the Christians themselves held this doctrine only as a mystery which was inherently beyond all human understanding, a unique miracle. (This may be a hidden reason why Christianity is so insistent on the singleness of the divine incarnation on Earth. Only if it is unique—and unique not only de facto but de jure—can it be a miracle, outside the established relation of God to creatures. If there were multiple instances of divine incarnation, this would argue some kind of principle at work, under whose regulation all the instances fell, and suggest a *natural* ability in the world to sustain such prodigies—and imply thereby something less than an absolute separation between God and the world.) Even in the Christian development of the Judaic tradition, therefore, which admitted a miraculous union of the divine with human nature in a single instance, it was unthinkable to go further still and unite God in a personal way with the whole world. The very suggestion has consistently raised with Christians the specter of pantheism and the threat of some kind of reversion to a paganism from which they have just escaped. This is why Teilhard had to thread his immense vision of cosmic divinity through the needle's eye of human personality, the one opening in the Christian theological dividing wall between God and the world.

There is a broad current—perhaps it is even the mainstream—in the Hindu religious tradition which does something very similar. It begins in the hymns of the Rig Veda, grows stronger in the late Upanishads, surfaces clearly in the great Epic, and swells to a definitive torrent in the Bhagavad Gītā. Teilhard had spoken of Christ acquiring His cosmic status by an expansion of the "aura" of the human personhood of Jesus. Compare the Rig Veda hymn to Puruṣa, the divine Person:

> Purusha is thousand-headed
> thousand-eyed, thousand-footed;
> And, pervading the earth on all sides,
> he exists beyond the ten directions.
>
> Purusha, indeed, is all this,
> what has been and what will be,
> And the Lord of immortality
> transcending by mortal nurture.
>
> Such is his magnificence, but
> Purusha is more than this;
> All beings are one-fourth of him,
> three-fourths—his immortality—lie in heaven.
>
> Three-fourths of Purusha ascended,
> the fourth part was here again and again,
> And diversified in form, it moved
> to the animate and the inanimate world.

From him was Viraj [splendour] born, and
from Viraj was born Purusha;
And as soon as born, he spread over
the earth from behind and in front.[119]

Later in the poem there is a description of how "Purusha, the first born" is made "the sacrifice" and from his dismembered being all created realities arose, both in the natural world and in the social world of men. "Sacrifice" is a central notion of the Vedic age. It is the great creative act which produces the whole cosmos, spiritual and material, reality and the rule of rightness.[120] The Rig Veda says that "the sacrificial altar is the utmost ends of the earth and the oblation is the navel of the earth,"[121] reminding us of Teilhard's beautiful "Mass on the World" in which he makes "the whole earth my altar" and offers as oblation "all the labours and sufferings of the world."[122] For the Vedic people, all human sacrifices are types of the archetypal divine sacrifice.[123] For Teilhard, the Eucharistic sacrifice "extends beyond the transubstantiated Host to the cosmos itself. . . . In a secondary and generalized sense, but in a true sense, the sacramental species are formed by the totality of the world and the duration of creation is needed for their consecration. . . . From age to age, there is but one single mass in the world: the true Host, the total Host, is the universe which is continually being more intimately penetrated and vivified by Christ. . . . Fundamentally . . . but one single thing is being made in creation: the body of Christ."[124]

Returning to the Puruṣa-sūkta, we see in it a weak parallel to the idea of expansion from a single person to a personal presence informing the whole cosmos. It does not yet include the notion of birth as a particular individual, and the sense of "personality" is diffuse. However, it gives the "great Person" (cf. "great Christ") both a mortal and an immortal nature, the former being subject to growth, and the latter transcendent of all form. It could easily be said of Puruṣa that he "invests himself with the whole reality of the universe" and that the universe "is illumined with his immortality,"[125] the consequence of which is that splendor or the glory of the world (Virāj), is born of him and also reveals him,[126] as Teilhard seems to suggest in the prayer, "Christ of glory," cited above. Puruṣa, the Sacrifice which forms the worlds, could also be described as "the living, the dead, the re-born . . . who gathers up in . . . superabundant oneness . . . every energy, every phase of existence."[127] As such, he is the Savior of those who know him:

> I have known this mighty Purusha, who is
> refulgent as the sun beyond darkness;
> By knowing him alone one transcends death,
> there is no other way to go.[128]

This is one of the most sophisticated pieces in the Vedic collection, but the theme of the cosmic divinity is seen also in hymns to the mythic gods, such as Varuna, Indra, or Tvaṣṭṛ. Varuna's breath is the wind, he upholds the heavens, the sun is his eye. He judges the actions of men against the standard of the Universal Order, Ṛta. He is called the "Universal Encompasser."[129] Indra succeeded Varuna as god of the heavens, taking over all of his functions. He is described as the creator of the world in the sense that he rearranged it, building it as one would a house, and like Varuna, he maintains it by upholding it. In the Vedic age he was the greatest of the gods.[130] Tvaṣṭṛ is praised as the divine artisan. He contains within himself the archetypes of all the forms of creation, to which he gives life.[131] He sustains the world as its nourisher and protector.[132]

All these can be seen as precursors of the notion of the one God as the "Pervader" of the universe. A late Rig Vedic song celebrates Prajāpati, Lord of Creatures, who is identified with the universe and also is the life-force which pervades it, ruling according to *satya dharma,* the true way of rightness. R. C. Zaehner calls this the first appearance of that "fusion of theism and monistic pantheism which is so utterly characteristic of Hinduism." Prajāpati, he says, "is both a transcendent God who rules according to law and an immanent spirit who is the life of every living thing: he is both God the Father and God the Holy Spirit."[133]

The concept of the Pervader becomes more clearly defined in those Upanishads in which the theistic trend of Hindu thought can be traced. In the Brihad-Āraṇyaka it is said that in the beginning this world was only the Self, as a person whose initial utterance was "I am."[134] To overcome his loneliness he first became a mated couple and then produced all creatures, whom he recognized as his own being. Later it is said that the "shining, immortal person" who is in the earth and in one's own body is Ātman, is Brahman, is all.[135] And finally this Ātman-Brahman is described as indwelling all beings as their "inner controller," while they constitute its (his) body:

> He who dwells in all beings, yet is within all beings, whom no beings know, whose body is all beings, who controls all beings from within, he is your self, the inner controller, the immortal.[136]

The Īśā Upanishad, which Gandhi said contained the whole of Hinduism,[137] opens with the words: "All this whatsoever moves in the universe, is pervaded by the Lord."[138] At the same time that it preaches immanence, the Upanishad maintains the transcendence of the Lord as both far and near, within all this and outside all this.[139] The intention of the Upanishad, Radhakrishnan says, is "to teach the essential unity of God and the world, Being and becoming."[140] As verse fourteen announces:

> He who understands the manifest and the unmanifest both together, crosses death through the unmanifest and attains life eternal through the manifest.[141]

The Upanishad ends with prayers to the Lord, addressed as Pusan and as Agni, for prosperity, remission of sins, the vision of truth and of the "loveliest form" of the Lord.[142]

Śvetāśvatara Upanishad is explicitly theistic, identifying God with Rudra, to whom Śiva has been assimilated. The Lord is not only the material and efficient cause of the world but also its protector and guide.[143] Lord Śiva is said to indwell all beings, to be all-pervading and omnipotent.[144] Himself "immortal and imperishable," he rules the perishable and the soul of man. The soul is not the Lord, but by meditating on the Lord and becoming united with him, the soul can be freed of its attachment to the perishable world.[145] "The God who pervades all regions . . . has been born and he will be born. He stands opposite all persons" and he is worthy of adoration.[146] The "Great Lord" is the maker (māyī) and the world is the made (māyā).[147] The one Lord "rules over every single source, over all forms and over all sources . . . over whatever creatures are born . . . over this whole world."[148] He is "higher and other than the forms of the world-tree."[149] "He is the maker of all, the knower of all, the self-caused, . . . the author of time, . . . the ruler of nature and of the spirit, . . . the lord of qualities, . . . the cause of worldly existence and of liberation."[150] He is "the Supreme Lord of lords, . . . the highest deity of deities, . . . master of masters, transcendent, . . . adorable."[151]

Śiva is one form of the personal God, who is recognized as having also a cosmic nature which unifies and sustains all this world. The other popular form of such a concept of God in Hinduism is Viṣṇu, whose name literally means (probably) "the Pervader."[152] He first appears as a relatively minor deity in the Vedic age, although even then he was regarded as the all-pervading god of light energy who takes three giant steps through the universe and manifests himself as the sun, lightning, and fire. He is a mediator between gods and men and is called "the kinsman," who welcomes men into heaven.[153] At one time he was identified with Śiva, but the two were separated and the god Brahmā added to complete a triad covering creation (Brahmā), preservation (Viṣṇu), and reabsorption (Śiva).[154] As Preserver, Viṣṇu is noted for his kindness and compassion; he is the friend of man, the personification of mercy and goodness. Independently self-subsistent, he pervades the whole universe by his sustaining power and rules it by the cosmic order of his own nature, dharma.[155] His rule as Preserver is significant in a world in which good and evil are engaged in a deadly struggle. When the balance tends too far in favor of evil, Viṣṇu sets it right.[156]

Obscure in the hymns, Viṣṇu becomes prominent in the Brāhmaṇas, where he is acknowledged as the supreme God.[157] The Śatapatha-brāhmaṇa says that Viṣṇu is the best of all the gods, superior to them all, and was Himself the sacrifice.[158] The Gopāla-uttara-tāpinī Upanishad offers a description of Viṣṇu which emphasizes his cosmic significance. He is represented as having four arms which may be related to a number of important tetrads in the Hindu tradition: the four directions of space, the four aims of life (pleasure, success, righteousness, liberation), the four stages of life (student, householder, recluse, renunciate), the four functions of society (teaching, protecting, producing, serving), the four ages of human history, and the four Vedas. The Upanishad explains the symbolic objects which Viṣṇu holds in his four hands as representing the creative tendency of being, the cohesive tendency, the dispersive tendency, and individual existence.[159] On his chest according to the Viṣṇu Purāṇa, shines a brilliant gem representing consciousness, "the soul of the world," composed of the totality of the consciousness of all living beings.[160]

Viṣṇu is identified with the Puruṣa of the Puruṣa-sūkta cited above and also with a deity called Nārāyaṇa. One meaning of Nārāyaṇa is "abode of man"; he is associated with the sacrifice by which the world gained its existence.[161] In the *Mahābhārata* Nārāyaṇa says "Being like the sun, I cover the whole world with my rays, and I am also the sustainer of all beings and am hence called Vāsudeva."[162] Vāsudeva is a name of Kṛṣṇa in the *Mahābhārata*; Kṛṣṇa is an avatar of Viṣṇu. By the time of the Epic, Viṣṇu had become prominent as the one God, and all these names—and some others, especially Hari, "remover of sorrow"[163]—were used interchangeably for Him. He is equated also with Prajāpati, Lord of living creatures, creator and supreme God who encompasses all three functions of creation, preservation, destruction.[164] According to the *Mahābhārata*. Viṣṇu indwells all, owns all, defeats all powers of destruction, "overcomes all."[165] From Him all gods had their being and the world is pervaded by Him.

In Alain Danielou's analysis Viṣṇu is related to the state of consciousness in which rest the prototypes of beings prior to their creation; as universal intellect, He plans the world. He is the inner cause by which things exist, the principle of duration, and the symbol of eternal life—the hope and goal of all who must die.[166] Even more interesting, in view of our search for parallels to Teilhard's ideas, is Danielou's treatment of Viṣṇu as the centripetal tendency of being which holds the universe together. The *Mahābhārata,* speaking of Viṣṇu, had called Him "the Lord and invisible cause of all, the unchanging and all-pervading soul, the center round which everything moves."[167] Danielou calls him therefore the cause of concentration, hence of light, of matter, and of life.[168]

> All that in the universe tends towards a center, towards more concentration, more cohesion, more existence, more reality, all that tends towards light, towards truth, is the Vishnu tendency.[169]

Because Viṣṇu is the Pervader and the Preserver, He is especially the God of avatāras, "descents" of the Lord into the human world, where He destroys evil, protects the good, and reestablishes right order. As this idea gains ground in the Hindu religious consciousness, the theistic tendency is, of course, strengthened and with it the experience of personal devotion to the God. His devotees acclaim Him as omnipotent and omnipresent and He vindicates their faith by manifesting His presence and answering their prayers. Dasgupta tells us that through the avatāra the "transcendent personality of God is realized not only as the culmination of spiritual greatness and the ultimate reconciliation of all relative differences, . . . but as the great deity, with a physical, adorable form, whom the devotee can worship not only mentally and spiritually, but also exteriorly. . . . The transcendent God is not only immanent in the universe, but also present before the devotee . . . in the personal form of the man-God."[170] The interesting thing for us will be to see how the Viṣṇu avatāra tradition combines the personal, even human, aspect of the Lord with His cosmic power and immensity. This is the note that is particularly relevant to Teilhard's concerns.

'Avatāra,' or avatar, as it is usually spelled in English, means literally a down-coming, from *ava,* down, and *tri,* to cross over, attain, or save. It is a late term, not occurring in the classical Upanishads and only a few times in some later Upanishads.[171] The doctrine is most evident in the *Mahābhārata,* especially in the Bhagavad Gītā, although the word itself does not appear. There Śrī Kṛṣṇa, an avatar of

Viṣṇu, insisting that he is eternal and Lord of beings, speaks of having passed through many births, coming into the world by His own power, age after age.[172]

Kṛṣṇa was, in some reckonings, the eighth avatar of Viṣṇu, in a series of ten, a third of which are in animal forms.[173] But the cult of Kṛṣṇa grew to such an extent, and the concepts of God and of avatarhood deepened so, that a distinction arose between the sense of the descent of the Lord in the series of avatars and the sense of the presence of the Divine Person Himself as Lord Kṛṣṇa. When Kṛṣṇa is considered according to the latter mode, the position of eighth avatar of Viṣṇu is filled by Kṛṣṇa's brother Balarāma.[174] Another name for Kṛṣṇa which appears frequently in the *Mahābhārata* is Vāsudeva, which was also Kṛṣṇa's father's name. But, according to Patañjali, "Vāsudeva" is not an individual person's name but an ancient name of God.[175] In the *Mahābhārata* the Supreme Person is represented as saying "as Vāsudeva I should be adored by all and no one should ignore me in my human body."[176] The Lord is also called "Bhagavan," from *bhaga,* shares. As meaning "the one who receives his share" it refers to any dignitary, holy man, god, and is applied to the creator, Īśvara. The syllable *va* indicates the mutual indwelling of the universal soul and all beings. Therefore "Bhagavan" means the being who is the "supreme Immensity, the resplendent Indweller."[177] Hence we have "Bhagavad Gītā" and "Bhāgavata Purāṇa."

Historically Kṛṣṇa was probably an ancient non-Aryan hero who became incorporated into the Aryan religious culture.[178] Stories of His life fall into four main periods: 1) childhood, marked by His escape from a king who seeks His death[179] and by feats of strength or mystic power; 2) youth, full of romantic affairs with the cowgirls of Brindāvan; 3) manhood, in which He has many adventures in the prosecution of His appointed task as an avatar of Viṣṇu, that of slaying demons, rescuing humanity, and establishing a kingdom of righteousness; 4) middle age, when He takes part in the great war described in the *Mahābhārata* by serving as Arjuna's charioteer, the occasion on which He delivers the discourse recorded in the Bhagavad Gītā.[180] He dies of an accidental poison arrow wound, forgiving the man who shot

Him. After death He ascends into heaven, returning to where He was before in His divine nature, filling the world with His glory.[181]

How much of His myth is legend and how much history cannot be said. Some scholars (Western) account for Him as a popular solar or vegetation deity. Others (including Indians) regard Him as a king who was elevated to divine status. There are several different strands to His legend, some speaking of Vāsudeva, others of Kṛṣṇa the warrior or Kṛṣṇa the sage. It is not absolutely certain that they all refer to the same person; but if they do, then He must have lived long before the Buddha, for He is alluded to in the Chāndogya Upanishad, which dates from the seventh or eighth century before Christ.[182] Certainly His position in His cult was already clear by the second century B.C. when a monument was erected to Him as "God of gods."[183]

The image of Kṛṣṇa that emerges is that of an embodiment of divine love, strength, virtue, wisdom, and universal majesty. Upanishad Brahmayogin, in his Commentary on the Kali-santaraṇa Upanishad, describes Him as an embodiment of divine joy that destroys pain, and the Gopāla-pūrvatāpinī Upanishad credits Him with destroying sin.[184] Dasgupta calls Him the incarnation of God on earth whom Arjuna treated as his friend.[185] Danielou says that since Kṛṣṇa is the incarnation of the Supreme Pervader, all the circumstances of His life and all His attributes must express cosmic significance and harmony, and he quotes the Kṛṣṇa Upanishad: "Action is his intellect, which enlightens all beings, for this visible world is neither distinct nor non-distinct from him. With him the entire heavenly world . . . manifests itself on the earth."[186]

This cosmic significance is expressed in a charming vignette from the Bhāgavata Purāṇa. Baby Kṛṣṇa is reported by some other children to be eating mud. His foster mother, Yaśodā, comes to investigate and asks Him to open his mouth.

> Krishna opened his tiny mouth, and wonder of wonders! Yasoda saw the whole universe—the earth, the heaven, the stars, the planets, the sun and the moon. and innumerable beings—within the mouth of Baby Krishna.[187]

In another story Yaśodā, vexed because the child breaks dishes and spills the food, tries to limit the range of his movement by securing Him with a rope. However, no matter how much rope she uses, it always proves insufficient to bind Him until Kṛṣṇa relents and allows Himself to be bound. Swami Prabhavananda's paraphrase of the Purāṇa text runs:

> He who has no beginning, no middle, no end, who is all-pervading, infinite, and omnipotent, allowed himself to be bound by Yasoda.[188]

The Bhāgavata Purāṇa has many other similar tales from all periods of Kṛṣṇa's life. But for our purposes the most important document is the Bhagavad Gītā. It comprises Book 6, sections 25-42, of the *Mahābhārata,* and there is some dispute as to its date. Troy Organ says it was "put together" between 100 B.C. and A.D. 100.[189] Zaehner judges that it was probably composed in the third or fourth century B.C.[190] Dasgupta declares that there is no influence of Christianity on it and that there are various reasons for putting it very early. He concludes that it is pre-Buddhistic.[191]

Kṛṣṇa is only infrequently addressed as Viṣṇu in the Bhagavad Gītā, but His qualities and characteristics have absorbed all the attributes of Viṣṇu and gone quite beyond them. For instance, Kṛṣṇa claims to uphold the world by His "work."[192] This is the function of Viṣṇu. The all-pervading nature of God and the fact that He is the essence and the sustainer of all things is repeatedly stressed in the Gītā. Kṛṣṇa declares Himself to be the "Life . . . by which this world is maintained. Beings spring from it, all of them. . . . On Me all this [universe] is strung, like heaps of pearls on a string. I am taste in water . . . light in the moon and sun . . . sound in ether . . . odor in earth . . . brilliance in fire . . . life in all beings. The seed of all beings am I, the eternal."[193]

> By Me is pervaded all this
> Universe, by Me in the form of the unmanifest.
> All beings rest in Me,
> And I do not rest in them.

And [yet] beings do not rest in Me:
Behold My divine mystery [or magic]!
Supporter of beings, and not resting in beings,
Is My Self, that causes beings to be.[194]

This is only one of many paradoxes of Kṛṣṇa's divine/human nature as represented in the Gītā. His transcendence and immanence are equally affirmed throughout. Kṛṣṇa identifies Himself, for instance, with all aspects of the holy sacrifice (the offering, the formula, the fire, the action), declares Himself to be the origin of the world and the object of knowledge, "the goal, supporter, lord, witness, the dwelling-place, refuge, friend, the origin, dissolution, and maintenance . . . both immortality and death, both the existent and the non-existent."[195]

Kṛṣṇa repeats, "Of the whole world I am the origin and the dissolution too."[196] "I know those that are past, and that are present, . . . and beings that are yet to be."[197] "I am the soul . . . that abides in the heart of all beings; I am the beginning and the middle of beings, and the very end too."[198] We may be reminded of Teilhard's enthusiastic exclamation to Lord Jesus: "I love you as the source, the activating and life-giving ambiance, the term and consummation, of the world . . . and of its process of becoming. . . . I love you for the extensions of your body and soul to the farthest corners of creation."[199]

The divine immanence in creation, however, is not a diffuse presence. Teilhard had said that the world expects to be united with the divine but it can do so only if Christ gathers it.[200] And Kṛṣṇa in the Gītā had declared Himself to be the cord on which the pearls of diverse beings are strung, held together in the unity of His superpersonal reality, higher than all creatures and eternal.[201] Few people can attain to this knowledge, He says, and so they worship partial forms of the divine being. But:

At the end of many births
The man of knowledge resorts to Me;
Who thinks "Vasudeva [Kṛṣṇa] is all."[202]

Without asserting that the intent is the same, let us just set alongside this text from Teilhard:

> From the most distant origin of things until their unforeseeable consummation, through the countless convulsions of boundless space, the whole of nature is slowly and irresistibly undergoing the supreme consecration. Fundamentally . . . but one single thing is being made in creation: the body of Christ.[203]

Another image which the Gītā uses to express the immanence and transcendence of the Lord is derived from the Rig Veda's Puruṣa-sūkta, which we have seen above. It was said there that "one fourth" of Puruṣa had become the universe while "three fourths" remained in heaven. This verse was repeated in the Chāndogya Upanishad (III.12.60). Now in the Gītā Śrī Kṛṣṇa says to Arjuna, "I support this entire world with a single fraction [of Myself]."[204] Anticipating that it is this "single fraction" which will expand into the immensity of the Vision of the Universal Form in Book XI of the Gītā, we can hear a kind of echo in Teilhard's acknowledgment to the Lord: "You came down into me by means of a tiny scrap of created reality; and then, suddenly, you unfurled your immensity before my eyes and displayed yourself to me as universal being."[205]

Book XI, entitled "Yoga of the Vision of the Universal Form," is the most dramatic of the Bhagavad Gītā's eighteen chapters, or books. Arjuna, given supernatural sight by Kṛṣṇa, sees all beings in the body of the Lord. Kṛṣṇa appears to have "many mouths and eyes . . . faces in all directions."[206] He is more luminous than a thousand suns and the whole world is united in the body of the God of gods.[207] Arjuna is filled with fear and reverence, and bowing to the Lord, says:

> I see the gods in Thy body, O God, . . .
> And the hosts of various kinds of beings too. . . .
> I see Thee, infinite in form on all sides;
> No end nor middle nor yet beginning of Thee
> Do I see, O All-God, All-formed! . . .
> Into Thee are entering yonder throngs of gods. . . .
> Together with our chief warriors likewise,
> Hastening enter Thy mouths, . . .
> As the many water-torrents of the rivers
> Rush headlong towards the single sea,

> So yonder heroes of the world of men into Thy
> Flaming mouths do enter. . . .
> Devouring them Thou lickest up voraciously on all sides
> All the worlds with Thy flaming jaws;
> Filling with radiance the whole universe.
> Thou art the Imperishable, the supreme Object of Knowledge;
> Thou art the ultimate resting-place [or treasure-store] of this universe;
> Thou art the immortal guardian of the eternal right,
> Thou art the everlasting Spirit. . . .
> By Thee the universe is pervaded, Thou of infinite form! . . .
> Thou art greater even than Brahman; Thou art the first Creator;
> O infinite Lord of Gods, in whom the world dwells,
> Thou the imperishable, existent, non-existent, and beyond both![208]

Compare with this Teilhard's description of two visions of Christ. One occurs on contemplating a portrait of the Lord in which he sees "on the unchanging face of Jesus . . . all the radiant hues of all our modes of beauty."

> Over the glorious depths of those eyes there passed in rainbow hues the reflection—unless indeed it were the creative prototype, the Idea—of everything that has power to charm us, everything that has life. . . . This scintillation of diverse beauties was so complete, so captivating . . . that the very core of my being vibrated in response to it. . . . Now while I was ardently gazing deep into the pupils of Christ's eyes, which had become abysses of fiery, fascinating life, suddenly I beheld rising up from the depths of those same eyes . . . an extraordinary expression [which] spread over the diverse shades of meaning which the divine eyes revealed, first of all permeating them and then finally absorbing them all. . . . This final expression . . . was *indecipherable.* I . . . could not tell whether it denoted an indescribable agony or a superabundance of triumphant joy.[209]

The other vision uses similar symbols as the narrator sees the exposed Eucharistic Host expand to fill the whole world. It "overran everything. At the same time everything, though drowned in that whiteness, preserved its own proper shape, its own autonomous movement." It "penetrated objects at the core of their being, at a level more profound even than their own life," and transformed, purified them. *"The white glow was active* . . . consuming all things from within itself."

> And now that it had established its hold on them it was irresistibly pulling back towards its centre all the waves that had spread outwards from it. . . . In fact, the immense host, having given life to everything and purified everything, *was now slowly contracting;* and the treasures it was drawing into itself were joyously pressed close together within its living light.[210]

Overwhelmed by the divine vision, Arjuna implores the Lord to resume his human shape and, horrified at the discovery that the one with whom he had been sporting as a boon companion was really the immeasurable God, he begs forgiveness. But even as he does so, he still trusts in the intimate relationship he has with Kṛṣṇa: "I beg grace of Thee, the Lord to be revered: As a father to his son, as a friend to his friend, as a lover to his beloved, be pleased to show mercy, O God!"[211] And Kṛṣṇa does resume His natural form, comforts Arjuna in his fright and reassures him of His grace. There are two similar visions of the Universal Form of God recorded in the *Mahābhārata*. In one of these the sage Utanka, to whom the Lord had manifested Himself, worshiped Him saying, "Thou art all this" and then entreated Him to "withdraw this supreme form, and show me thine own [human] form, which is also eternal."[212]

Teilhard, too, finds in his God a combination of "personal love and cosmic Power"[213] and addresses Him thus: "Lord Jesus, you who are as gentle as the human heart, as fiery as the forces of nature, as intimate as life itself. . . ."[214]

But now Arjuna has a new problem, very similar in its way to Teilhard's problem of his two loves. Arjuna has had two very different experiences of God. How is he to know which is the more "real" one? Should God be worshiped as a person with loyal devotion, or dispassionately sought as the "imperishable unmanifest"?[215] Both ways lead surely to the end, Kṛṣṇa tells him, but the way of devotion is easier. Those who cast their burdens on the Lord and fasten all their thoughts and affections on Him, speedily find Him to be their Savior.[216] To justify this answer a new concept of God is announced which reconciles the personal and the impersonal by transcending and including them both.

> Here in the world are two spirits,
> the perishable, and the imperishable;
> The perishable is all beings;
> the imperishable is called the immovable.
>
> But there is a highest spirit, other [than this],
> called the Supreme Soul [or Supreme Person: Puruṣottama]
> Which, entering into the three worlds,
> supports them, the undying Lord.
>
> Since I transcend the perishable,
> and am higher than the imperishable too,[217]
> Therefore in the world and the Veda I am
> proclaimed as the highest spirit.[218]

It is Kṛṣṇa as this Supreme Person who is worthy of devotion,[219] who loves His devotees and reveals Himself to them by His grace.[220] And because He reconciles in His being the values of the transient world, which He indwells with His own life, to the values of the transcendent, one of the chief ways of worshiping the Lord is by righteous action. This Kṛṣṇa never neglects to encourage, and we shall have more to say about it later.

Let us pause a little at this point to reflect briefly on the outlook of the Bhagavad Gītā. As Dasgupta points out, it is largely unlike the later philosophy of absolute monism, that philosophy which Teilhard had supposed characterized the whole of Indian thought. It is, on the contrary, very close to the Upanishads, and it is they, not the speculations of a single philosophical school, which can be said to represent the thought of the Hindus. "Māyā," for instance, the much misunderstood term for this temporal world, does not mean an illusion but simply that which is made by the Creator. And Brahman itself, which had been the supreme being in the Vedic literature, and was to be made the sole Reality in the Advaita, is inferior to the superpersonal God in the Gītā.[221] Zaehner adds to this that the Gītā is as far from a dualism of matter and spirit as it is from a pure monism. Either of these systems would end in a salvation of the spirit alone, but the Gītā reunites spirit with matter, which it molds and elevates.[222]

The theology of the Gītā continues that of the Śvetāśvatara Upanishad, says Zaehner. God transcends both time and eternity and because He is a person, the souls of men cannot become absolutely identified with Him,[223] although they can "go to him"[224] or "enter into him."[225] They merit this union with the Lord by their devotion. The Gītā is one of the great scriptures of that religious attitude which the Hindus call "bhakti," personal love for a personal God. It is a new approach, compared with those described in the Vedic hymns and the classical Upanishads. The people of the Vedic period sought to gain heaven by righteous living and properly performed sacrifices. The sages of the Upanishads sought to gain release from the round of births by the practice of yoga. Now the Gītā values above both a loving union with an infinite Person attained by devotion on the human side and grace on the divine side.

This attitude is represented in the great religious movement of Vaiṣṇavism—devotion to Viṣṇu and His avatars. It first appeared around the fifth century B.C. as part of a general movement of protest by the warrior (Kṣatriya) caste against the ruling Brahmins and their complicated rituals which were no longer significant to the people. Buddhism and Jainism were other aspects of this same movement. The movement is sometimes called Bhāgavata—devotion to Bhagavan, the benevolent Lord, or Ekāntika, monotheism.[226]

The popular cult of Kṛṣṇa was spread by the Alvar poets. They celebrated the union of the great God with a humble man, the "cowherd who thought no scorn to graze the cows, who overpaced the world in his two strides!"[227] During the middle ages the movement produced many popular saints who stressed the distinction between God and the soul, some of them insisting that they did not wish to be liberated or ontologically linked with God. They preferred to think of themselves as the Lord's lowest servant or as his dearest sweetheart.[228] The love of bhakti was not all on the worshiper's side. The Lord also loved his devotees[229] and became incarnate for their sakes.[230]

But out of the welter of excessive emotionalism which these sects generated, some clear ideas also emerged. Relative to our topic we may notice Baladeva Vidyābhūṣaṇa, of the school of Caitanya, who wrote that "when God is worshiped in a limited form as Krishna, he reveals himself in his limited form to the devotee, and such is the supralogical nature of God that even in this form he remains as the All-pervasive."[231]

The greatest of the Vaiṣṇavite philosophers was Rāmānuja (1017-1137), whose system is called Viśiṣṭādvaita, qualified nondualism. It is an attempt to hold together the ideas of the Absolute One, the immanent cosmic deity, and the personal God of love. Rāmānuja bases himself on the Upanishads and the *Vedānta Sūtras* which summarize them. He teaches that the Absolute is an embodied whole consisting of Brahman, individual souls, and the world. The world and the individuals stand to Brahman in the relation of body to soul. "All three are different, distinct, eternal, and inseparable. The oneness of the Absolute is a unity of differences which together form a living organism." Here Brahman means "the highest Person (Puruṣottama), who is essentially free from all imperfections and possesses numberless classes of auspicious qualities of unsurpassable excellence."[232] To solve the problem of how God can have good qualities but no evil ones, Rāmānuja holds that all actions on the cosmic plane belong to the "body" of the Lord which is distinct from his "essence." As a devotee of the "Pervader," Rāmānuja believes that God is all-pervading in space and time, but he insists that this does not mean that God is the only reality, everything else being illusion, or on the other hand that God is identical with the cosmos. It does mean that He is immeasurable and that His goodness is without limit. And inasmuch as all finite beings constitute His "body," it may be said that by His "body" God pervades the world.[233]

The concept of the divine "body" is of particular interest to us because Teilhard also tried to lock the various elements of his synthesis together by the concept of the body of Christ. Rāmānuja considers individual souls and the material universe as forming the "body" (śarīra) or God.

One of his commentators, Anantārya, defines "body" as "that which is liable to be held or controlled in its entirety for the purpose of spirit," which fits well with Teilhard's conception of how Christ as the Center holds the whole world together and draws it to its goal. Another member of Rāmānuja's school, Sudarśanācārya, adds that "when the movement of anything is wholly determined by the . . . will of any spirit . . . , the former is said to be the 'body' of the latter."[234] The assumption, which this doctrine requires, of some level of willfulness in animal and even vegetable forms offers an interesting parallel with Teilhard's notion of the "within" possessed by every element in a conjugal, if not always a governing, relation with its "without." A further refinement in the definition, to the effect that "a body is a substance which is wholly dependent upon and subservient to a spirit," where "dependence and subserviency are to be understood in the sense of productivity of a special excellence," would seem to require also the assumption of evolution when applied to the world's relation to God. The only excellence that the world could produce in God would be to determine Him as its cause when it is serving His purpose. But these conditions can be realized only when something happens that can be construed as a furthering of a divine (good) purpose. However, this view runs into the tangled problem of predestination, something that Teilhard also has to guard against in his moments of overwhelming conviction that the pattern of evolution will inevitably be followed.[235]

It would appear, then, at first glance that there are many points of similarity between Teilhard's thought and the structures developed over the centuries by Hindu religious thinkers. The conception of the human avatar, in particular, would seem to unite the most important elements of religious concern, the infinite transcendent being, the cosmic immanent being, and the personal related being. "This doctrine of the incarnation of God," says Dasgupta, "though not dealt with in any of the purely speculative systems, yet forms the corner-stone of most systems of religious philosophy and religion."[236]

Geoffrey Parrinder, in *Avatar and Incarnation,* has enumerated twelve characteristics of the Hindu avatar doctrines. Summarizing and collapsing them somewhat, we may say that: 1) the avatar is real, not a mere appearance, even a genuine historical person, who is born of human parents and dies upon the completion of his/her particular divine purpose; 2) the avatar displays both human and divine qualities and demonstrates the reality of the world and the value of action by setting an example of moral and religious significance; 3) the avatar brings God into direct communication with men by delivering a special revelation of the God of grace who loves men dearly.[237]

Is this really the same notion as the Christian concept of the Incarnation from which Teilhard was working? Parrinder does not discuss Teilhard, but he points out several differences between the Hindu conception and the Christian, all of which add up to saying that the avatars are not adequately conceived as genuine human beings, i.e. incarnations. They are weak on historicity, their personalities a montage of legends in which they are either too supernatural or too abstract or (rarely) all-too-human (as Kṛṣṇa's affairs with the gopis). Comparing them with Christ, Parrinder notices that they always retain their consciousness of themselves as God, not really having a human consciousness, never entering as one human being among other human beings, and always being triumphant—or at least absolutely imperturbable—thus failing to identify themselves with humanity at its most characteristic and critical point; where it suffers. They are rightly called avatars, "descents" of the God, he concludes, for they are essentially theophanies rather than full incarnations in human flesh: man-Gods, not God-men.[238]

This analysis presents some interesting points and is probably largely capable of being sustained. From our point of view, it serves to bring out the range of possibilities for the elemental anchor points of any world-picture: Absolute Being, cosmic being, personal being, and the various combinations of these. As Parrinder says, when stressing that Christ was not just another theophany, there had been theophanies in the Old Testament. And he might have added that the difference between them and the avatars is just as great as the difference he has indicated between the avatars and the Incarnation. The avatar of the Hindu tradition represents a certain position in the range of combinations of absolute, cosmic, and human qualities. Perhaps it is weak on historicity and on identification with suffering humanity.[239] But it is strong on the link between the personal and the absolute through the cosmic. And since it was just this link that Teilhard was struggling, with great difficulty, to establish in a tradition which had stressed heavily the human and divine almost to the exclusion of the cosmic, it is not unreasonable to suggest that a sympathetic acquaintance with the Hindu tradition of the avatar might have been of some advantage to him.

Pantheism and the Personal God

The fear in the West of introducing a cosmic aspect into the conception of God is the fear of pantheism, and the fear of losing the personal aspect. Teilhard understood this fear and himself railed against certain systems of thought—including the Hindu tradition—which he thought fostered a false view of the divine. He speaks of "the pantheisms of the inanimate" which cling to "formless energy" as the basis of stability[240] and of "the degraded form of godless pantheism."[241] He warns against "the perverse pantheism and materialism which lie in wait for our thought whenever it applies to its mystical concepts the powerful but dangerous resources of analogies drawn from organic life."[242] "Pantheism," he says in *The Divine Milieu,* "seduces us by its vistas of perfect universal union. But ultimately, if it were true, it would give us only fusion and unconsciousness; for, at the end of the evolution it claims to reveal, the elements of the world vanish in the God they create or by which they are absorbed."[243] "All non-Christian pantheisms have this in common," he claims; they surrender to the great mother and permit themselves to be passively rocked in her arms.[244] "Effortless enjoyment and Nirvana" characterize this attitude which Teilhard denounces as the "philosophy of the lowest degree of consciousness."[245]

Teilhard himself went through such a period, he tells us, sinking into a contemplative life, away from men and from struggle and responsibility. But it was his experience that as he withdrew from human society—even lost his taste for it—and drifted into "primordial consciousness," "the light of life was dimmed" in him.[246] Succumbing to this same temptation, he believes, has led astray "many a system of pantheism . . . to the cult of a great All in which individuals were supposed to be merged like a drop in the ocean or like a dissolving grain of salt."[247] This is "that destructive fusion of which all the pantheisms dream."[248]

But at the same time he understands the attraction: "I had always been by temperament a 'pantheist.' "[249] "The attraction of the All . . . set everything in motion in me. . . . I can never aspire to . . . less than the All itself."[250] "I become aware of the growing light of this truth . . . that God is all."[251] "Resonance to the All—the keynote of . . . pure religion."[252] And so Teilhard undertook to show that there is a legitimate, even a peculiarly Christian, pantheism. He is almost always working on this problem, in one way or another, but he has one essay specifically devoted to it, "Pantheism and Christianity,"[253] in which, instead of emphasizing the differences between pantheism and Christianity, as Christians usually do, he tries to narrow the gap between them. He means to bring out "the Christian soul of pantheism or the pantheist aspect of Christianity," he says.[254] "Pantheism" need not carry only the unacceptable connotations it has accumulated from monists, theosophists, and philosophers such as Spinoza and Hegel, he concedes. Beneath these "heterodox forms of the pantheist impulse," Teilhard believes, there lies "a psychological reality and an intellectual need which are much vaster and more enduring than any system of Hindu, Greek, or German thought" and which "can be fully satisfied only in Christianity."[255]

The root of Teilhard's argument for a legitimate pantheism is his concept of the Sense of the Whole. This will come up again presently when we make some remarks about Teilhard's aspirations for collective humanity. It is a pivotal concept for him, as we have already suggested, because it is the mediator between his two loves, that of the transcendent God and that of the material world. He means by it the world in its totality and its immensities of space, time, complexity, and consciousness. He argues that we are inescapably bound to the Whole: intellectually, because we cannot understand except by unifying, and affectively, because our aspiration reaches for some sufficient value which is everywhere present. Ultimately, if we analyze it, only the Whole as such has any meaning or any worth.[256] And it is the mediator, because "with its attributes of (at least relative) universality, unity, and infallibility, the Whole cannot reveal itself to us without our recognizing in it God, or the shadow of God. And on his side, how can God make himself manifest to us otherwise than by passing through the Whole, by assuming the features or at least the outward integument of the Whole?"[257]

In the article on "Pantheism and Christianity" Teilhard is addressing himself more to those who might be attracted by modern scientific pantheisms, to those who have "abandoned Christianity," than to those who might turn to the traditions of the Eastern cultures. Ancient as the concern for the Whole is, it is highly peculiar to our own time, he says, in which it is going through a "crisis of awakening."[258] It is science which has awakened us, revealing, from the electron to the galaxy, one continuous energy-system,[259] and in the biological sphere, a unity of matter and consciousness in a growing world, a cosmogenesis. These ideas and images surround us. We are living *in our secular lives* "in the presence of the All."[260] This "humanist pantheism" is a youthful religion as yet, Teilhard remarks. It is not systematized, has no theology, proclaims no revelation. But it has a "contagious faith in an ideal": it believes that "the supreme value of life" is "universal progress." It is "the religion of evolution."[261]

Both pagan pantheisms and scientific pantheisms, in Teilhard's view, are liable to the same error. They are apt to conceive the unity of the world as being at the bottom of the scale of complexity, where the "All" is a vast undifferentiated homogeneous, uniform, and diffuse being in which all individuality or difference is absorbed and obliterated.[262] It should rather be sought at the peak of the cone of converging complexity, where the organizing unity becomes most intense. Fundamentally, says Teilhard, there are two kinds of pantheism: 1) that in which the unity of the Whole is born from the fusion of the elements which disappear in it, and 2) that in which the elements are fulfilled in their individual qualities by entering a centered and organized unity which both dominates and differentiates them. Only the second, he argues, is "intellectually justifiable and mystically satisfying."[263] When the total Christ is conceived as the whole complexity of a personalizing and converging universe, centered on the transcendent divine, then Teilhard finds that his "deepest 'pantheist' aspirations are satisfied, guided, and reassured."[264] This, he says, could be "a very real 'pantheism.' "[265]

> Unlike the false monisms which urge one through passivity into unconsciousness, . . . 'pan-Christism' . . . places union at the term of an arduous process of intellection. I shall become the Other only by being utterly myself. I shall attain spirit only by bringing out the complete range of the forces of matter. The total Christ is consummated and may be attained, only at the term of universal evolution: . . . a personalized universe, whose domination personalizes me.[266]

Elsewhere Teilhard says that our goal is a cleaving to God which makes us one and the same complex thing with him[267] and that the Body of Christ should be conceived as a physical reality.[268] He complains that the theologians of his day did not put any more physical reality into the bonds that unite the mystical body of Christ than some common moral agreement and a little affection. The powerful religion of the Whole cannot be Christianized on those terms![269] The trouble with Christianity, Teilhard admits, is that it has not had a strong connection from earth to heaven. "The reason for this," he says, "was that, as a result of seeing only 'personal' relationships in the world, the average Christian has ended by reducing the Creator and creature to the scale of 'juridical man.' " He has regarded the soul as "a transient guest in the cosmos and a prisoner of matter." Salvation, reduced to "a matter of personal success, developed without any reference to cosmic evolution. Christianity . . . has never developed the *sense of the earth*."[270] But by expanding the sense of the Incarnation and tracing out the unfolding of personal relationships in the context of cosmic evolution, such a sense of the earth and such a middle ground between earth and heaven could be developed. The belief in the unification of the world in God through the Incarnation was present in Christianity from the beginning but it could not be expressed except in juridical terms until science fabricated new metaphors. Now we can say that to be God, Christ must be coextensive with space and time, and to be Omega, center and goal of evolution, He must "superanimate the world."[271]

God must enter the world, assume control of its evolution, transform and unite all, and then rejoin Himself. Thus God becomes "all in all." This would be a superior form of pantheism, with no annihilation of the elements in order to achieve unity.[272] In order for the whole universe to be united with God, the Incarnate God must "enter into contact with" every level of reality.[273] This is achieved through what Teilhard calls *creative and differentiating union.* In the course of evolution the elements of any given level of reality are united by their incorporation into an entity of a superior level, with these conditions observed: 1) The superior entity is a genuine novelty unpredictable from the constitutive elements. Its characteristics are not reducible to those of the inferior level; the synthesized entity is called "superior" because it is more complex and more conscious than its constituents. Greater complexity means that a greater variety of different kinds of elements have been subjected under a single governing principle, all of their characteristic activities now channeled to contribute to one new function. Greater consciousness means that the organizing and governing principle of the new entity is capable of thus subduing a greater variety of elements within the unity of its being and of carrying on a wider range of activities with other entities of its own level. This is the *creative union.* 2) However, the composing elements do not lose their own individuality and particular character. Indeed, their several peculiarities are enhanced by their position in the new union because of the diversity of relationships now established with a greater variety of other elements. The union is established by activities and functions, what we might call unity of purpose, rather than by unity of substance. This is the *differen-*

tiating union. These two laws are the keys to Teilhard's conception of the evolving universe.

As evolution advances, the complexity, of course, becomes compounded. Animals are composed of cells which are composed of molecules which are composed of atoms, etc. The unifying principle of the animal, then, for instance, may be said to be "in contact with" every level of reality represented in its own being, and every element of each level may be said to be united to the animal in the physical reality of its living being. Now when we arrive at the level of human persons, considered in the fullness of their complexity and their consciousness, the situation becomes even more complicated, because each of these person-elements is a self-conscious being, a kind of absolute principle of organization and unity for all of his own elements. When the persons therefore are superorganized into yet another entity above their individual level of being, it becomes difficult for us to conceive it. It is something like trying to visualize the four-dimensional hypersphere which we are told is the shape of our astronomical universe. Its "surface" is the three-dimensional space with which we are familiar. The total Christ is a kind of hypersphere whose three-dimensional "surface" is composed of the quasi-absolutes of our own self-conscious beings. Christ as "head" of this "body" is the organizing and governing principle, the source of its unity. The elements which compose it are human persons. Each person is a union of elements of inferior level, in a descending order of complexity. But since Christ is the final principle of unity of the whole, He is *the* principle for all the elements on all levels. In this way He is "in contact with" every level of reality, and the whole universe may be said to compose only the one Christ. This is "pan-Christism."[274]

This Christic synthesis reconciles pantheism with personal values, both of God and of human beings, because the unifying "activities" and "functions" which relate the elements within the new entity of the Body of Christ are personal activities and functions, such as sympathy, shared intellectual interests, common joys, ideals, and dedications. And the organizing rule of the governing principle, Christ, which holds them together in this new "Body," is also a personal act, that of divine love. Teilhard sees the whole movement of evolution as a tending toward these higher and higher unities, culminating in this last one centered on Christ by personal bonds, and therefore he calls ours a "personalizing universe."

This structure, Teilhard believes, represents a legitimate pantheism, not of simple identification with a homogeneous whole, but of unification within a highly complex whole.[275] God is all in every being in the universe because he is the ultimate principle of the differentiating unification.[276] Such a conception of pantheism does not lead to slackness or to a sense of diffusion or dissolution. The elements of the union are not dispersed but center themselves, with other centers, on the Ultimate Center. It is "union by differentiation and differentiation by union . . . sole definition of true pantheism."[277] Souls mutually transparent to each other in perfect self-possession constitute the only pantheistic fusion that is logically conceivable for self-conscious persons who are not to fall to a lower level of reality when they are united, says Teilhard.[278] This is the highest type of unity, he believes, and the only pantheism that can finally satisfy human aspirations.

> It is *only* in fact the 'pantheism' of love or Christian 'pantheism' (that in which each being is super-personalized, super-centered, by union with Christ, the divine super-center)—it is only that pantheism which correctly interprets and fully satisfies the religious aspirations of man, whose dream is ultimately to lose self consciously in unity. That pantheism alone agrees with experience, which shows us that in every instance *union differentiates*. And finally, it alone legitimately continues the curve of evolution, on which the centration of the universe upon itself advances only through organic complexity.[279]

Recognizing that this pan-Christic model which Teilhard has proposed is significantly different from any "pantheism of the inanimate"[280] in which "the elements vanish in the God . . . by which they are absorbed"[281] and from systems which recommend an effortless surrender to the inscrutable forces of life,[282] we may still ask whether Teilhard is justified in insisting on such a total gap between his thought and that of the Hindus. We may recall (see Introduction) that Teilhard had claimed in his essay "The Spiritual Share of the Far East" that all the Indian systems had in common "a very particular conception of Unity" according to which "below all conceivable determinations, a universal essence . . . awaits your return to it to absorb you and identify you with itself."[283] "The Hindu religions," says Teilhard, "give me the impression of a vast well into which one plunges in order to grasp the reflection of the sun."[284] They are deceptive, he feels, because they speak much of the spirit. But actually they reduce everything to one and that one is matter.

> At first it would appear that in the eyes of . . . the Hindu *everything is animated; in reality, everything is materialized.* The luminous destiny of things, the paradise of souls they dream of, *become one with their dim source;* they are absorbed in the fundamental reservoir of homogeneous ether and latent life, from which everything has emerged and by returning to be lost in which it is destined to attain its beatitude. *Life is understood and experienced as a function of matter.*[285]

Elsewhere Teilhard lumps all the Eastern religions together in their distinction from Christianity and calls them, for convenience, "Buddhism"![286] He grants that "never perhaps has the sense of the Whole, which is the life-blood of all mysticism, flowered more exuberantly than in the plains of India," and describes his "own individual faith" as "peculiarly sensitive to Eastern influences" of whose "attraction" he was "perfectly conscious."[287] Nevertheless, he was amazingly ill informed about these attractive systems, not even being aware of the tremendous differences within the vague boundaries of "Hinduism" itself. He supposes that, for any true Hindu, "spirit is the homogeneous unity in which the complete adept is lost to self, all individual features and values being suppressed."[288]

> For the East, the One is seen as a suppression of the multiple; for me, the One is born from the concentration of the multiple. Thus, under the same monist appearances, there are two moral systems, two metaphysics, and two mysticisms.[289]

He notes in this connection that he is referring only to "Eastern religions as they *should rightly be regarded* in virtue of their fundamental concept of spirit, and *not in the form they assume in fact.*" Systems which do not conform to the pattern he is criticizing he dismisses as being "under the influence of an approximation to Western types of mysticism"[290]—the same answer he gave Maryse Choisy when the latter pointed out to him that absolute monism was only one school among many in India.[291]

It is a remarkable forcing of the argument to attain the desired conclusion. One can only suppose that Teilhard's own struggles with the problems raised in his Catholic thought-world by the sense of the Whole, which he felt so strongly, caused him later to overreact and reject prejudicially any non-Christian approach to the same problems. Even acknowledging that his own scheme is different and does go beyond anything to be found explicitly in the Hindu traditions, this is still an inexcusably unfair assessment of a great body of diverse turns of thought. As Zaehner says, what Teilhard is attacking is only the system of Śaṅkara and that of Theravāda Buddhism—less than half of Indian religion.[292] One way of realizing this disproportion is to observe that in Dasgupta's five-volume *History of Indian Philosophy,* twelve pages are devoted to Theravāda Buddhism, and the Śaṅkara School of Vedānta is treated in eighty-nine. Even after subtracting the considerable coverage given materialistic and naturalistic schools, debates on points of logic and epistemology, this means that more than half of this standard work is concerned with the theistic philosophies of India.

Śaṅkara's Advaita Vedānta *is* monistic and impersonal, as in Teilhard's description, although even here it is by no means the case that the Unity as conceived by Śaṅkara is essentially "materialistic" in the sense of being "homogeneous" and "absorbing" differences into itself. In a highly simplified way, one might grant that Śaṅkara "suppresses" the many to achieve his assumed perfect unity, but this very point is rejected by the philosophers who follow Śaṅkara: Rāmānuja, Madhava, Vallabha, Nimbarka, the disciples of Caitanya, and others.[293] And this is not a question of Western influence, as Teilhard claims, because the *Vedānta*

Sutras themselves, on which Śaṅkara wrote his commentaries, contain passages which quote recognized authorities of still earlier date who denied the precise doctrine on which the whole system of Śaṅkara depends: the doctrine of the absolute identity of the individual soul with Brahman.[294] The successors and opponents of Śaṅkara, as well as Western scholars, have shown that Śaṅkara's doctrine on this point is not faithful to the Upanishads or to the *Vedānta Sutras*.[295]

Moreover, most of Indian religion, beginning long before there could have been any influence from Christianity, is theistic and personal. The Śvetāśvatara Upanishad, the Epics, the Purānas, the teachings of the medieval saints, Vaiṣṇavism, Śaivism, Śaktism, all testify to the personal God of grace. In the general doctrine of the Upanishads, in which the two trends—toward monism and toward theism—begin to be differentiated, Brahman is described both as transcendent and as the material and efficient cause of the universe. Insofar as the human soul is eternal, it is at one with Brahman, but insofar as it lacks the creative power, it must be clearly distinguished from Brahman. "In Western terminology," says Zaehner, this means that the soul "partakes of Absolute Being, but is not for that reason God."[296] For instance, the human soul is sharply distinguished from the grace-extending divine Soul in the Kaṭha Upanishad, where it is said that the latter is not to be "attained by instruction, nor by intellect, nor by much learning. He is to be obtained only by the one whom he chooses; to such a one that Soul reveals his own person."[297]

The personal God is first identified with the Absolute in the Śvetāśvatara Upanishad. There Śiva indwells the human soul but is not identical with it. Worship is due him and his grace may be sought.[298] He is represented as the Lord who transcends both the finite and the infinite, as the one who creates the world, protects it for a time, and gathers all into final unity at the end of the age. He is both immanent and transcendent; as immanent, He may be known by yoga (jñāna),[299] and as transcendent He is to be worshiped with devotion (bhakti).[300]

Worship of a personal God is very old in India, Dasgupta tells us. The Bhāgavata forms of worship, involving images, were not Vedic in origin but at some point coalesced with Vedic religion, so that their advocates felt it necessary to claim that this worship was Vedic. Viṣṇu seems to have been the link. He was a Vedic god and he was also the supreme God and object of worship of the Bhāgavatas.[301] Two of the main sources for Bhakti religion, the attitude of devotion to a personal God, are the *Bhāgavata Purāṇa (Śrimad Bhāgavatam)* and the Bhagavad Gītā.[302] These documents are to be accepted as authoritative expositions of mainstream Hindu religious positions long before there could have been any question of a "Western influence" such as Teilhard suggests. "It may be believed," Dasgupta assures us, "that the views of the Vedānta, as found in the Purāṇas and the Bhagavad Gītā, present, at least in a general manner, the oldest outlook of the philosophy of the Upanishads and the *Brahmasutra.*"[303]

In the Gītā, the multiple world—which is a real universe, not an illusion—is considered as rooted in a transcendent Unity which is free of all differences. This is the Brahman of the Upanishads. But God, as the Puruṣottama, or Supreme Person, is higher still. Human souls, the physical world, and the Brahman may all be regarded as "constitutive essences" in the "complex personality of God," as Dasgupta puts it. It is God's own super-personality which is the principle of unity in all existence. His will "gives a unity and a purpose to all the different elements that are upheld within Him"[304]—surely an idea not so alien to Teilhard's conception of the cosmic Christ, principle of his "pan-Christism." The Gītā makes it clear that devotion to Kṛṣṇa is better than contemplation of the Absolute[305] and also warns that it is sincerity of love that counts, not outward elaboration of ritual.[306]

In the Gītā abstract philosophy is made concrete through the intimate personal relationship of Kṛṣṇa and Arjuna, which may be taken as a type of the relationship between God and man.[307] This relation is clearly one of difference; there is no question of some absorption of the individual into an unconscious One—the characteristic of all genuine Hinduism, according to Teilhard. As Parrinder says, "Religiously the Gita is not monistic, there is an abiding difference between God and man and this is not merely a matter of the present limited knowledge of [man]."[308] In fact, the greatest teaching of the Gītā—the "most secret" thing Kṛṣṇa has to tell Arjuna—is just that the highest attainment is a union of love with God in which the individual's personality is retained as distinct. The devotee finds his happiness in total love of the Lord and the Lord also is turned toward His devotee, whom He "loves dearly."[309]

This doctrine of loving communion with God, Zaehner tells us, constitutes a "decisive turning point in the history of Hinduism."[310] It is seized upon by later theistic philosophers and theologians as their central thesis. From this time on it constitutes the mainstream of the Hindu religion. Somehow Teilhard remained in complete ignorance of this obvious fact. In 1950, speaking of the Hindu renaissance and the interest in it shown in the West, he remarked, "An odd thing, this fascination with a religious attitude so faintly marked by the love of God." Without Christianity, he claimed, "the presence of a loving God would disappear from the psychological equipment of the world—darkness and coldness beyond any we could even begin to imagine. . . . The Church . . . is alone now in effectively preserving the idea and the experience of a *personal Godhead*."[311] Let us bear these remarks in mind as we now exhibit from Hindu religious history only a few of the most prominent refutations of this charge.

Rāmānuja, the great theologian of Vaiṣṇavism, delights in pointing out that God is the friend of all beings, a companion, one who loves men[312]; the highest goal of human life is the union of love with the Lord.[313] Rāmānuja represents God as saying that the one who loves Him "though he has come to possess me, is not himself destroyed, and though I give myself to one who worships me in this wise, it seems to me that I have done nothing for him."[314] Liberation, as conceived by Śaṅkara, that disappearance of the human soul in the abyss of the One which Teilhard attributed to all Hinduism, is spurned by Rāmānuja. It is the goal of selfish men who cultivate only their own souls; as an aim in life it is fit only for those who do not know how to love.[315] And, in fact, such destruction would not be courted even by one who truly loved himself. We seek liberation from the sufferings of this world, Rāmānuja admits, but not at the price of our own personal being. If someone realized that the effect of his effort to avoid pain "would be the loss of personal existence, he surely would turn away as soon as somebody began to tell him about release. . . . No sensible person exerts himself under the influence of the idea that after he himself has perished there will remain some entity termed 'pure light!' "[316]

Rāmānuja's conception of God is much more positive than an abstract "pure light." He says in his Commentary on the *Vedānta Sutras*:

> We know from Scripture that there is a Supreme Person whose nature is absolute bliss and goodness; who is fundamentally antagonistic to all evil; who is the cause of the origination, sustenation and dissolution; who differs in nature from all other beings, who is all-knowing, who by his mere thought and will accomplishes all his purposes; who is an ocean of kindness . . . for all who depend on him; who is all-merciful, who is immeasurably raised above all possibility of anyone being equal or superior to him.[317]

This is not an attitude so opposed to the genuine "fundamental concept" of Hinduism that it can be accounted for only by "the influence of an approximation to Western types of mysticism."[318] On the contrary, it clearly tallies with the description of God given in the Bhagavad Gītā, as we have already seen.

Vaiṣṇavism is not the only school of theism in India. In fact, the Śaiva Siddānta of South India is, in Zaehner's opinion, Hinduism's highest form of theism. It is the worship of Śiva, who is represented so as to give a very strong impression of transcendence and otherness. According to this system, the world is real and can be used by God to bring souls to their goal. God is transcendent and independent; the world and souls are dependent on Him. The soul is destined to be united with God but is not simply identified with Him. The soul and God must remain distinct from one another in order that they may love one another. God Himself is a Person, active but peaceful, having only one desire, to do good to His creatures. His law is summarized in love. Love is the indispensable virtue; no amount of other virtues can save one from sin if love is lacking.[319]

The theistic schools of India do not only encourage men to love God; they represent God as loving men. Typical of their descriptions would be such qualities as these:

> He gives knowledge to those who are ignorant, power to those who are weak, pardon to those who are guilty, mercy to the sufferers, paternal affection and overlooking of guilt to those who are guilty, goodness to those who are wicked, sincerity to the crooked, and goodness of heart to those who are wicked at heart. He cannot bear to remain separated from those who do not want to be separated from Him, and puts Himself within easy reach of those who want to see Him. When He sees people afflicted, He has mercy on them and helps them. Thus all His qualities are for the sake of others and not for Himself.[320]

Tulsidasa, the author of the Hindi *Rāmāyaṇa,* describes Rāma as "full of compassion, and of loving kindness for the destitute, disinterested in his benevolence."[321] And Rāmānuja emphasizes:

> We need not fear that the Supreme Lord, when once having taken to himself the devotee whom he greatly loves, will turn him back to samsara [transmigration]. For he himself has said, "To the wise man I am very dear, and he is dear to me."[322]

The avatar especially is an expression and embodiment of God's love for man, as the famous verse of the Gītā indicates: that it is for the sake of making Himself available to men and correcting the imbalance in their lives that the Lord descends into human flesh. Rāmānuja comments:

> [By his incarnation] he can be seen by the eyes of all men, for without putting aside his [divine] nature, he came down to dwell in the house of Vasudeva, to give light to the whole world with his indefectible and perfect glory, and to fill out all things with his own loveliness.[323]

All this is God's grace—an ancient doctrine much stressed in all forms of Hindu theism. In the *Mahābhārata* it is said: "That person upon whom Nārāyaṇa looks with compassion succeeds in becoming awakened. No one . . . can become awakened through his own wishes."[324] That the goal is attained through God's grace is mentioned in the later Upanishads (e.g., Kaṭha), it is clearly enunciated in the Śvetāśvatara, and of course, the doctrine is strong in the Bhagavad Gītā.[325] According to the Gītā, grace is the only final way to release. And, interestingly enough, it is not limited to devotees of Kṛṣṇa.[326] The doctrine of grace is emphasized by Rāmānuja, who was fond of quoting the Kaṭha Upanishad:

> This Ātman is not to be attained by instruction, nor by intellect, nor by much learning. He is to be obtained only by the one whom he chooses; to such a one this Ātman reveals his own person.[327]

Man's response to God's grace is *bhakti,* love and loyalty.[328] The bhakti movement has been present in India from the earliest days and became especially strong after the compiling of the Bhagavad Gītā. The Gītā ends by saying that the devotee should give up all duties (dharmas) and seek God as his refuge; he is not to fear, God will save him.[329] Why should not Teilhard appreciate this, who also said: "Have unbounded trust, and may all your thoughts and searchings end in a feeling of complete abandonment to the infallible and loving guidance of God. And, that this may be so, reject every other feeling and even every other personal pseudo-evidence."[330]

The fifteenth century poet Kabīr is one of India's great spokesmen for bhakti. It was the whole of religion, as far as he was concerned. No caste, no scriptures, no sectarian allegiance, no ceremonies or special modes of life, no philosophy had any importance for him. God is found in the depths of one's own consciousness: "Search in thy heart, search in thy heart of hearts; there is his place and abode."[331] Tulsidasa also rejected learning as a means of reaching God and urged worship and total devotion: "I have but one faith, O Ram, that I am called yours: —Yours, O friend of the wretched, is the compassion, and mine the wretchedness."[332] Perhaps Tukārāma took the strongest stand in this direction. The story is told that rather than listen to a reading on Advaita Vedānta, he put his fingers in his ears, afterward explaining:

> I cannot listen to the doctrine that God and His worshipper are one. . . . Between Himself and His worshipper God has drawn a line; this line we must recognize. A man may have perfect insight into God's nature, but he does not acquire God's power to create, preserve, and destroy; these attributes belong to God alone. So long as God in His three forms exercises these powers Himself let us mortals be humble and claim no identity with Him.[333]

Looking back, now, we can thoroughly appreciate the invalidity of Teilhard's criticism of all of Hinduism—even of all "Eastern religions"—under the blanket of a common notion of unity as a universal essence, ultimately material in nature, which absorbs everything into itself, destroying all individual features. It is also overwhelmingly clear that Hinduism is anything but a "religious attitude so faintly marked by the love of God" that without Christianity "the presence of a loving God would disappear from the psychological equipment of the world." Perhaps, drawing together a composite image of the religious/philosophical attitude which the Hindu traditions described here do offer, we can even see how congenial they are to Teilhard's own themes.

The cosmic divinity is a towering image for Hindus. The most important "missing piece" in the explicitly developed Christian tradition, the link which Teilhard most needed is here available in a form which protects simultaneously the infinitude and transcendence of the Absolute Being, His immanence in the creation which is dependent upon Him, His own personhood, and the intimacy and intensity of the personal relationship between Him and human persons. Consequently, there is no conflict between devotion to the personal God and to the material world, and cooperation with the progress of the universe is a religious duty.

The goal is a gathering of all creatures into union with God, but a union which preserves their distinction from Him and from each other. This is especially true of Rāmānuja's Viśiṣṭādvaita, the nondualism with distinction contained within the unity. It is not worked out expressly in terms of personalization, as Teilhard did it, but still it is not far from Teilhard's differentiated union. Teilhard proposes an organic union of the elements in Christ's Body—the unity of the "body" deriving from the "control exercised."[334] In the Viśiṣṭādvaita, the world and human souls also make up the "body of God," and the work done on the definition of "body" by the school of Rāmānuja might well have been useful to Teilhard. In no Hindu system does God "blend with" creation; He always remains transcendent and independent of the world. But, for the theists, through His avatars He touches the world personally and gathers it all into Himself cosmically. The mystical union is the final synthesis, and all one's own active efforts must be crowned by surrender to God's grace as the only way ultimately to arrive at the goal.[335]

There is a freedom in these Hindu conceptions which could have been of much value to Teilhard if he had taken the trouble to study them carefully and without preconceived judgments. As he himself remarked, the average Christian conception of the relation of God to the world was exceedingly narrow, being reduced to "the scale of 'juridical man.' "[336] This makes his hasty dismissal of the Indian philosophical systems all the more of a "pity," as Zaehner says, "since he might have found there insights akin to his own and used them to strengthen his position against the legalist postures of Rome."[337] These legalist postures of the Roman authorities in dealing with their subjects are intimately related to their whole juridical imagery in conceiving the relation of God to the world. This is the main obstacle which Teilhard had to overcome.

The Incarnation is clearly Teilhard's key to the reconciliation of the transcendent God and the evolving world, but it must be an Incarnation that is a genuinely *cosmic* event. "If . . . Christ is to be *able* to be the saviour and the life of souls . . . he must first satisfy certain conditions in relation to the world, apprehended in its experiential and natural reality."[338] What Teilhard needs is a strong doctrine of a God who reveals Himself as the cosmos. He does not really have this in Christianity as developed in his tradition. He has two or three texts from St. Paul and he makes maximum use of them. But what if he had also had the Bhagavad Gītā, in which God is equally transcendent, cosmic, and personal? Its very freedom from the juridical harness would have allowed him the scope he needed and would have supported him in holding together those seeming extremes which he felt must somehow be joined. Teilhard recognized that his difficulty in trying to assimilate the "religion of the Whole" into Christianity was due to "the antagonism between the God of supernatural revelation on one side and the great mysterious figure of the universe on the other."[339] But the Gītā rises imperturbably above these fine theological distinctions. As Dasgupta says:

> It is evident that the Gītā does not know that pantheism and deism and theism cannot well be jumbled up into one as a consistent philosophic creed. And it does not attempt to answer any objection that may be made against the combination of such opposite views. The Gītā not only asserts that all is God, but it also again and again repeats that God transcends all and is simultaneously transcendent and immanent in the world. The answer apparently implied in the Gītā to all objections to the apparently different views of the nature of God is that transcendentism, immanentism, and pantheism lose their distinctive and opposite characters in the melting whole of the super-personality of God.[340]

It is possible that by adopting the outlook of the Gītā and of Indian theism, Teilhard might have gotten more of a cosmic God than even he would have bargained for. He tells us that he rejects anything like a "hypostatic union" of God and the whole universe, such as was suggested, he says, by Eckhart and Spinoza. This would destroy "individual freedom and personal salvation."[341] Translating theological concepts from one tradition to another is not a practice to be recommended, but in a rough way we might grant that the Gītā does envision a kind of hypostatic union of God with the cosmos—at least the union is in the very substance of God, although it does not involve the whole of the Divine Being and in no way compromises His transcendence. But the unvierse does have its own *direct* union with the Lord, not merely an indirect union achieved only through the mediation of the personal being, as in Teilhard's system. This is an outstanding difference between Teilhard's Whole and that grasped by the Indian theocosmic traditions.

Teilhard acutely sensed this difference, but, in my view,

did not analyze it correctly. He accused the Hindus of reducing everything finally to matter, because they did not organize the universe and its tendency toward its end exclusively around human personal energies, as he did, conceiving it as a "personalizing universe." Perhaps what he never actually succeeded in doing is what the Hindu mainstream tradition has always done, that is, work in a genuinely *triadic* conceptual framework of God as transcendent, God as cosmic, and God as personal. Teilhard's third—the "cosmic nature" of Christ—never really stands as an independent dimension. His system has to fall back to a dyadic model: only two basic elements to be dealt with, God and man. In the final analysis *cosmos* is subsumed under *human person* and enters into the ultimate unity only under this form.

The further syntheses which Teilhard himself could not make, others may make after him. He had felt that the large currents of the Eastern, the Christian, and the humanist pantheisms were already starting to flow together.[342] In the formation of the cosmic sense, a collective task, "the nebula of ancient pantheisms condenses and takes shape at the heart of the modern world."[343] Each one has its special contribution to make: the transcendent and immanent cosmic person who is already a synthesis of several streams of Hindu thought; the personalizing union in which Christ, God and man take possession of the evolving universe; and the pragmatic sense of a great natural unity which may be subject to human intelligence by a cooperative effort of research, reflection, and action. This could be a great vision. Teilhard himself did not see quite so far. He even had a blind spot that deprived him of views useful to him. But he saw so much so well that it is difficult to blame him heavily for what he did not see.

REFERENCES

[1] Ainslie T. Embree, ed., *The Hindu Tradition* (New York: Modern Library, 1966), p. vii.

[2] Troy Wilson Organ, *The Hindu Quest for the Perfection of Man* (Athens: Ohio University, 1970), p. 3.

[3] A. C. Bouquet, *Comparative Religion* (Baltimore: Penguin fifth ed., 1956), p. 112.

[4] Cf. K. M. Sen, *Hinduism* (Baltimore: Penguin, 1961), p. 15.

[5] Cited by Sen, p. 21.
[6] Cited by Sen, p. 39.
[7] Bhagavad Gītā IV. 11 (Edgerton).
[8] Bhagavad Gītā IV.11 (Prabhavananda and Isherwood).
[9] See also the ninth hymn.
[10] Madeleine Biardeau, *India,* tr. F. Carter (New York: Viking, 1965), p. 149.
[11] Rig Veda X. 148. 4 (Bose).
[12] Sama Veda 231 (Bose).
[13] Rig Veda VII. 66. 16 (Bose); cf. Atharva Veda XIX. 67.
[14] Atharva Veda XIX. 60 (Bose).
[15] Yajur Veda 3. 17 (Bose).
[16] Rig Veda IV. 31. 1 (Bose).
[17] Sen, p. 18.
[18] *Ibid.,* pp. 46, 51.
[19] Rig Veda IV. 2. 11 (Bose).
[20] Rig Veda X. 121. 8, 10 (Bose).
[21] Rig Veda VI. 9. 5 (Bose).
[22] Rig Veda VI. 9. 6 (Bose).
[23] Atharva Veda X. 8. 43.
[24] Dorothea Jane Stephen, *Studies in Early Indian Thought* (Cambridge University Press, 1918).
[25] Organ, p. 99.
[26] Rig Veda I. 164. 46 (Bose).
[27] Atharva Veda X. 31 (Bose).
[28] Satischandra Chatterjee and Dhirendra Mohan Datta, *Introduction to Indian Philosophy* (University of Calcutta, 1968), p. 352.
[29] Atharva-Veda X.
[30] Franklin Edgerton, *The Beginnings of Indian Philosophy* (Cambridge: Harvard University Press, 1965), pp. 21-22.
[31] Atharva Veda X. 7. 4 (Bose).
[32] Atharva Veda X. 7. 15 (Bose).
[33] Atharva Veda X. 7. 22 (Bose).
[34] Cf. Abinash Chandra Bose, *Hymns from the Vedas* (New York: Asia Publishing House, 1966), p. 319.
[35] Rig Veda X. 90. 1-3 (Bose).
[36] Rig Veda X. 129. 1, 7 (Bose).
[37] Rig Veda X. 129. 3 (Bose).
[38] Subala Upanishad I (Radhakrishnan).
[39] *Ibid.*
[40] Chāndogya Upanishad 24. 1 (Radhakrishnan).
[41] *Ibid.,* 24. 1-2.
[42] *Ibid.,* 25. 1.
[43] Muṇḍaka Upanishad 3 (Radhakrishnan).
[44] Rig Veda X. 129. 2 (Bose).
[45] Atharva Veda X. 7. 7 (Bose).
[46] Atharva Veda X. 7. 4 (Bose).
[47] Atharva Veda X. 7. 1 (Bose).
[48] Chāndogya Upanishad 25. 1-2 (Radhakrishnan).
[49] Atharva Veda X. 7. 17 (Bose).
[50] Cf. R. C. Zaehner, *Hinduism* (New York: Oxford University Press, 1962), p. 18.
[51] Cf. Sisirkumar Mitra, *The Vision of India* (New York: Jaico, 1949), pp. 9-10.

[52] *Tagore for You,* ed. Sisirkumar Ghose (Calcutta: Visva-Bharati. 1966), pp. 19-20. Cf. Īśā Upanishad, verses 10 and 12.

[53] R. R. Diwakar, *Mahayogi Sri Aurobindo* (Bombay: Bharatiya Vidya Bhavan, 1962), p. 123.

[54] Atharva Veda XIII. 4 (Bose).

[55] Biardeau, p. 153.

[56] Mitra, p. 56, quoting Aurobindo's *A Defence of Indian Culture,* published in *Arya,* a periodical. Cf. A. C. Bose, *The Call of the Vedas* (Bombay: Bharatiya Vidya Bhavan, 1960), p. 79.

[57] Cf. Embree, pp. 27-28, 51-52; Bose, *Call,* pp. 62-64.

[58] Bhagavad Gītā IV. 24 (Prabhavananda-Isherwood).

[59] Rig Veda IV. 33. 11 (Bose).

[60] Rig Veda VIII. 70. 3 (Bose).

[61] Bhagavad Gītā V. 7, 8, 10, 6 (Edgerton).

[62] Kaṭha Upanishad II. 3. 1 (Radhakrishnan). Cf. Maitrī Upanishad VI. 4: "The three-footed Brahman has its root above. Its branches are space, wind, fire, water, earth, and the like." (Radhakrishnan).

[63] Rig Veda I. 24. 7 (Bose).

[64] Pierre Teilhard de Chardin, *The Divine Milieu* (New York: Harper & Row, 1960), p. 161.

[65] Teilhard, "The Spiritual Share of the Far East."

[66] Teilhard, *The Phenomenon of Man* (New York: Harper Torchbook, 1961), p. 296.

[67] Rig Veda X. 158. 4 (Bose).

[68] Yajur Veda 36. 24 (Bose).

[69] Rig Veda VIII. 54. 2 (Bose).

[70] Atharva Veda X. 8. 44 (Bose).

[71] Rig Veda IX. 84. 1 (Bose).

[72] Rig Veda VII. 41. 4 (Bose).

[73] Rig Veda X. 103. 13 (Bose).

[74] Atharva Veda XII. 2. 27 (Bose).

[75] Teilhard, *Writings in Time of War,* tr. René Hague (New York: Harper & Row, 1968), p. 59; cf. Teilhard, *The Future of Man,* tr. Norman Denny (New York: Harper & Row, 1964), p. 305.

[76] Henri de Lubac, *Teilhard de Chardin, The Man and His Meaning* (New York: Hawthorn, 1965), pp. 40 ff.

[77] *Ibid.,* pp. 35-36.

[78] *Ibid.,* p. 20.

[79] Col. 1: 15-18 RSV.

[80] Eph. 1: 17-23 RSV.

[81] Col. 1: 27-29 RSV.

[82] Rom. 8: 22-23 RSV.

[83] Teilhard, *Science and Christ,* tr. René Hague (New York: Harper & Row, 1968), pp. 165-66.

[84] C. C. Martindale, "Thy Labour under the Sun" in *Teilhard de Chardin: Pilgrim of the Future,* ed. Neville Braybrooke (New York: Seabury, 1964), p. 94.

[85] Pierre Smulders, *La Vision de Teilhard de Chardin* (Paris: Desclee de Brouwer, 1964), pp. 249-50.

[86] de Lubac, p. 41.

[87] *Ibid.*

[88] Teilhard, "Le Christique" (unpublished, 1955), p. 9; cf. de Lubac, pp. 40-41.

[89] Teilhard, "Comment je vois" (unpublished, 1948), no. 31; cf. de Lubac, p. 41.

[90] Christopher Mooney, *Teilhard de Chardin and the Mystery of Christ* (London: Collins, 1966), p. 79.

[91] Teilhard, *The Making of a Mind,* tr. René Hague (New York: Harper & Row, 1965), p. 300.

[92] Teilhard, *Hymn of the Universe* (New York: Harper & Row, 1965), p. 151.

[93] Ibid., p. 75.

[94] Teilhard, *The Divine Milieu* (New York: Harper & Row, 1960), pp. 154-55.

[95] Teilhard, *Writings in Time of War,* p. 175.

[96] Teilhard, *Hymn of the Universe,* pp. 152-53.

[97] Teilhard, *The Divine Milieu,* p. 127.

[98] *Ibid.*

[99] *Ibid.,* p. 128.

[100] Teilhard, *Writings in Time of War,* p. 253; cf. Mooney, p. 79.

[101] Teilhard, *Hymn of the Universe,* p. 153.

[102] Teilhard, *The Making of a Mind,* pp. 282-83.

[103] Teilhard, *The Future of Man,* tr. Norman Denny (New York: Harper & Row, 1964), p. 23.

[104] John 10: 16.

[105] Teilhard, *The Divine Milieu,* p. 65.

[106] Teilhard, *Writings in Time of War,* p. 299.

[107] *Ibid.,* p. 220.

[108] Teilhard, *The Divine Milieu,* pp. 121-22.

[109] *Ibid.,* p. 122.

[110] Teilhard, *Writings in Time of War,* p. 58.

[111] Teilhard, *Christianity and Evolution,* tr. René Hague (New York: Harcourt Brace Jovanovich, 1971), p. 96.

[112] Teilhard, *Letters from a Traveller* (New York: Harper & Row, 1962), p. 88.

[113] Teilhard, *The Divine Milieu,* p. 123.

[114] Teilhard, *Letters from a Traveller,* pp. 133, 305.

[115] Teilhard, *The Divine Milieu,* p. 117.

[116] Teilhard, *The Future of Man,* p. 24.

[117] *Ibid.,* p. 224.

[118] The passage is from "The Mass on the World," Teilhard, *The Hymn of the Universe,* p. 34, but I prefer this translation from Pierre Leroy's introductory essay in *The Divine Milieu,* p. 26. Cf. Rev. 1: 14-16.

[119] Rig Veda X. 90. 1-5 (Bose).

[120] Cf. Atharva Veda XI. 7.

[121] Rig Veda I. 164. 35 (Zaehner).

[122] Teilhard, *Hymn of the Universe,* p. 19.

[123] Cf. Rig Veda X. 130.

[124] Teilhard, *Christianity and Evolution* (New York: Harcourt Brace Jovanovich, 1971), p. 73-74; *The Divine Milieu,* p. 104.

[125] Cf. Teilhard, *The Future of Man,* p. 224.

[126] See Bose, *Hymns from the Vedas,* p. 285, note to stanza 5.

[127] Teilhard, *The Divine Milieu,* p. 26.

[128] Yajur Veda 31. 18 (Bose).

[129] Veronica Ions, *Indian Mythology* (London: Hamlyn, 1967), p. 15.

[130] *Ibid.,* p. 17.

[131] Cf. the New Testament, John 1: 3-4.

[132] Ions, p. 18.

[133] Zaehner, p. 41.

[134] Brihadāraṇyaka Upanishad I. 4. 1 (Radhakrishnan).

[135] *Ibid.,* I. 4. 3-5; II. 5. 1.

[136] *Ibid.,* III. 7. 15.

[137] Zaehner, p. 180.

[138] Īśā Upanishad, vs. 1 (Vasu and Thirlwall).

[139] *Ibid.,* vs. 5.

[140] S. Radhakrishnan, *The Principal Upanishads* (London: Allen & Unwin, 1953), p. 565.

[141] Īśā Upanishad, vs. 14 (Radhakrishnan).

[142] *Ibid.,* vss. 15, 16, 18.

[143] Radhakrishnan, p. 707.

[144] Śvetāśvatara Upanishad III. 11 (Radhakrishnan).

[145] *Ibid.,* I. 8, 10.

[146] *Ibid.,* II. 16; IV. 11.

[147] *Ibid.,* IV. 9-10.

[148] *Ibid.,* V. 2, 4, 5.

[149] *Ibid.,* VI. 6.

[150] *Ibid..* VI. 16.

[151] *Ibid.,* VI. 7.

[152] Derivation seems to be from *viṣlṛ,* to spread in all directions. Alain Danielou, *Hindu Polytheism* (New York: Pantheon, 1964), p. 149.

[153] Ions, pp. 22-23.

[154] Some call this the Hindu Trinity, pointing out similarities to Christian symbols in Brahmā, the Origin and Creator of all, Viṣṇu, the one concerned to promote human life, acting as Mediator between God and man, especially in his human avataras, and Śiva, the deity associated with wind and flame, giver of fertility (cf. "Vivificator," a name of the Holy Spirit). Alain Danielou (*op. cit.,* p. 24 n.7) suggests another arrangement in which Śiva corresponds to the Father because of Śiva's symbol, the linga, the male organ of procreation, and Brahmā represents the Holy Spirit, interpreted as the link between Father and Son, because Brahmā is associated with the force in the universe which reconciles contrifugal and centripetal forces. Viṣṇu again corresponds to the Second Person because of his function as protector, mediator, redeemer. However, Zaehner remarks, and rightly, I think, that if one is looking for Hindu parallels to the Christian Trinity, a much better one can be found in the conception of the Absolute as Sat (Being) Chit (Consciousness) Ānanda (Bliss). R. C. Zaehner, *Evolution in Religion* (Oxford: Clarendon Press, 1971), p. 55.

[155] Cf. Ions, p. 46.

[156] *Ibid.,* p. 47.

[157] Cf. Organ, p. 264.

[158] Śatapatha-brāhmaṇa XIV. 1. Cited in Surendranath Dasgupta, *A History of Indian Philosophy* (Cambridge University Press, 1968), II. 536.

[159] Gopāla-uttara-tāpinī Upanishad 55-57 (Danielou, p. 153).

[160] *Viṣṇu Purāṇa* 1. 22. 68 (Danielou, p. 157).

[161] Dasgupta, II. 537.

[162] *Mahābhārata* XII. 341. 41 (Dasgupta, II. 541).

[163] Danielou, p. 151.

[164] Ions, p. 46.

[165] *Mahābhārata* V. 70. 13 (Danielou, p. 149).

[166] Danielou, p. 150. Cf. some Christian Logos theologies.

[167] *Mahābhārata,* Adi Parva 58. 51.

[168] Danielou, p. 149.
[169] *Ibid.*
[170] Dasgupta, II. 532.
[171] Parrinder, p. 19.
[172] Bhagavad Gītā IV. 5-8.
[173] These ten are called Yuga avatāras, because they appear according to the great ages of the world. There are also partial descents of the Lord into many saints and devotees, and there are two other lists of mythic avatāras, the *Bhāgavata Purāṇa* (1. 3. 6-25) naming twenty-two and the *Ahirbudhya Saṁhita* (5. 50-57), thirty-nine. See Danielou, p. 165.
[174] Ions, p. 61.
[175] Dasgupta, II. 539. It occurs in the *Ghatajataka* II. 542.
[176] *Mahābhārata VI.* 66 (Dasgupta, II. 543). Compare John 5: 23: ". . . that all may honor the Son, even as they honor the Father. He who does not honor the Son does not honor the Father who sent him." Bhagavad Gītā IX. 11 (Edgerton): "Fools despise Me, that have assumed human form, not knowing the higher state of Me, which is the great lord of beings." John 6: 52. 60-62: "The Jews then disputed among themselves, saying, 'How can this man give us his flesh to eat?' . . . Many of his disciples, when they heard it, said, 'This is a hard saying; who can listen to it?' But Jesus, knowing in himself that his disciples murmured at it, said to them. 'Do you take offense at this? Then what if you were to see the Son of Man ascending where he was before?' "
[177] *Viṣṇu Purāṇa* 6. 5. 74-78 (Danielou, p. 36).
[178] John Dowson, *A Classical Dictionary of Hindu Mythology* (London: Trübner's Oriental Series, 1891), p. 160.
[179] Cf. the massacre of the innocents in Matt. 2: 13 ff.
[180] Ions, p. 61.
[181] *Mahābhārata* XII. 340.
[182] Dasgupta II. 544; Radhakrishnan, p. 22.
[183] *Epigraphica Indica,* Vol. 10, Inscription No. 669.
[184] Cf. Danielou, p. 175.
[185] Dasgupta II. 532.
[186] Kṛṣṇa Upanishad 1. 26, Danielou, p. 178.
[187] Swami Prabhavananda, *The Wisdom of God* (Hollywood: Vedanta Press, 1943), p. 190, a paraphrase of the *Śrimad Bhāgavatam,* or *Bhāgavata Purāṇa,* X. 2.
[188] *Ibid.,* p. 191, *Bhāgavata Purāṇa* X. 3. Anyone familiar with Christian liturgical literature will recognize the parallels.
[189] Organ, p. 265.
[190] Zaehner, *Hinduism,* p. 93.
[191] Dasgupta II. 551.
[192] Bhagavad Gītā III. 24.
[193] *Ibid.,* VII. 5-10 (Edgerton). Cf. also Gītā X, where Kṛṣṇa identifies Himself with a long list of beings and categories of being.
[194] *Ibid.,* IX. 4-5 (Edgerton).
[195] *Ibid.,* IX. 16-19 (Edgerton).
[196] *Ibid.,* VII. 6 (Edgerton).
[197] *Ibid.,* VII. 26 (Edgerton).
[198] *Ibid.,* X. 20 (Edgerton).
[199] Teilhard, *Hymn of the Universe,* p. 76.
[200] *Ibid.,* p. 152.
[201] Bhagavad Gītā VII. 13 (Edgerton).

[202] *Ibid.*, VII. 19 (Edgerton).
[203] Teilhard, *Christianity and Evolution*, p. 74.
[204] Bhagavad Gītā X. 42 (Edgerton).
[205] Teilhard, *Hymn of the Universe*, p. 91.
[206] Bhagavad Gītā XI. 10-11, 16, 23, 24, etc. (Edgerton).
[207] *Ibid.*, XI. 12-13 (Edgerton).
[208] *Ibid.*, XI. 15, 16, 21, 26, 27, 28, 30, 18, 37 (Edgerton).
[209] Teilhard, *Hymn of the Universe*, pp. 44-46. The visions are fictions, but accurately express Teilhard's own feelings and perceptions.
[210] *Ibid.*, pp. 48-49.
[211] Bhagavad Gītā XI. 44 (Edgerton).
[212] *Mahābhārata* XIV. 55; cf. V. 13.
[213] Teilhard, *Hymn of the Universe*, p. 54.
[214] *Ibid.*, p. 76.
[215] Bhagavad Gītā XII. 1 (Edgerton).
[216] *Ibid.*, XII. 5-8 (Edgerton).
[217] Kṛṣṇa had already declared Himself to be the ground of Brahman: "I am the foundation of Brahman, the . . . imperishable." *Ibid.*, XIV. 27 (Edgerton).
[218] *Ibid.*, XV. 16-18 (Edgerton).
[219] *Ibid.*, XV. 19 (Edgerton).
[220] *Ibid.*, IV. 3; VII. 25; XI. 52-54; XVIII. 56-58. 62-64. Cf. the New Testament, John 14: 22-23.
[221] Cf. Dasgupta II. 478.
[222] Zaehner, *Evolution in Religion*, p. 70.
[223] Zaehner, *Hinduism*, p. 93.
[224] Bhagavad Gītā XVIII. 68 (Edgerton).
[225] *Ibid.*, XVIII. 55 (Edgerton).
[226] Cf. Organ, pp. 263-64.
[227] J. S. M. Hooper, *Hymns of the Alvars* (Calcutta: Association Press, 1929), p. 86. The references are to Kṛṣṇa's early days with his foster parents, when He herded cows (whence He is frequently called Govinda) and sported with the cowgirls (gopis). and to the myth of Viṣṇu, whose avatar He is, in which the god takes giant steps through the heavens.
[228] Cf. Zaehner, *Hinduism*, pp. 144-45.
[229] Cf. Bhagavad Gītā XVIII. 64.
[230] Dasgupta IV. 410.
[231] *Ibid.*, IV. 442.
[232] *The Vedānta-Sutras with the Commentary of Rāmānuja*, 2. 1. 33. *Sacred Books of the East*, Vol. 48, p. 477.
[233] Cf. Dasgupta III. 156.
[234] See Dasgupta III. 298.
[235] Cf. Dasgupta III. 299.
[236] Dasgupta II. 525.
[237] Parrinder, pp. 120-26.
[238] *Ibid.*, pp. 233-37.
[239] It may be pointed out, however, that these two charges cannot be made against Śrī Rāmakrishna and Śrī Sārada Devi, who lived in the second half of the nineteenth century and are today widely accepted as avatars.
[240] Teilhard, *Human Energy*, tr. J. M. Cohen (New York: Harcourt Brace Jovanovich, 1969), p. 152.
[241] Teilhard, *Writings in Time of War*, p. 121.
[242] Teilhard, *The Divine Milieu*, p. 57.

[243] *Ibid.*, p. 116.

[244] Teilhard, *Writings in Time of War*, p. 28.

[245] *Ibid.*, pp. 32-33.

[246] *Ibid.*, pp. 30-31.

[247] Teilhard, *The Phenomenon of Man*, p. 262.

[248] Teilhard, *Hymn of the Universe*, p. 22.

[249] *Ibid.*, p. 53. The words are put in the mouth of a fictitious character but it is evident from the context that the character is expressing Teilhard's own ideas and feelings.

[250] Teilhard, *Science and Christ*, pp. 43-44.

[251] Teilhard, *The Making of a Mind*, p. 84.

[252] Teilhard. *The Phenomenon of Man*, p. 266.

[253] Teilhard, *Christianity anl Evolution*, pp. 56-75.

[254] *Ibid.*, p. 56.

[255] *Ibid.*, pp. 56-57; cf. *The Making of a Mind*, p. 91.

[256] *Ibid.*, pp. 57-58.

[257] *Ibid.*, p. 60.

[258] *Ibid.*, p. 60.

[259] Cf. *ibid.*, p. 62.

[260] Teilhard, *Human Energy*, p. 130.

[261] Teilhard, *Christianity and Evolution*, p. 123.

[262] Cf. Teilhard. *Human Energy*, p. 67, and *Christianity and Evolution*, p. 75.

[263] Teilhard, *Christianity and Evolution*, pp. 136-37; cf. p. 171.

[264] *Ibid.*, pp. 128-29.

[265] Teilhard, *The Phenomenon of Man*, p. 308.

[266] Teilhard, *Christianity and Evolution*, p. 129; cf. *The Divine Milieu*, p. 118.

[267] Teilhard, *The Divine Milieu*, p. 122.

[268] Teilhard, *Writings in Time of War*, p. 51.

[269] Teilhard, *Christianity and Evolution*. pp. 68-69.

[270] *Ibid.*, pp. 125-26.

[271] Teilhard, *Human Energy*, pp. 90-91.

[272] Teilhard, *The Phenomenon of Man*, p. 294.

[273] Teilhard, *Christianity and Evolution*, p. 71. Cf. Ephesians 4. 9-10.

[274] It is also called by Teilhard the "Pleroma." Cf. Donald P. Gray, *The One and the Many:* Teilhard de Chardin's Vision of Unity (New York: Herder, 1969), pp. 123-25.

[275] Cf. Teilhard, *Letters from a Traveller*, p. 302 n.3.

[276] Cf. Teilhard, *The Phenomenon of Man*, p. 308, and *Christianity and Evolution*, p. 75.

[277] Teilhard, *Human Energy*, p. 93.

[278] Cf. *ibid.*, p. 69.

[279] Teilhard, *Christianity and Evolution*, p. 171; cf. p. 117.

[280] Teilhard, *Human Energy*, p. 142.

[281] Teilhard, *The Divine Milieu*, p. 116.

[282] Teilhard, *Writings in Time of War*, p. 28.

[283] Unpublished manuscript.

[284] Teilhard, *Christianity and Evolution*, p. 124.

[285] Teilhard, *Writings in Time of War*, p. 29.

[286] Teilhard, *Christianity and Evolution*, p. 121.

[287] *Ibid.*, p. 122.

[288] *Ibid.*, p. 122.

[289] *Ibid.*

[290] *Ibid.*, n.9, italics added.

[291] Maryse Choisy, *Teilhard et l'Inde,* Carnets Teilhard 11 (Paris: Ed. Univ., 1963), pp. 12-14.

[292] Zaehner, *Evolution in Religion,* p. 23.

[293] Cf. Zaehner, *Hinduism,* p. 100.

[294] Cf. *The Vedānta Sūtras of Bādarāyaṇa, with the Commentary by Śaṇkara,* tr. George Thibaut, *The Sacred Books of the East* (New York: Dover, 1962), I. xx.

[295] Cf. P. M. Modi, *A Critique of the Brahma-Sūtra* (Bhavnagar: Modi, 1943).

[296] Zaehner, *Hinduism,* p. 55; cf. p. 80.

[297] Kaṭha Upanishad 2. 32 (Hume).

[298] See Śvetāśvatara Upanishad III.13; II.17. Cf. Zaehner, *Hinduism,* pp. 83-84.

[299] *Ibid.,* V. 13 (Radhakrishnan).

[300] *Ibid.,* VI. 23 (Radhakrishnan); cf. Zaehner, *Hinduism,* pp. 81, 84.

[301] Dasgupta II. 547.

[302] Cf. Organ, p. 270.

[303] Dasgupta III. 496. *"Brahmā-sutra"* is another name for the *Vedānta-sūtras* referred to earlier as the authoritative statement of Vendānta philosophy.

[304] Dasgupta II. 477.

[305] Bhagavad Gītā XII.

[306] *Ibid.,* IX. 26. Compare IX. 27 with the New Testament, I Cor. 10: 31:

Whatever thou doest, whatever thou eatest,
Whatever thou offerest in oblation or givest,
Whatever austerity thou performest, . . .
That do as an offering to Me. (Edgerton)

So, whether you eat or drink. or whatever you do.
do all to the glory of God. (RSV)

[307] Cf. Dasgupta II. 525.

[308] Parrinder, p. 225.

[309] Bhagavad Gītā XVIII. 65.

[310] Zaehner, *Hinduism,* p. 98.

[311] Teilhard, *Letters from a Traveller,* n. 302 p.3. Cf. *Christianity and Evolution,* p. 90.

[312] Cf. Bhagavad Gītā V. 29, XI. 41, XVIII. 64.

[313] Cf. Organ. p. 273, referring to Rāmānuja's commentary on the Bhagavad Gītā.

[314] Rāmānuja, *Commentary on the Bhagavad-Gītā,* 9. 2 (Zaehner, *Hinduism,* p. 100).

[315] *Ibid.,* 12. 11-12.

[316] *The Vedānta-Sūtras, with the Commentary of Rāmānuja, The Sacred Books of the East* Vol. 48, p. 70.

[317] Rāmānuja, *Commentary on the Vedānta-Sūtra,* 4. 4, 22.

[318] Teilhard, *Christianity and Evolution,* p. 122.

[319] Cf. Zaehner, *Hinduism,* pp. 88-91.

[320] Dasgupta III. 158, discussing the thought of Lokacarya.

[321] Tulsidasa, *Rāmacharitmānasa,* Book 7.

[322] Rāmānuja. *Commentary on the Vedānta-Sūtras,* 4. 4. 22.

[323] Rāmānuja, *Commentary on the Bhagavad-Gītā,* 6. 47.

[324] *Mahābhārata* XII. 349.

[325] See, *e.g.,* Bhagavad Gītā XI. 50, 53. Cf. Zaehner, *Hinduism,* p. 96.

[326] Bhagavad Gītā VII. 21.

[327] Kaṭha Upanishad 2. 23 (Hume).

[328] See Organ, p. 273 and Zaehner, *Evolution in Religion,* p. 33. Compare *pistis* in the Christian tradition and the thesis of Bishop Nygren *(Agape and Eros)* that *pistis* is the believer's response to God's initial love *(agape).*

[329] Bhagavad Gītā XVIII. 66.

[330] Teilhard, *The Making of a Mind,* p. 283.

[331] Kabir, *Adi Granth, Prabhati* 2.

[332] Tulsidasa, *Kavitavali,* tr. F. R. Allchin (London: Allen & Unwin, 1964), p. 154.

[333] J. N. Fraser and J. F. Edwards, *The Life and Teachings of Tukārām* (Madras: Christian Literature Society for India, 1922), pp. 102-3.

[334] Teilhard, *Christianity and Evolution,* p. 70.

[335] To see that these are the very points with which Teilhard was concerned, see again pp. (15, 28, 36-37).

[336] Teilhard, *Christianity and Evolution,* p. 125.

[337] Zaehner, *Evolution in Religion,* p. 17.

[338] Teilhard, *Christianity and Evolution,* p. 127 n.10.

[339] *Ibid.,* p. 65.

[340] Dasgupta II. 527.

[341] Teilhard, *Christianity and Evolution,* p. 69.

[342] *Ibid.,* p. 130.

[343] Teilhard, *Human Energy,* p. 158.

3

THE EVOLUTION OF CONSCIOUSNESS

Complexity/Consciousness and Sāṃkhya

Some of the Hindu traditions, as we have just seen, could have been of considerable help to Teilhard in the elaboration of his thesis of the "cosmic Christ." They would also have been most congenial to the whole idea of evolution—with which he and others had so much difficulty in the Christian West—and particularly congenial to his special idea of the evolution of consciousness. In this chapter we want to look at several topics in this general area: first, the notion of evolution itself in the setting of the immensity of space-time; then in greater detail at Teilhard's "law of complexity/consciousness" and some parallels in the Hindu duality of Prakṛti/Puruṣa; more generally again, we shall examine Teilhard's central conception of the unicity of psychic energy which nevertheless takes various forms, compared with the Hindu notion of Śakti; finally, we will spend some time on Teilhard's idea of the future evolution of consciousness in some collective form, where we will find a very similar projection in the philosophy of Śrī Aurobindo.

Evolution has never been a problem for the Hindus as it has been for the Christians. Even those schools which regarded the phenomenal world as "unreal," when compared with the absolute and eternal Brahman, considered that evolution took place within this phenomenal world in a phenomenal way. In fact, the image of one form arising from another, forms passing into one another, the continuity of life underlying the inconceivably intricate shifting patterns of "name and form"—this is the characteristic Hindu image of the world. It is true that "evolution" does not always mean in an Indian system exactly what it means today in the scientific language of the West. There are similarities and dissimilarities, sometimes important ones. But a basic notion of evolution as "a course of change of what is real, a change from one state into another of what always exists as a positive entity" is common to a broad tradition of Hindu thinkers.[1]

Unfortunately, Teilhard was either unaware of this or unable to situate its positive significance. Take, for instance, the notion of great stretches of time, which the idea of evolution necessarily involves. The realization of the immensity of the past had come as a great shock to the West. Teilhard remarks in wonder that "less than two hundred years ago, the world's leading thinkers did not imagine a past and would not have dared to promise themselves a future of more than six or eight thousand years."[2] It was only, he says, "from the eighteenth century onwards" that we began to accept the idea that the world was much older than that. Even then the estimates of the world's age were "still very modest." But gradually, "under the unceasing pressure of facts," our conception of the time span has increased and increased, and still has not come to rest.[3] "The most magnificent discovery of our time," Teilhard proclaims, "is that we have become conscious of the abyss of the past."[4] And, oddly enough, considering the terrific battles that have been fought over the issue of evolution in the Christian churches, Teilhard felt free to state broadly that every religion other than Christianity has been halted in its tracks by the obstacle of the universe perceived as evolution.[5]

But "the abyss of the past" is not a "discovery of our time" at all. It was quite familiar to Hindus centuries before the opening of the Christian era. It is a presupposition of the Purāṇas (scriptures dealing with ancient history) that, as Professor Ainslee Embree says, "human existence must be seen against a background of an almost unimaginable duration of time."[6]

> In contrast to other civilizations which have been content to see man's history in terms of thousands of years, Indians—Buddhists and Jains as well as Hindus—speak of billions of years.[7]

In the Bhagavad Gītā Kṛṣṇa tells Arjuna that they really understand what "day" and "night" are who understand them as the "day" and the "night" of Brahmā, each "compassing a thousand world-ages."[8] (The Gītā is here repeating what was originally said in the *Manu-Smṛti,* a much older document.) A "world-age," or *yuga,* is a historical period. The Hindus speak of four yugas: *Kṛita,* lasting 1,728,000 years; *Tretā,* 1,296,000 years; *Dvāpara,* 864,000 years; and *Kali,* 432,000 years. A "day of Brahmā," or *kalpa,* is considered to be 4,320 million years long—which does not compare badly with modern science's estimate of the age of the earth. Moreover, there is an even vaster time span, the "year of Brahmā," calculated by some at 311,040,000 million years.[9]

These enormous ages supported continuous processes of evolution—and of devolution, according to the Hindu concept. Human social relations and virtues, for instance, are supposed to have deteriorated from the Kṛta (golden) age to the Kali (iron) age. On the other hand, in the mythology of the Yuga Avatars of Viṣṇu we see a progression of life.

We may recall that in the last chapter, when we were discussing the avatars of Viṣṇu, we noted that they formed a series and that some of them were in animal forms. These are the Yugavatars, the avatars who come appropriately for each age of the world. It is worth pointing out that the series follows in general form the sequence uncovered by scientific evolutionists: marine life (Fish), amphibians (Tortoise), mammals (Boar), the "missing link" from animal to man (Man-Lion), the most primitive type of man (Dwarf), stone-age man (Rāma with Ax), feudal man (King Rāma), romantic man (Kṛṣṇa), scientific man (Buddha), and the man or superman of the future (Kalki).

The Hindu mind was capable of expansion not only with respect to time but also in regard to space and diversity of worlds. The Vedic people felt that the universe was much greater than they could experience. They spoke of three worlds, two of which were unseen by men, only one of them lying within our experience.[10] The Rig Veda sings of "a hundred earths," "a thousand suns."[11] And a recommended yogic practice was meditation on the infinitude of space.[12]

Somehow Teilhard must not have known these things or not have been able to appreciate their potentials for his thought, for he says that the "cosmic outlook" of modern science has caused such a crisis in "the ancient religions," (among which we may be confident that he numbered Hinduism) that "if they have not yet been killed by it, it is plain they will never recover." In their "pessimistic and passive mysticism" they are unable to "adjust themselves" to the "immensities . . . of space-time."[13]

But now let us go into the matter of evolution in more detail, considering in particular Teilhard's "Law of Complexity/Consciousness." We have touched on most of the central ideas in Teilhard's theory of evolution already, of course. It is impossible to say anything about Teilhard without mentioning and explaining it to some degree. However, our point now shall be to explore just how complexity and consciousness are related, how consciousness guides evolution, and finally how in the unity of psychic energy, it turns out that the evolution of the cosmic stuff is actually the evolution of consciousness itself. Each of these topics will offer opportunities for Hindu parallels which we will point out as we proceed.

The first general principle of organization of the universe which Teilhard notes is that of "corpusculization." The cosmic "stuff" is not continuous but tends to clump, to gather itself into discrete entities. Only so can it begin the business of synthesizing unions of the diverse multiple. "Fuller being consists of closer union," Teilhard had said, enunciating what he took to be a fundamental principle of the cosmic organization. But this presupposes a variety of items to be united as well as a uniting principle. And these conditions can be realized only in a universe which orders itself in terms of corpuscles. If reality were simply an evenly distributed homogeneous continuum of energy, there would be no structure: no differences, and hence no unions. This is an important point, for on it depends Teilhard's further principle that *union differentiates,* the foundation for his mysticism of personal union, as against a mysticism of total absorption.

Early Hindu philosophy, too, affirmed the atomic nature of matter. The Vaiśeṣika system reduced all finite beings to nine substances, four of which were material (earth, water, light, and air) and composed of unitary particles which could be neither produced nor destroyed. The Vaiśeṣikas argued that although an atom cannot be perceived, one can validly conclude that it must exist in order to account for the existence of composed beings. Composed beings are made up of parts; but if they are taken apart, one must eventually come to certain basic units which do not have parts. These are the atoms (paramāṇus). But the atoms are diverse in quality in order that their many different combinations may account for the variety of observable things in the world.[14] The physical world is made up of these atoms organized as structures of structures of structures; that is, more complex beings are organizations of less complex beings which in turn are organizations of the basic atoms.[15]

This principle of using previously composed structures as units in further building is what Teilhard calls a "recurrent pattern" in nature. It is not merely a matter of binding smaller units into larger ones. The trajectory of cosmic evolution does not run from the atomic nucleus to the supergalaxy. It runs rather from the inorganic to the organic to the living to the thinking: the path of increasing complexification.[16]

This is the kind of unification which is creative, Teilhard contends. Indeed, it is the only kind of unification which is genuinely progressive, that is, in which the unification process itself advances. By complexification the *quality of the unity* produced increases rapidly. A chunk broken off a crystal of salt does not change the quality of the whole —in fact, it is not clear what a "whole" crystal would be— but what happens to a molecule of hemoglobin if the iron atom is removed? And a limb or an organ removed from an animal obviously mutilates and may even destroy the unity of its being. The elements bound in an organic union *do* constitute a "whole" in a more and more precise sense as we go up the scale. Each element becomes more and more essential to this wholeness, so that the "unity" itself becomes more and more intense. Seeing reality in terms of such "wholeness" is one of the perspectives which Teilhard recommends as vital to our understanding of the past and our grasp of the energies which are drawing us into the profounder unities of the future.

In Hinduism's Sāṃkhya theory of evolution, it is also a matter of producing more and more integrated wholes. It is a rather intricate system, and we will have to build up to an understanding of its conception of graduated complexity in evolved beings. Along the way, though, we may note several points of interest for Teilhard.

Sāṃkhya may be the world's oldest theory of evolution, its ideas first starting to take shape about the seventh century B.C. or earlier.[17] It holds that there are two fundamental principles in the universe: Puruṣa, or person, sometimes translated "soul," and Prakṛti, the cosmic stuff, usually—and misleadingly—rendered "matter."[18] The evolution takes place in Prakṛti only, the Puruṣas (who are many) remaining uninvolved. This would seem to be a basic disagreement with Teilhard's scheme in which consciousness plays such an essential role, but we must first look more closely at what is included in Prakṛti to see how consciousness is contained in it, and then look at the relation of Puruṣa to Prakṛti, which may also be seen in a certain parallel to Teilhard's ideas.

Prakṛti is said to be composed of three distinct types of reality, called *guṇas.* The word does not translate easily; most scholars settle for "qualities." Literally *guṇa* means "strand," the image being drawn from spinning and weaving, in which different strands are twisted or woven or tied together to compose a variety of products. The world's guṇas are *tamas, rajas,* and *sattva.* Tamas is the quality of inertia. On the physical level it accounts for mass, with its characteristics of impenetrability and heaviness. Of the three guṇas it most closely corresponds to what the West calls "matter." It is the principle of passivity and negativity; it manifests as indifference and as obstruction. On the vital level it relates to sleep and lethargy. On the psychic level it produces ignorance, confusion, and mental and moral opaqueness. Rajas is the quality of activity. Physically it is energy, the dynamic principle in things. Vitally it is stimulation, sensation, even pain. Psychically it is restlessness of mind, curiosity, drive to achieve. Sattva is the quality of light. In inanimate objects it is associated with brilliance, buoyancy and expansion. Among the living it brings consciousness and pleasure. On the level of thought it is reflection, intelligence, intuition, luminosity of insight, and it produces contentment, happiness, and bliss.[19]

The guṇas are not perceived in their pure state. The phenomenal world is composed of various complex corpuscular arrangements of them. Without this corpusculization, the world would have no form; Prakṛti would be one vast undifferentiated homogeneous plenum. And indeed, Sāṃkhya postulates that "in the beginning" the world was such a homogeneous indeterminate unity. Teilhard supposes something rather similar. Although from the outset the world must have been particulate, he says, the particles were so alike as to constitute a unity of homogeneity in which differentiation was totally lacking.[20] According to Sāṃkhya, the original equilibrium of the guṇas is disturbed and they begin to enter into various combinations with one another. The process of gradual aggregation results in more and more heterogeneity, interrelatedness, and organized unity.[21] According to Teilhard, some principle of organization begins to work within the primeval homogeneity, arranging the original particles and ordering their several energies in terms of "collective bonds."[22] And it is true to say for both what B. N. Seal says in his *Positive Sciences of the Ancient Hindus* of the Sāṃkhya system:

> The order of succession is neither from parts to whole nor from whole to the parts, but ever from a relatively less differentiated, less determinate, less coherent whole to a relatively more differentiated, more determinate, more coherent whole.[23]

If we are to understand Teilhard's world in terms of a gradually increasing unification, we may also notice that the world at any given moment always constitutes a total unity with respect to any particular degree of organization. As inorganic, it is not just a random collection of atoms, but a stellar universe ranked in systems, galaxies, and supergalaxies. As living, it is a biosphere in which the living organisms are not separate from one another but form a network of vital links of increasing intricacy.[24] And as thinking, the world is a noosphere of intercommunicating psychic energies.[25] Each of these spheres is built up on its predecessors without displacing them.

In the Sāṃkhya system, Dasgupta tells us, the "guṇas once thrown out of balance begin to group themselves together first in one form, then in another, then in another. . . . But . . . not . . . in such a way that the later aggregations appear in supersession of the former ones. . . . For . . . one stage is produced after another; this second stage is the result of a new aggregation of some of the reals of the first stage."[26] By a process of integration of previous stages, successive distinct levels of being are evolved.

The impulse toward more intense unions is conceived by Teilhard as a kind of interior pressure which gradually builds up until certain "critical points" or "thresholds," are reached at which significant changes take place. This pressure represents the universal effort to "grow and fulfill itself," which Teilhard feels lies at the root of the living universe. The mechanism involved here rests on the principle that "no reality in the world can go on increasing without sooner or later reaching a critical point involving some change of state."[27] A favorite example of Teilhard's is the boiling of water. If heat energy is constantly added to liquid water, the temperature of the water will increase at a constant rate until the boiling point is reached. Then, as more energy is added, no change at all takes place for a while, until a sufficient quantity of energy as been added, when suddenly the liquid water at boiling temperature changes into gaseous water at the same temperature. From a change in *degree* (increase in temperature), there has been a passage to a change of *state* (from liquid to gas). This rule can be verified on all levels of reality, Teilhard contends. Critical speeds produce changes in mass. Critical masses of radioactive materials set off nuclear explosions. Critical size of embryonic cells stimulates cell division. Critical buildup of electrical charge on a neuron triggers discharge to neighboring cells.[28] Extending this image to the evolutionary process,

Teilhard suggests that an accumulation of elements organized in a given way will persist only to a certain point, at which there will be a sudden leap or breakthrough to a new *type* of arrangement which will assimilate the former arrangement as an element in the new organization. Because the pressure to expand and to unify is always present and never decreases, it is inevitable that such leaps should occur, Teilhard says.[29]

Similarly, in Sāṃkhya, according to Dasgupta:

> Evolution (tattvantaraparinama) . . . means the development of categories of existence and not mere changes of qualities of substances. Thus each of the stages of evolution remains as a permanent category of being, and offers scope to the more and more differentiated and coherent groupings of the succeeding stages.[30]

Teilhard points out that the new being is substantially composed of the earlier arrangements of matter, and so if it is taken apart, these earlier arrangements will be discovered. But the way in which these elements were structured in the more complex being will thereby be destroyed and its distinctive nature lost. A given pattern of arrangement is always irreducible to the elements which it arranges. It cannot therefore be "explained" by analysis into these elements and their modes of activity. This is why evolutionists say that the novel level of being "emerges" from the earlier stages.[31] Again it is a question of realizing that to understand our world composed of internally differentiated unities, we must understand phenomena as *wholes.* The intelligibility of the being lies precisely in its organization as a whole and not in its reduction to component elements.[32] This means that its reality lies in its mode of organization, in the very pattern in which its constituent energies are arranged. To some minds this may be frustrating, because "nothing we are able to touch is the real *consistency* . . . while . . . the real consistency of the world we are unable to touch."[33]

Evolution thus is seen to advance by stages, acquiring in the course of time more and more complex levels of arrangement of the various types of corpuscles. These levels are like rings on the tree of life, revealing its history even while constituting its substance.[34] Life is neither a confusion nor a simple continuity, but it is an accumulation of corpuscles arranged in tiers.[35] It is a single organized unity: "*Everything is classified; therefore everything holds together.*"[36]

Not only is there unity on any one level of complexity, but there is an over-all unity of the whole evolutionary reality. Far-spread in time, as dissimilar in the details of its productions as one can imagine, it still constitutes, Teilhard claims, one single unified movement from the greatest homogeneity to the highest complex unity.[37] There is continuity in the evolutionary event, Teilhard says, because the properties of the end are already present in a certain way during the process.[38] Nothing can appear as final which has not already existed primordially in some way.[39]

This is an interesting intersection of Teilhard's thought with Sāṃkhya, for, according to Mircea Eliade, "No new form, Sāṃkhya affirms, goes beyond the possibilities of existence that were already present in the universe." For this reason Eliade warns that "to compare 'evolution' in the Indian sense with Western evolution is to be guilty of great confusion."[40] Yet here is Teilhard, apparently saying something more or less equivalent to that Sāṃkhya affirmation.

But, in Teilhard's view, it is not a substance or a finished form which is already present. It might more nearly be called a desire, or just an impulse. "To grow and fulfill oneself to the utmost . . . that is the law immanent in being."[41] And he sees the world as a whole subject to this interior pressure to grow and fulfill "itself," as if it is possessed of a unified "self" capable of "fulfillment." There seems to be a kind of "gravity" of complexity that draws cosmic matter into more and more intricate forms of ever deeper unity, thereby achieving greater freedom.[42] The more complex anything is, the more alive it is; the greater its physical plurality, the greater its psychic unity.[43]

We suggested above that this line of development might be clearer if we considered it in terms of a sort of unity of "purpose" rather than a unity of substance, a unity of activity and of what underlies activity—call it "intention." Teilhard calls it even more vaguely simply "the within."[44] Sometimes Teilhard equates the principle of creative union with the principle of vitalization and says that "life" is *the* phenomenon of the universe.[45] And vitalization he descrbies as a modification of the universe's stuff in its most fundamental condition, its degree of interiorization. *Increasing interiorization is what is behind increasing complexity.*[46] There is a "double aspect" to the "structure" of the "stuff of the universe": "coextensive with their Without, there is a Within to things."[47] These are the two sides of corpusculization, the formation of discrete individuals.

The "within" is granular, or corpuscular, just as is complex matter, and it is intimately connected, both qualitatively and quantitatively, with complexity.[48] Everything is conscious according to its complexity and complex according to its consciousness.[49] Experimentally the two terms are inseparable, says Teilhard.[50] He has crystallized this relationship in what he has called the Law of Complexity/Consciousness:

> Left long enough to itself, under the prolonged and universal play of chance, matter manifests the property of arranging itself in more and more complex groupings, and at the same time in ever-deepening layers of consciousness; this double and combined movement of physical unfolding and psychic interiorisation (or centration) once started, continuing, accelerating and growing to its utmost extent.[51]
>
> Spiritual perfection (or conscious 'centreity') and material synthesis (or complexity) are but the two aspects or connected parts of one and the same phenomenon.[52]

This law is Teilhard's "primal intuition," Wildiers says,[53] and the originality of his expression of it lies in his expansion of the relationship to universal significance. Everything is conscious, i.e. has a "within," down to the least corpuscle.[54] What is evolving in our world, is not simply matter (whatever that is, for we do not really know) but is complexity/consciousness: *it* is the unit of world-stuff. The two factors advance as one. When there is a critical change in the arrangement of elements on the complexity side, there is a corresponding transformation in the nature of the consciousness.[55] They must increase together; evolution is a movement toward "an increasing amount of spiritual energy in matter that is ever more powerfully synthesized."[56]

> From the lowest and least stable nuclear elements up to the highest living being, we now realize, nothing exists, nothing in nature can be an object of scientific thought except as a function of a vast and single combined process of 'corpusculization' and 'complexification,' in the course of which can be distinguished the phases of a gradual and irreversible 'interiorization' (development of consciousness) of what we call (without knowing what it is) matter.[57]

Now, what is similar in Sāṃkhya to this view of Teilhard's that the cosmic stuff is a "complexity/consciousness"? It is the correlation of the "without" and the "within" in all the compounds of nature. The similarity is not perfect and it must not be pushed too far. But we are interested only in showing that there are fundamental attitudes or orientations of thought among the Hindu traditions which are congenial to Teilhard's. When Teilhard proposed in the West that "consciousness" was present in all beings, down to the inanimate stone and the least subatomic particle, the idea was not well received. There was no traditional mode of thought about the world which had prepared the way for this suggestion. But such a proposal, made against the background of the Sāṃkhya system, would not have seemed so strange.

Sāṃkhya hypothesizes that from the beginning of the evolution of Prakṛti—in which exist the three guṇas of "light," "action," and "inertia"—there are two sides to each production. The first reality to be formed is called *Mahat* (Great One) in its cosmic aspect and Buddhi (Intellect) in its psychic aspect. It is the principle of determination, distinction, and formation.[58] The second product is *Ahaṃkāra* (the "I"-maker). Eliade says that its basic reality is a "uniform apperceptive mass," from which the process of evolution "bifurcates in opposite directions, one of which leads to the world of objective phenomena and the other to that of subjective phenomena (sensible and psychomental)."[59] According to the predominance of one or another guṇa, Ahaṃkāra in turn gives rise to *Manas* (the coordinating mind), the five senses of knowledge, the five organs of action, and the five subtle elements (*tanmātras*). From the last come finally the five gross elements which form themselves into atoms (*para-*

māṇus) and molecules (*sthūlabhūtāṇi*), from which arise vegetable organisms (*vrikṣa*) and animals (*śarīra*). The psychical branch of this evolution is called *buddhi-sarga* and includes the mind and the organs of perception and action. The physical branch is called *tanmātra-sarga* and comprises the tanmātras, the gross elements, and their products. There are complex relations between the two branches, senses responding to elements and organs acting on gross bodies, but elements, senses, and bodies alike are composed of the same three guṇas, though in different proportions.[60]

As Eliade says, the Ahaṃkāra has "created a two-fold universe—inner and outer—these two 'worlds' having elective correspondences between them."[61] Kunhan Raja claims that it is a concept "common among all the thinkers" in the history of Indian philosophy that "the world has evolved from within,"[62] and Troy Organ points out that a key Upanishadic teaching is that the ultimate reality composes harmoniously outer and inner qualities: matter, life, mind, intelligence, and bliss.[63] Danielou reminds us that when a Hindu identifies the universe with the "Cosmic Being, it is not the physical universe only that is meant, but the entire universe with its mind, its guiding energies, the laws which rule its development, and the consciousness which pre-exists its appearance."[64] The modern Indian can easily say, in the bosom of his tradition, what Teilhard found so difficult to say:

> Those who consider the sun merely as a sphere and know nothing of the life that animates it, those who see the sky and the earth as two worlds but do not know their presiding consciousness, possess, indeed, a limited knowledge. A science which studies only the inanimate part of things and does not reach their inner life, their presiding consciousness, is incomplete and leads to no stable knowledge.[65]

There is another point on which Sāṃkhya bears a rather interesting resemblance to Teilhard's scheme. This concerns the relation of Puruṣa to Prakṛti, which in a curious way is somewhat like the relation of Omega to the evolving world-stuff. Let us look again at the way Teilhard has marshaled his arguments. Directing our attention to the facts of evolution, Teilhard can legitimately point out that growth (over the long term) does not simply spread randomly or equally in all possible directions. Variations group themselves within certain fields and develop with more intensity in certain selected orientations.[66] This shows especially in the growth of nerve tissue and the emphasis in evolution on producing larger and more convoluted brains.[67] What Teilhard calls the "groping," or inventive, power of nature appears as a "continuous and dominating influence" over the elementary arrangements of matter, urging them in the direction of "always more improbable mechanical groups" and corresponding "astonishing expansions of spontaneity."[68] A related observation is that when, in the course of this groping productivity of spontaneity, a new species *is* formed that is more conscious, the evolutionary pressure seems to be reduced on the less spontaneous levels of life. This indicates, to Teilhard's mind, that there is some unitary tendency over the whole of life.[69] There is a continuous psychic chain going back to the beginning of life, he feels[70]; the universe can be seen as a composition of spontaneities, all seeking to expand.[71] The steady ascent toward greater consciousness throughout life convinces Teilhard that consciousness cannot possibly be a mere secondary effect of cosmic forces, a subordinate feature of the universe.[72] Evolution does not merely *happen* to result in greater consciousness, evolution *is* an ascent toward ever greater consciousness.[73]

We had already established that in Teilhard's view the cosmos is one single evolution and that its goal is the completion of the body of Christ. Christ acts on the evolutionary movement as a kind of "soul," organizing, forming, directing and guiding it by drawing it into His final and perfect unity in the Point Omega. Furthermore, the Point Omega has a very peculiar feature in that it is not only conceived as the goal of the evolution, and therefore as a terminal point in a series, but it is also conceived as a living reality outside the series altogether. This comes about because of the nature of evolution itself as an evolution *of consciousness*. Reflexive consciousness seeks as its goal not only a final unity but a transcendent and indestructible value. There must be something which is secure from any tendency of the material universe to fall back into the grip of ever-increasing entropy. The end of evolution, simply because it is an end for *consciousness,* must escape the process of evolution. Christ-Omega, in His divine nature, satisfies this condition. So although Christ is the guiding spirit of the evolution, drawing it to its destination, and is Himself, through His Incarnation, most intimately involved with it, there is also a sense in which He is outside it, was never involved in it, and remains untouched by it.

In the Sāṃkhya system, Puruṣa covers many of these same functions. In the first place, there is a recognition on the part of the Indian philosophers that nature displays "a design or purpose . . . and this suggests also the presence of an Intelligence behind the process."[74] Sāṃkhya says that the evolution of the world begins and continues only as there is an influence on Prakṛti by the presence of Puruṣa. Puruṣa is not so much distinguished from Prakṛti as consciousness is distinguished from unconsciousness, but as freedom is distinguished from determinism. Puruṣa—or rather the puruṣas, for they are many—are the selves, the ultimate persons who are the perceivers or experiencers of the world evolved from Prakṛti. They themselves do not evolve and they are not efficient causes of Prakṛti's evolution, but, like Teilhard's Omega, they are final causes. Under the guidance of the puruṣas, the differentiated elements of Prakṛti play out the history of the universe in such a way as to serve the ends of the spiritual life. "The history of the world must be . . . the progressive realization of the life of the spirit," according to Sāṃkhya.[75] As Troy Organ puts it,

> The creation of the concept of *puruṣa* by the *Sāṅkhya* philosophers must have been the result of their awareness of the purposiveness of the world. A world in which there is a design is a world in which there must be reference to an end not inherent in the world processes themselves. *Puruṣa* is the principle for the sake of which *prakṛti* evolves. *Puruṣa* does not evolve; but by being what it is, it causes *prakṛti* to evolve.[76]

At the same time, like the Incarnate Christ, Puruṣa is wedded to Prakṛti, both for the evolution of Prakṛti and for the development and eventual liberation of Puruṣa from Prakṛti.[77] (Teilhard also will have something surprising to say about the liberation of souls from the material universe; we will return to this point in the next chapter.)

In the Yoga school of Hindu philosophy, which absorbed the bulk of the Sāṃkhya theory, this view is amended to cover the criticism that the merely "transcendental (non-mechanical)" influence of Puruṣa on Prakṛti is insufficient to account for the multitude of intricately harmonious movements of Prakṛti, and requires too heavy an assumption of a prearranged teleology on the part of Prakṛti. The amended view holds that the evolution of Prakṛti is under the personal guidance of God (Īśvara).[78] This arrangement would make an even closer approximation to Teilhard's theory.

We see, now, that the whole notion of a temporally immense evolution in which both material and conscious elements are active, which proceeds toward greater complexity and greater consciousness (a higher spiritual life), and which is both guided by and drawn to a Divinity beyond the evolution itself, is a fundamental part of the Hindu tradition. Sāṃkhya first introduced the view, as a pure philosophy, based on reasoning alone, but in the synthesizing atmosphere of the Indian mind it was adopted by all schools of religious thought as well and even incorporated into scripture (the Bhagavad Gītā).[79] It is therefore a mainstream theme in the Hindu consciousness. Teilhard's thought is well received among religious thinkers in India today because they find his conception of the evolution of consciousness through long periods of time a congenial idea. It would seem, then, too abrupt a judgment on Teilhard's part to have condemned "the ancient religions" as unable to "adjust" to the modern perspectives of space-time and the constructions of evolution. On the contrary, Hinduism would seem to be in a most favorable position, not quite for "adjusting" to these "new" perspectives—for it had them all along—but for continuing to carry forward its own traditional insights into the evolution of the cosmic stuff from which the spiritual glory of free consciousness is gradually emerging.

Śakti: Evolving Psychic Energy

One of the most interesting conjunctions of Teilhard's thought with the Hindu traditions lies in the area of their considerations of energy. The Hindus call energy *śakti* and have a whole system of philosophy, theology, and spiritual practice built around it, as well as a variety of conceptions of it entering into systems whose central value is otherwise defined. In one or another of these systems there can be found something amenable to almost every point that Teilhard makes in his discussions of energy. In this section we will take up several of these topics: entropy and evolution; the evolution of consciousness-energy; the unicity of energy; the radial and tangential forms of energy; centers of energy; and evolutionary levels of energy, continuously advancing through series of discontinuities. In each case the Hindu complements will be presented. Finally, we will look at the whole picture of the evolutionary energy-universe as diagrammatically presented by both Teilhard and Śakti-vada, and see that the axis of development is a path of steady ascent toward the highest Being and Consciousness.

In any consideration of energy and evolution, one has to face the fact of entropy, the great enemy of evolution. "Entropy" is a measure of the disorganization—or homogenization—of the energy in a given physical system. In a "closed" system, one with no energy exchanges with the outside, it will always increase. In order for "work" to be done, i.e. for events to take place, in a physical system, the energy must be of different kinds and different levels; it must be structured in some way. If it is all of the same kind and the same level, nothing can happen. This is what is back of Teilhard's fierce rejection of any philosophical-theological theory which glorifies the unity of the homogeneous. It means inaction—which, of course, those philosophies which praise it admit—but which means, in Teilhard's book, death, nonbeing, destruction of all values.

Now, the problem for the proponent of evolution is this: We live in a world which seems to be behaving like a closed system. This is not perfectly sure, according to present knowledge, but there is a good deal of evidence that physical transactions at least are indeed governed by the law of ever-increasing entropy. This should imply that the universe is "running down," and will eventually die, cease to be active any longer. It is as though the universe started with a certain amount of available energy which is gradually being exhausted.[80] At our moment in history there are both progressive (organizing) currents in the world-energy and regressive (disorganizing, entropic) currents.[81] But for every synthesis that the organizing current achieves, something is "burned" to pay for it, says Teilhard, and this limits the world's development.[82] Entropy is the ultimate threat to life.[83] (When we come to talk about Teilhard's view of death, in the next chapter, it should be remembered that these ideas are very much part of the problem for him.)

Life, of course, especially evolving life, is the great anti-entropic movement. It is the organizer, the builder of more and more improbable structures (from the physicist's point of view). Consequently, it is a mystery, if one believes that the laws of physics are the norm of all being. If all being were to be understood by taking it apart into its constituent elements and reducing its functions to the physical laws which govern these, then life would be strictly unintelligible and should be impossible. This is why Teilhard argues that this whole methodology in science is wrong. Complex systems are not to be understood by reducing them to simple systems. Each level of the advancing synthesis has to be understood in its own terms.

The general terms in which evolving life is to be understood, Teilhard claims, are the terms of increasing complexity and consciousness. Just as the increase in entropy defines the irreversibility of the physical universe and determines its orientation in time, so the increase in interiorization, in consciousness, ultimately in personality, defines the directionality of the living universe, and its orientation with respect to values.[84] It is clear from the evidence of life that it is better to be more conscious than less conscious.[85] Since we usually think of consciousness as "mind"—what the Greeks call *nous*—the single name of the antientropic movement then may justly be "noogenesis."[86]

What about the relation between the two currents of entropy and consciousness? If they conflict, which will conquer? Teilhard suggests that the lower orders of being are indeed governed by entropy, but that it disappears at the top of his hierarchy, where it is replaced by the highest consciousness as the essential function of the universe.[87]

Turning now to the Hindu tradition for parallels, we think of Brahmā and Śiva as the contrary currents in the universe. Brahmā is the energy of creation, the constructive, synthesizing tendency. Śiva is the energy of destruction, the simplifying, homogenizing tendency. Brahmā is evolution, in our scheme, while Śiva is entropy. Or, in a slightly different version, Viṣṇu, representing the power of cohesion, plays evolution to Śiva's entropy, while Brahmā is the principle of space-time in which they are balanced, and the tension between them is Śakti. Śakti is femininely imaged power, and it is from Her that all the manifest universe comes.[88]

Another scheme opposes Śakti as the source of all movement to Śiva as the absence of all movement. In this formation, Śiva would be not so much the tendency toward increasing entropy as the perfection of maximum entropy, the state of energy in which it is perfectly homogeneous and inactive. Śakti, then, would be all moving energy, both constructive and destructive, and She is so represented in Hindu mythology.[89] Some images of the Goddess are beneficent, as Bhuvaneśvarī, "Lady of the Spheres," who, as the Power of Knowledge, rules the evolution of the world. Others, as Bhairavī, the Power of Death, are destructive. One is as true as the other, and both are constant in their work: all that Bhuvaneśvarī builds up, Bhairavī tears down.[90] Still other images of Śakti include both aspects of the moving energy. Typical of these would be Kālī, the Power of Time, whose four hands display emblems of both life and death. And corresponding to each of these active feminine images is a passive masculine image representing the energy at rest, neither creating nor destroying.[91]

Both Teilhard and these Hindu traditions thus recognize that there is considerable ambiguity in the ways of energy in our world. Even when it is engaged in organizing, in building up life-forms, it is dogged by disintegrating tendencies, and even when it succeeds in reaching a higher level of consciousness, it has done so by a circuitous route which Teilhard calls "groping"[92] and which is related to the anti-entropic character of life.

By the law of increasing entropy a composed being should tend to decompose and its constituent particles to come to a common energy level. The final state of this process is universal homogeneity. There is, so to speak, only one way of practicing increasing entropy. So we do not speak of matter "groping" its way to this single, simple state. But there are a multitude of ways to move in the opposite direction, toward increasing organization and complexity. Life has "tried everything," Teilhard says.[93] Not all of these arrangements have been equally harmonious with their neighbors in the organic and inorganic worlds. The consequent failure of some forms and success of others is what gives rise to the image of "groping."

The tentativeness of Nature's experiments is also exemplified in the phenomenon of mutation, one of the ways by which new arrangements are introduced into the living world. With each new individual produced there is not only the opportunity for *variation* supplied (among most of the higher plants and animals) by the device of sexual reproduction, but there is the chance of a genuine *change* in the genetic material. Such changes are usually slight, but if successful, they are then cumulative, and by this slow but persistent process a quite revolutionary change may eventually become established.[94] It is the large number of such experiments and tests against the environment which insures that some forms will succeed. And, interestingly, it also insures that some will fail. (This factor will play a central role in Teilhard's treatment of the problem of evil, as we shall see.)

It may seem an uncertain way of proceeding for an evolution which is supposed to be governed by an overarching unity and drawn forward by a definite divine end. When we see the trial and error movement of Nature, so often ending in blind alleys, we may be tempted to dismiss the idea that the world process has any real sense of direction. But Teilhard compares this groping activity with the process of invention on the human level—"Organic life, like our consciousness, is an infinite fumbling and perpetual discovery"[95]—and he points out that it passes through the same distinct stages. First, a tentative sketch, or working model, undergoes a great deal of modification until it is fairly satisfactory. Then, the new creation goes into mass production and few changes are made thereafter. Its "vertical" rise has leveled off and its "horizontal" spread has begun.[96] It is a combination of "blind fantasy" and "precise orientation." It is "directed chance."[97]

So the presence of both success and failure in the evolutionary advance is not an argument against Teilhard's conception of evolution as a single unity, or even as a gradually divinizing one. We must remember that evolution, for Teilhard, is a creative union, a cumulative organization of elements in which the principle of the organization is always immanent to the organized unity. The arrangement is not imposed from the outside. Teilhard had rejected the arbitrary intervention of a Creator-God. Yet if all the attempted arrangements of matter had succeeded, or only successful forms had been tried—i.e. if there had been no groping in evolution—that would be tantamount to an external intervention; for there is never anything in a biological situation itself, prior to an attempted synthesis, by which to determine whether or not a projected form will succeed or fail. Such judgments would have to be extrinsic to the evolutionary process at every stage of its advance.

Evolution, for Teilhard, even an evolution ultimately divine, must be free to make mistakes. Otherwise it would not be inwardly directed. And if it were not inwardly directed, it could not establish the progressively tighter unions of differentiated elements which it is observed to establish. The divine tendency in the evolution, therefore, shows not in protection from failure but in preservation of the successes in an additive fashion, so that over the ages there develops a steady "drift" toward more complexity, more unity, more consciousness, and more freedom.

Vitalization is the autonomous process par excellence. Its spontaneity is what makes it the apt metaphor that it is for divinity. Life is a metamorphosis of matter controlled by no external cause, a modification of the universe's stuff in its most fundamental condition: its degree of interiorization.[98] Inward direction, immanent government, spontaneity—in other words, *consciousness*—this is the force in the universe which opposes increasing entropy. It is this "persistent advance of consciousness towards always more spontaneous and finally reflective forms" which allows us to trace the "continually ascending advance of a single fundamental greatness."[99] Teilhard emphasizes it, for this is an important discovery:

> *Energies of a psychic nature everywhere control the development of life; and man by his thought has renewed the face of the earth.*[100]

Evolution itself is ultimately of a psychic nature, Teilhard concludes; it is "primarily psychical transformation."[101] It is not only "Spirit that is now evolving,"[102] but life itself is really a matter of the evolution of the spirit.[103] This idea, Teilhard says, the idea that "the universe, partially expressed in our individual consciousness, continuously sustains a growth in being which increases its quality" is an idea "so vast and rich in consequences that we are only just beginning to assimilate it."[104]

No doubt this is true for Western consciousness, and for any other cultural consciousness which never knew or which has forgotten this amazing view of the world. It is not so clear that it is true of the Hindu consciousness, particularly the Śakta consciousness. That evolution is primarily, even essentially, a psychic process, is a theme that is central in the Śaktas' literature. Even their word for "consciousness" is closer to Teilhard's concept than the usual meaning of this word in Western languages and philosophies. *Chit* does not mean merely "thought," or "awareness," or "mind." It is "the psychic" in its broadest sense, a "Spiritual Principle" which is simultaneously Being and also Bliss,[105] thus referring to appetitive and affective experiences as well as to cognitive ones. Ordering and unifying principles of all levels are included, even those which we would rank as "unconscious." The "subconscious," the directly conscious, the reflectively conscious are likewise included, as are any imaginable levels of the "superconscious." Our reflective consciousness in the waking state—what we usually mean exclusively by "consciousness"—is a band in the Chit spectrum about equivalent to the band of visible light in the electromagnetic spectrum, the rest of it being occupied by forms of psychism above or below our mental consciousness. And this Chit is energy; in fact, it is frequently called "Chit-Śakti." As such, it is of the essence of Reality; it is "Reality-Power."[106]

It is Chit-Śakti whose evolution we are witnessing in the world, the Śakti-vādins say. It unfolds from unitary simplicity to complex forms embodying highly structured internal differentiation.[107] Evolution takes place through a series of levels in which gradually increasing freedom from constraint is a measure of the progress attained.[108] Individuals existing on the various levels possess their own appropriate concentrations of Chit-Śakti which must cooperate with one another, or enter into corporate forms, in order for higher level entities to be evolved.[109] The higher level beings are those which have the greater ratio of spontaneity, or deliberate goal-seeking, to their degree of determinism.[110] Śakti-vāda is in perfect agreement with Teilhard when he says that "energies of a psychic nature everywhere control the development of life"; and in describing the human being rising through the grades of evolution to "become controller and creator of wider and wider phases of creation,"[111] it echoes Teilhard's word that "man by his thought has renewed the face of the earth."

The energies of the lower levels are transmuted into energy-forms of the higher levels under pressure from the evolutionary force of Chit-Śakti. Particular forms and even particular levels suffer disintegration when the organizing consciousness relinquishes them (entropy), but the basic Chit-Śakti itself is imperishable.[112] Teilhard holds something quite similar, as will come out in his discussion of death. He and the Śakti-vādins are also in close agreement in saying that a given form of consciousness-energy tends to escape entropy to the extent that it acts as an organizing force which unifies lower forms into instrumentalities for itself. That is to say, the more a being is conscious, the more it is antientropic and the more apt it is for survival. This view results in coincidence with Teilhard's dictum that the world holds together from above, not from below. That which unifies and supports in existence all other beings is that *for whose sake* they are ordered, not that *out of which* they are composed.[113]

Śakti-vāda and Teilhard, then, are agreed in saying that "consciousness," in their broad sense of the word, is "the substance and heart of life in process of evolution."[114] It is the guide for evolution's unidirectional arrow of progress.[115] Because everything is conscious, consciousness can always be expected to emerge and to accumulate from generation to generation.[116] Most of the great principles of Nature are reversible; they can be read in either direction on the axis of time. Also, most of them have some limitation of size or of applicability. Not so consciousness. Consciousness cannot fall backward, says Teilhard, and consciousness cannot have any limit. Every increase in interiority is the stimulus for a further increase which will assimilate and integrate its predecessors. Consciousness is "unique . . . among all the energies of the universe."[117]

And now we come to a great central concept in Teilhard's thought, one which will find parallels among the Hindu traditions which it cannot find in the West. It is the *unicity of energy.* All through the progress of evolution we are observing the development of "collective bonds"—those which hold the world together. The bonds in different arrangements consist of different types of activities and relationships. But they are all forms of *energy.* Energy is the capacity for interaction, the expression of structure, the most primitive form of the universal stuff.[118] In some ways of looking at the world there appear to be two forms of energy, physical and psychic, but as the universe is one and its whole tendency is to become more intensely one, Teilhard concludes that "in last analysis, *somehow or other,* there must be a single energy operating in the world."[119] Foreswearing a simple reductionism, Teilhard nevertheless opts for the psychic as the basic reality of all being.[120] What really holds the cosmos together, he urges, is not so much the "without" as it is the "within." If we want to understand being, we must seek a base of the most highly unified interiority rather than a base of the most finely divided matter. Furthermore, if it is to account for ourselves, who are thinking beings, the universal energy must be something that includes the energy of thought.[121] That energy, of course, is the universal companion of complexity, Teilhard's broadly defined "consciousness." Consciousness, as conceived by Teilhard, is not a curious epiphenomenon attached to one or a few species of animal, but is a great natural force, a cosmic energy in its own right.[122] Not only so, but it subsumes all other energies as special cases of itself. Modified by certain internal distinctions, one of Teilhard's nuclear principles is the staggering conception: "All energy is psychical in nature."[123]

This is an enormous idea, and Teilhard is understandably excited about it. What a pity he did not know of the Śakta appreciation of the same concept! The very notion of "Śakti" is that of an energy which can include everything. The word is derived from the root, *śak,* meaning "to be able, to be possible." It is "power, ability, capability, faculty, strength, energy, prowess; regal power; the power of composition, poetic power, genius; the power or signification of a word or term; the power inherent in cause to produce its necessary effect."[124]

Śakti appears in many places in the various Hindu traditions. We have already mentioned a few of them. In some of the Hindu schools, particularly the Śaivite, Śakti functions in a way as a solution to a theological problem. The Śvetāśvatara Upanishad, for instance, refers to the "self-power of the Divine," which is said to be the cause of the world.[125] It further says that this God pervades the whole world and is in every being.[126] In fact, this God (a personal God) *is* the whole world.[127] Yet, the Upanishad also holds that the divine Self is actionless, infinite, and eternal.[128] How are these two positions to be reconciled? This is the problem— very like Teilhard's own problem which we analyzed in Chapter I— and the answer is, through His Śakti the actionless Transcendent is the cause, the substance, and the pervading energy of the world.[129] The Divine is one, yet by its Śakti it is manifold.[130] She, the Śakti, is Herself unborn and produces manifold offspring.[131] She is the Evolver of all differentiated beings.

This thought is developed in somewhat varying ways in the different Śaivite schools. One says that God's energies (Śakti) are the means of creation and that Māyā is the material.[132] Another says that there is no separation between Brahman (God) and Śakti; even the produced world is of the nature of God, who nevertheless transcends it.[133] Another clarifies this by saying that God Himself is not transformed into the form of the material universe, but the energy (Śakti) of God which manifests itself as the material universe is *part* of the entire being of God.[134] According to another view, the Supreme Being is a union of Śiva, the inactive transcendent principle, with Chit-Śakti. When, in the beginning of creation, the creative Māyā comes out of the Chit-Śakti, then the energy becomes the material cause of the world, and from it the various categories of finite being evolve.[135] Śakti is not an instrument for creating the world, but Śakti pervades all and itself undergoes the transformations which constitute the creation of the universe. This Chit-Śakti is the original force of life that manifests itself in the activities of life on lower and higher levels.[136]

The *Rudra-saṃhita* of the *Śiva-mahāpurāṇa* says that prior to creation there is no energy, neither being nor non-being, neither name nor form, only pure Consciousness. Then arises will, or desire, spontaneous activity *(Līlā),* and the universe begins to take form. This is the all-creating pure Energy, and the form produced by it is Īśvara (the personal God). This Energy creates its own eternal body, *Māyā,* which creates all else. This Energy is also called *Kāla,* time, the "ordering power of God," and from its body, Māyā, proceeds the evolution of the world.[137]

According to Vīra-Śaivism, Brahman is Sat-Chit-Ānanda (Being, Consciousness, Bliss), limitless, beyond knowledge. The whole world of consciousness and unconsciousness rests in It and becomes manifest from It. God delights in His manifestation through His power of Sachchidānanda. But Sacchidānanda is Śakti.[138] Through His Śakti God creates, and loves what He has created.[139] In Śaiva Śiddānta God's action in the world is līlā, play, but it is līlā with a purpose, the divinization of man, in which the soul is not annihilated but fused into the likeness of God.[140]

In general the Śaivite schools hold that Śiva, through Mahāmāyā (Śakti), produces Māyā and its products and creates the world which is the basis of bondage for souls. Also through Mahāmāyā souls are liberated. This movement of the diverse energies for the production and dissolution of the universe is called *anugraha* (action without a cause, or grace): "By these energies both the souls and the inanimate objects are brought into proper relation and the work of creation goes on."[141]

An image of Śakti that emphasizes the unicity of energy is that of the *bindu,* the "metaphysical Point of Power," into which all the energies of the universe are concentrated at the beginning of the evolution of the world.[142] According to this imagery, the inactive or contemplative spirit is reflected in the concentrated energy and, inspired by this presence, the energy begins to dilate.[143] An indistinct sound (*nāda*) or generalized vibration (*spanda*) arises. The bindu expands and releases the various energies. First to appear is Chit-Śakti, the power of consciousness, and from it Ānanda-śakti, the power of joy, then Icchā-śakti, will-power, Jñāna-śakti, power of knowledge, and Kriyā-śakti, power of action.[144] The same Energy is also Vimarsa-śakti, the deliberating, planning, reasoning energy of creation which "measures out" (hence, "māyā") the world as its architect. She is the origin of objectivity, relative to the inactive transcendent principle, Her consort, with whom She is nevertheless perfectly united.[145] Again, the same Śakti takes the form of "Kuṇḍalinī" in all breathing creatures. "Kuṇḍalinī" is "coiled up" energy, which, when it unfolds, lifts the individual creature to successively higher levels in the evolutionary hierarchy.[146] The one Śakti is thus the source of all defined beings: devas, human beings, animals—the whole universe.

There is a story in the *Markandeya Purāṇa* which illustrates this conception of the unity of all energy. It seems that the gods had been unable to subdue their enemy, a bull-demon. Gathered in council with Viṣṇu and Śiva, they gave vent to their rage and frustration. The flames of wrath issuing from all of them joined in a single fiery cloud, in the midst of which appeared the Goddess, the primeval Energy. With Her many arms She reassumed the various powers differentiated as the several emblems and weapons of the assembled gods, and going forth, She destroyed the demon. The fact that the gods surrendered to Her their individual powers reveals that whatever power they possessed was originally derived from Her;[147] and that when the Power is reunified no evil can stand against it. All the powers of the gods (i.e., all the powers of the world) are in fact but a single Śakti, in whom the essence of divinity is to be located.[148] Śakti, therefore, say many hymns in Her honor, should be worshiped above Viṣṇu and Śiva, for they are but Her creatures.[149]

In the *Devī Bhāgavata* it is said that Śakti is "eternal, primeval, and everlasting." Nothing can move without Her. Each individual's energy is a part of the divine Śakti.[150] Eliade tells us that according to the Sāṃkhya philosophy, which is taken over almost intact by Śakti-vāda, states of consciousness are refined products of the same substance that is at the basis of the physical world.[151] And in the *Tantra-sara,* Sarasvatī (a personification of Śakti, especially as Wisdom) is hymned both as "Destroyer of Ignorance" and as "Substance of the World."[152] Danielou, citing Vijñāña Bhikśu, adds that sometimes *Śakti* is taken as synonymous with *"Pradhāna,"* the first basis of the world.[153]

Because of this unicity of substance and energy, the entire universe, with the totality of diverse phenomena, forms one single whole in which the smallest element has an effect on the largest through the union each has with the eternal ground.[154] All forms are transmutable into one another because all are in essence the one Consciousness-Power.[155] It is in and through Chit-Śakti that all transformations take place and that the world evolves and reaches its goal.[156] She pervades the entire universe. She is the author of creation, preservation, and destruction.[157] The *Mahānirvāṇa Tantra* affirms that everything in the world owes its existence to Her,[158] and the *Devī Purāṇa* declares that the universe is but a part of Her.[159] A Rig Vedic hymn has Her say:

> My sphere is wide. I dwell in all things. From me comes the food you eat, all that you see, all that has prana [vital

> energy], and all the words you hear [i.e. both physical vibration and intelligibility]. . . . I make everyone whatever he wishes to be [inwardly directed evolutionary pressure]. . . . I blow like the wind, creating the worlds. My greatness expands beyond the sky and the earth [transcendence].[160]

We can see from this sampling that the Hindu traditions, once awakened to the idea of the single energy from which all finite beings, both material and spiritual, are derived, enlarged and developed the notion with characteristic extravagance and splendor. But even Teilhard, though usually adopting fairly scientific language and refraining from personification, makes it clear that energy is one and that that energy is consciousness. It is a basic assumption in *The Phenomenon of Man* that the psychic holds the primacy as the stuff of the universe and that consciousness is the reality which is evolving.[161] The universe is "noodynamic," Teilhard says; it has the "dynamic of spiritual energy."[162] Just as Śakti-vāda teaches that the inanimate world is inoperative without the act of the conscious being,[163] so Teilhard asks, "Is it not the Spirit that animates everything, . . . even the stones?"[164]

Teilhard, however, does not always confine himself to scientific and impersonal language. He has an intense feeling for the primal and universal energy. He often refers to it under the image of Fire and equates it with the divine presence in the world: It is "the devouring fire . . . [identified] with the Divine" and pointed out by science in the form of the various energies of the world, from nuclear fusion in the stars, to life, to soul. In all these ways, "*See, the universe is ablaze!*" he cries.[165] Fire is, for Teilhard, the archetypal energy; it represents the ultimate energy of which all other energies are special manifestations[166]: "I pray you, divine milieu, already decked with the spoils of quantity and space, show yourself to me as the focus of all energies."[167]

Everything is illumined and animated from within by this divine Fire.[168] God is in the world as "a universal transparency aglow with fire."[169] This fiery energy, which, passing through various stages of its evolution, at length shows itself as personal consciousness, does not come into being as a product of matter. As far back as we care to go, we always find it. In the very beginning "there was the *Fire*."[170] And the Fire is also our model for the future. We ought to seek out "the hidden powers" in "the ocean of energy," developing our thought, expanding our love, intensifying our activity.[171] Evolution is but the convolution of the creative energy which kindles life and implodes as a convergent Noosphere. Teilhard often speaks of the "psychic warmth" in the world,[172] of the rise in tension and "psychic temperature" in the Noosphere, which "heats as it contracts,"[173] and says that "human creative energy" is to be measured "according to the degree of temperature generated within it."[174] For we ourselves are now the fuel of this living flame. We must open our arms to "call down and welcome the Fire."[175] It is not enough to contemplate this "super-substantial, personal Fire" which solicitously preserves what it consumes.[176] We must resolutely give ourselves to it as its food.[177]

The Hindus, too, have used heat and Fire (the god Agni) as symbols of the divine energy which creates the world, operates all its transformations, and guides the consciousness of the human beings into spiritual fulfillment. The *Tiruvatar Purāṇa* says, "Our Lord is the dancer, who, like the heat latent in firewood, diffuses his power in mind and matter and makes them dance in their turn."[178] The Rig Veda declares:

> The whole world was swallowed and concealed in darkness; Agni was born, and it became manifest. The deities, the earth, the heavens, the waters and the plants gloried in his friendship.[179]

Fire is the first birth of life in inanimate matter,[180] and he is the conscious thinker in human beings, illumining what is dark to them.[181] Fire is full of energy, strength, and wealth, and "has power for a large Immortality."[182] He "fills the world," he is the "guardian of the laws of all workings and he kept safe the laws of his action and motion" even as he "measured into shape the middle world [Earth]."[183]

Embree remarks that like Christ, Agni is represented as an intermediary between gods and men, being identified with the mediating and world-creating sacrifice, and being himself the priest of it. He is called "Messenger," "Illuminator of darkness," and "Custodian of Ṛta [universal law; cf. Logos.]."[184] A. C. Bose tells us that Agni is "Priest, Sage, Father, Brother, Friend, Guest, and finally the Light of lights, the Soul within our soul, and the Deva who is identified with . . . the Ultimate Reality."[185]

Agni unifies all the energies in the singleness of his consciousness:

> A steady Light, swifter than thought, is stationed
> among the moving things to show the way;
> all the Devas, of one mind and like wisdom,
> proceed devoutly to that One Intelligence.[186]

And, as Teilhard had said, it is by "fire" in man's consciousness that he comes to his destiny in the evolution, and enters with all the energies into the sacrifice and into the Divine Fire with decision and with joy.

> When mortal man by his musings comes to take pleasure of work and thought in the Fire, he shines with light and is one supreme; he receives the impulsion that leads him to safety.[187]

> Create for yourselves in the sacrifice with a common joy in him the divine Fire along with all the fires, . . . who is in mortals the possessor of truth, inwardly permanent, whose food is Light.[188]

According to Teilhard in *The Phenomenon of Man,* "all energy is psychical in nature," but he adds that "in each particular element this fundamental energy is divided into two distinct components: a *tangential energy* which links the element with all others of the same order [of complexity/consciousness] . . . and a *radial energy* which draws it towards ever greater complexity and centreity."[189] Although the two types of energy, which correspond to the "without" and the "within," are not directly transformable into one another,[190] they do react on one another in such a way as to stimulate the evolutionary process by a kind of leap-frogging.

Tangential energy is energy of relations with other entities on the same level, as atoms with atoms, or cells with cells. Now, as these energy relations begin to assume a certain *arrangement,* as for instance, when the tangential bonds between atoms of sodium and atoms of chlorine order themselves in geometric patterns, there comes a moment of "change of state" when the *arrangement* constitutes a new *level* of entity, the crystalline molecule. And the molecule has a higher degree of *radial* energy than had the atoms, that is, it has more internally unified complexity and therefore more "consciousness," or more "centreity." But, stimulated by this more intense interiority, the new molecule promptly sets about establishing new *tangential* relations with other molecules, which will lead in turn to a further level of *radial* energy when the cell is formed, and so on.[191] Teilhard also calls tangential energy "peripheral" energy, and says that it is "constant and reversible," that is, it is the energy described by the laws of physics. Radial energy he also calls "axial"—energy of the axis—which is increasing and irreversible. It is the actual energy of evolution.[192]

The custom among scientists, Teilhard says, and therefore among the rest of us, has been to regard the tangential energy as the basic reality, the radial energy being only a "subsidiary effect or a fragile super-structure." But evolution would make much more sense, he suggests, if we were to invert this perspective and consider the radial energy as the "primitive and consistent, the tangential being only a minor product statistically engendered by the interactions of the elementary 'centres' of consciousness."[193] If the great energy of the universe, that is, the energy of evolution, which we have seen earlier can be identified as the drawing power of Omega, acts on even the pre-living corpuscles as a stimulus to their "within" to advance to more intensely centered levels, then, says Teilhard, the physical energy studied by physicists and governed by the law of increasing entropy could be "interpreted as the statistical 'by-product' of a great number of elementary psychic energies (energies of atoms) which combine tangentially . . . just as the regularity of physical laws (the determinism of matter) is explained by the statistical play of a great number of . . . free impulses." Under this view, he says, it would be clear that "everything in the universe . . . moves in one and the same internal stream, emanating from Omega: *physical energy* being no more than *materialized psychic energy*."[194]

Teilhard speaks of psychic energy, or consciousness, as interiority, or as "centreity." It will be of some interest to notice this, because this image, together with the analysis of energy into tangential and axial, will find a remarkable support in Śakti-vāda's conception of "centers" and its image of the universe of energy in the pattern of the *yantra.* First, let us see what Teilhard means by "centreity." It is one of the ways in which he reinforces his "law of recurrence." "Centeredness" is a characteristic of the universe of energy on all levels. It means simply the granular character of the "within" aspect of all being, corresponding to the corpuscular character of the "without." Each corpuscle of matter has a *center* "within," which is its principle of organization. More complex corpuscles have more highly centered "withins," or a greater degree of *centreity.* We might also say that they have thereby—through the principle of organization that is their *center*—a greater definition of their own being, or more "selfhood." (This extension of Teilhard would seem to be legitimate and will enable us presently to pinpoint an interesting coincidence with a Śākta doctrine.)

Centreity, says Teilhard, is the "true, absolute measure of being in the beings that surround us," the only "basis for a truly natural classification of the elements of the universe."[195] The axis of advancing evolution stretches from the lowest degree of centreity to the highest. Entities having the same degree of centreity constitute what we may call levels of reality, or what Teilhard calls "isospheres," because they form universal units of the same type of being. For instance, the pre-living entities are ordered on Earth in the lithosphere, the hydrosphere, and the atmosphere. The living compose the biosphere, and the thinking, the noosphere. The universe as a whole, therefore, assumes the appearance of a *"centred universe,"* says Teilhard; and he goes on to affirm that when ranked in their natural order, "the whole family of isospheres" will define "at the heart of the system" a "focus-point of universal synthesis, Omega."[196] It will be, as he often calls it, the Center of centers.[197] And this idea also will find among the Śāktas a companion in the concept of the Point at the center of the energy-system.

Śakti-vāda begins by affirming that That Which Is is a

unitary Being-Consciousness-Bliss (Sachchidānanda) which is Divine Energy (Śakti). Far from holding—as Teilhard considered all "genuine" Hindu traditions to hold—that the universe is an illusion, Śakti-vāda proclaims that if there is any mirage in our experience, it is the pragmatic appearance of unreality, unconsciousness, or unhappiness, that real blissful Consciousness-Energy constitutes not only the universe as a whole but also each individual being in it. Each such being is a "Center" of the divine Śakti, a focus and principle for the finite organization of energy. Sir John Woodroffe, one of the earliest Western students of the Śākta doctrines, defines "Center" this way:

> Evolution and history have become possible because the Power [Śakti] has manifested itself as Centres. A Centre is Cosmic Power . . . condensed into a point in a certain stage of evolution.[198]

We had suggested above that Teilhard's "centreity" might usefully be interpreted as "self-hood," in the sense of definition of one's own being. Woodroffe relates the two concepts thus, in terms of Śakti-vāda:

> Being is *Chit,* or consciousness. It becomes or evolves as Power. In becoming It finitizes and centralizes Itself as the selves, whereby different Centres with finite "fields" of being appear. . . . Ātman (selfhood) is everywhere—in man, in the amoeba, and in a particle of dust. . . . It is [there] as Power, the Centre-making Principle, and it must be there, where there is a centre of being and operation.[199]

Elsewhere he says more summarily, "All Centres . . . down to the cells and even their elements . . . must have their own consciousnesses and selves."[200]

It is the supreme consciousness, *Chit,* says Śakti-vāda, which forms itself into all levels of reality,[201] including those which seem to us to be "unconscious," such as stones. The aspect of the stone which we call "matter" is constituted by its relations with other entities on its own level, the "conditions of the province of inter-central convention" (*Vyavahāra*), and by the contrast of these relations with those of the human level.[202] Says Woodroffe:

> To Vedantism, and the Śākta form of it in particular, every object down to the material particle, is a . . . form of Conscious-Power. . . . A particular thing, A, by virtue of its position in the stress-system in relation to another thing, B, may behave as though it were devoid of Consciousness, Bliss, and Play (i.e. free, spontaneous action): but that does not mean either that A is in itself . . . devoid of these, or that it is necessarily devoid of them in relation to a third centre, say C.[203]

We see here Teilhard's thesis that consciousness is the primal reality, of which tangential energy is the epiphenomenon, and his view of being as consisting of "centers" which granulate the radial energy and relate to one another by the laws of tangential energy—the "inter-central convention" of which Woodroffe speaks.

Teilhard distinguishes his own "inter-centric links" in three categories: 1) tangential solidarity, the bonds on the surface of any given isosphere; 2) the radial solidarity by which entities of a given isosphere share in the totality of tangential links of the isospheres inferior to their own (as all cells in a body share in the united tangential energies of the molecules of which they are composed and in the bonds of the atoms of which the molecules are composed) ; 3) the radial solidarity by which a given isosphere moves forward, drawing with it all the inferior isospheres of which its members are composed, tending to produce the next higher isosphere.[204]

In Śakti-vāda a being, or level of being, may be imaged as a point (bindu) of concentrated potential energy which expands in such a way that it is analyzable (among other ways) as a triangle of forces (*Trikona*), the Polar Triangle.[205] Woodroffe calls these three dimensions "Base," "Index," and "Coefficient" of the Fact. One interpretation, given in the terms of subjective consciousness, is that Base refers to a "substratum of immediate, intuitive feeling," Index refers to a "superstructure of ideas and memories suggested by the Base," and Coefficient refers to a "store of possibilities or tendencies which makes the fact change and grow."[206] The same characteristics, properly reinterpreted, apply to all levels of reality.[207] In general, Base refers to the present tense of time, Index to the past, and Coefficient to the future.[208]

Now, since Teilhard himself maintains that the fundamental energy relations are relations of consciousness, the most mature form of which is known to us as our own subjective experience, it may not be inappropriate to point out here the correlation between these two analyses: 1) the superficial bonds of tangential energy certainly exist only in the present and are of the nature of immediate, direct experience for the entity concerned. 2) The radial solidarity by which elements assimilate the tangential bonds of their inferiors is necessarily a reference to the past. Tangential bonds of inferiors are in a way "memories" for the superior entity. Also, the "organization" which the superior entity has made of the tangential energies which it has assimilated constitutes an "idea" of them and is, relative to them, a "superstructure." 3) The radial solidarity by which the isosphere moves forward, of course, refers to the future, and expresses the "store of possibilities and tendencies which make" the given entity or isosphere "grow." It may be only coincidence, but it seems a rather close parallelism, and may be considered another small weight in the pan of the opinion that Teilhard would have found Hinduism more congenial than he thought.

The Centers, so linked, further organize themselves in groups of like kind, so that we have in Śakti-vāda "a world of correlated Centres," an "Order of Centres"[209]—corresponding to Teilhard's "isospheres"—all subtly connected with one another in virtue of their being all parts of one single system of Being-Consciousness[210] within which they are ranked. "The World shows Centres in different stages of growth: they appear to constitute an hierarchy from 'dead' matter to the highest Spirit,"[211] according to the degree of internal comprehension attained,[212] says the Śakti-vādin, recalling Teilhard's words that centreity is the absolute measure of being and the basis for the only truly natural classification of the elements of the world.[213] Consequently, the Śakti-vādin continues, the positions of these elements and their actions within the one "cosmic dynamic system" are different, and we separate them roughly as Matter, Life, and Mind.[214]

"Matter, life, thought," Teilhard echoes: "three zones . . . the distinction between which must reappear, and must be accounted for, in any explanation, however learned, of the universe."[215] Having insisted as strongly as he has upon the unity of all reality and the continuity of the Earth's development, Teilhard is also careful to underline the complementary fact of the discontinuities within the evolutionary process. The structures of these different levels are immensely different, of course, and their whole way of behaving is different. There is a physics of atoms, a chemistry of proteins, a biology of genes, and a logic of thought, to say nothing yet of an aesthetics of feeling and a morality of deliberate action.[216]

Likewise, the transitions from one order to the next, as we have already indicated, are not perfectly smooth. A major evolutionary advance is more like an abrupt "change of state"; after a period of building up tangential energy, there is a sudden shift in the status of the radial energy. Either by a new arrangement of its parts (on the lower planes), or by the acquisition of a new dimension of activity (on the higher planes), consciousness—the cosmic reality—is enabled to jump a level.[217] This history of consciousness in evolution, therefore, shows itself in "successive leaps," based on "psychic quanta."[218]

Within the order of living creatures we also find that there is no simple transformation from one species to another in a perfectly continuous line. When we look back along the path evolution has taken, what we see is more like a "bundle" of related forms which overlap one another in the temporal sequence. Successive forms do not prolong their predecessors; one type does not "pass into" another. Rather, one group replaces another, and the displacement is lateral rather than direct.[219]

Evolution is a pattern of discontinuities immersed in an underlying continuity: this view is common to both Teilhard and the Śāktas. Śakti-vāda tends, perhaps, to emphasize the continuity, in conformity with its philosophical position as a school of the nondualist Vedānta. But it conceives the *continuum* of Chit-Śakti as also "finitised, broken into discontinuities which are centres or points in it."[220] These "discrete centres . . . are in action and reaction" relative to one another,[221] so that "the universe is an infinite stress-system. All centres, near or distant, are in constant interaction."[222] The differences among the discrete elements are due to the fact that "the stress-system is different in each" of them, "because in each the ultimate units . . . are configured and are moving differently."[223] These different elements range, as suggested by the Chāndogya Upanishad, from that which is "greater than the greatest" to that which is "smaller than the smallest."[224] Woodroffe comments:

> Between the uppermost limit and the lowermost we have a series of *continua* and *discontinua* arranged in ascending and descending orders; and all these intervening orders of largeness and smallness, continuity and discontinuity are susceptible to strain and stress in a varying degree. The . . . "Elements" arise out of this variable stress-and-strain attitude.[225]

One conclusion from this system which is of special interest is that the units of matter, which are "stress-and-strain centers" of Chit, can change their position in the system by changing their action, and thus evolve into other types of centers: nonliving into "living," into "feeling," into "thinking" matter.[226] The ascent passes through "higher vegetable, lower animal and higher animal forms until we arrive at Man," and within the Man-type there is still a further ascent "from the rudest of primitive men to the Yogin whose consciousness is united with the Supreme Consciousness."[227]

This is, of course, highly agreeable to Teilhard's view of evolution as "the appearance of progressively more luminous centers of consciousness,"[228] despite his judgment that Hinduism could not support a doctrine of progress in the world.[229] But we will have more to say on this issue presently under the head of determinism and freedom.

The most crucial moment in the evolution, and in its progress toward the divine consciousness to which the Śaktivādin aspires, is the appearance of reflective thought. Just as Life is of a "higher" level than physics or chemistry because it assimilates by synthetic arrangement the determinisms of those levels, so also there is a discontinuity between the world of Life and the world of Thought, between the biosphere and the noosphere.[230] Humanity is not just a more interesting form of life, it is an entire new level, a new world characterized by the breakthrough into reflection. By possessing a consciousness which "doubles back on itself"—is conscious of being conscious—humanity constitutes a completely new sphere of existence.[231] Teilhard cannot stress this too much. The appearance in the world of the power of thought, he says, is a "discontinuity of the first order, comparable to the first appearance of organic bodies."[232] It is the greatest phenomenon "since the condensation of matter and the first appearance of life."[233] It is a "transformation affecting the state of the entire planet."[234]

As with other species, it is impossible to trace man's ancestry in a continuous line. The trajectory, clear as to direction, is broken into segments. It is a "curve concealed by a number of tangents."[235] Mankind is not descended from any known ape, for instance, and yet the quality and intensity of consciousness must have been growing steadily in the line of mammals and especially among the primates.[236] That consciousness could not continue to increase indefinitely without undergoing a change of state.[237] When it came, it was probably a very small leap, from one point of view—just a chromosome mutation, like any other[238]—but in this case a "mutation from zero to everything."[239] A whole new zoological division was born.[240] The discontinuity is so profound that no intermediate stage is imaginable: either you reflect, or you do not.[241]

Reflection inaugurates what Teilhard calls life of the second degree, life characterized by consciousness of being conscious, and like every great level of development before it, it spreads rapidly over the Earth and forms its own world, the noosphere.[242] The noosphere is not simply a greater degree of an energy-form already present on the Earth. It is a new *kind* of being, a network of intercommunicating self-conscious centers. Reflection is so fundamental that from the time of its appearance there is a new form of biological existence, and biological evolution begins to change its general mechanisms. Morphological changes slow down. Factors of internal choice become superior to factors of external influence; the organism begins to have more control over itself. Genuine love and rejection in their full psychic sense emerge from the attractions and repulsions of lower levels. Synthetic arrangement of whole groups begins to be as significant as the synthesis of individual elements had previously been. And finally the question of survival itself, of the limitations of life, comes very strongly to the fore in a most crucial way.[243]

Now we must correct the picture a bit by renewing our understanding that while Teilhard stressed the discontinuity created by the appearance of Thought, he did not mean to say that it interrupted the evolutionary current. There are in the West two extreme interpretations of the human way of being: one can "bury man among the animals," holding that humanity differs from them only in degree, not in kind; or one can separate mankind completely from all the rest of Nature, accounting for its origin by a special intervening creation, or simply leaving the question unanswered. Both of these interpretations are equally wrong, says Teilhard, and are due to an imperfect understanding of the movement of evolution through stages and levels, in which the most general principles of cosmic development are uniformly reverified, but in which the qualities and dimensions of the achieved levels are totally new and different.[244]

Śaktism gives Teilhard strong support of this reconciling view. The " 'lines' of the Grand Cosmic Evolution," in its system, "are repeated in the details of creation."[245] Both see evolution as a union of discontinuities. Teilhard argues that the fact that the universe grows by passing through steps characterized by irreducible novelty does not imply any break in the phenomenal, physical, or psychic unity of the world. It is one great cosmogenesis which expands from geogenesis to biogenesis to psychogenesis to noogenesis to Christogenesis. And Śaktism reaffirms that "all that exists, all whether as Mind, Life and Matter, are forms and products of the one fundamental Substance Power which is *Chit-Śakti*, or unlimited Being-Consciousness as Power which is also Bliss."[246]

Teilhard has made an attempt or two to express graphically his conception of evolution as a series of discontinuities embedded in the great unity of the universal consciousness-energy. For instance, he has the image of "the cone of time."[247] The base of the cone represents the perfect homogeneity of unorganized particles from which the universe arises. If the cone is then divided into sections by cutting it with horizontal planes, the lowest section can represent "Pre-life," in which are situated all those transformations which lead up to the emergence of living matter. There is some contraction, or increase in centreity, even in this section—some tendency toward tighter organization into unity. The next section, "Life," is separated from Pre-life by a gap, yet it rests upon Pre-life. Its organized beings are more compact, more unified, more interior and spontaneous, having greater control over their own behavior. Above another gap defining the section representing "Thought," this interiority and spontaneity become reflexive, and the unity condenses powerfully, while the differentiation intensifies enormously. The topmost section represents whatever convergent forms are to emerge in the future, and the apex symbolizes the perfect unity of all. The arrow of time runs upward through these sections as an axis, giving an irreversible direction to complexity, unity, and spontaneity. Dynamically, it is one single genesis in which all the levels cohere.

Another image appears in Teilhard's essay "Centrology." The lowest levels of cosmogenesis are shown here as arcs of circles being "pushed" toward the center by arrows. At the level of Life, when easily definable "selfhood," or functional unity of differentiated elements, appears, the "surface of centration" is closed and the arrow shifts to the inside; the energy of evolution is now "pulling" the elements toward the center. The "pushing" arrow represents chance, the "pulling" arrow, immanent action, spontaneity. The isosphere of Life then contracts under the force of psychic attraction and forms the more strongly centered unity of the Noosphere at the critical surface of Reflection. At the heart of the Noosphere is the most intense unity of all, the Point Omega.[248]

In Śaktism, the universe of energy, with its discontinuities held in the unity of the single Chit-Śakti, is represented by various figures called *yantras.* The word "yantra" is from *yam,* "to gain control over energy," and the suffix *-tra,* meaning "an instrument for." A yantra, then, is an instrument for gaining control over energy. Devotionally it can refer to any object used in worship, such as a picture or statue. But in particular it means a diagram or chart for guiding meditation on the Reality, as God, or world, or self. It pictures the space-time development of evolution and simultaneously represents the One transcending space and time: the transformations of Śakti, who is also Brahman.[249]

There are a number of these diagrams, but the most famous one is called Śrī Yantra. It consists of nine intersecting triangles set in two lotuses, surrounded by three circles, enclosed within a triple wall having four gates. There is no need to go into all the intricacies of interpretation of the various elements of the diagram. It is sufficient for our purposes to draw attention to the interlocking triangles and their center. The triangles represent the creative polarized energies of the universe, distinct from one another, interacting with one another, setting up tensions along many lines and creating different perspectives with a variety of patterns. The diagram as a whole displays the levels of order in the world, the planes of consciousness attained at different stages in the evolution. It shows order, symmetry, variety, dynamism, hierarchy, and unity.

Most important, there is at the center a small point, the *bindu*. As Teilhard's Omega presents the most intense unity of centered beings, so "when Power [Śakti] becomes infinitely intensive or concentrated, its condition is called *Bindu*."[250] As "the Perfect Dynamic Point," it "has a tendency to evolve as a series of Lower 'Centres,' and yet remain as the 'Point' at the base of them all: it is thus, 'the Centre of all centres.' "[251] This point is the transcendent element, the unity to which all the variety is referred, the center of resolution of all tensions. Its function in the yantra is in some respects the same as that of Teilhard's Omega in his diagrams, which he also calls, as we have noted, the "Centre of centres." It presides over the transformations of energy going on all about it and also stands as the terminal point sought by those advancing and contracting energies. However, Bindu more often figures as what Teilhard would call Alpha, the beginning of the evolutionary process, the original potency of the universe, "condensed massed Power."[252] From one point of view, nevertheless, this can mean that the Bindu is "the Perfect Universe, the state of maximum manifestation . . . Complete Being-ness."[253] And Teilhard also admits: "Omega, in which all things converge, is reciprocally that from which all things radiate. . . . Impossible to place it as a point at the peak of the universe without at the same time diffusing its presence within each smallest advance of evolution."[254]

Passage from one plane to another in the evolutionary sequence represented by the yantra requires a kind of "change of state," or change of "pattern," yet takes place within the unity of the Whole.[255] The yantra itself is a way of saying that there is a Whole, which holds together both the universe of dynamic multiplicity and the transcendent realm of eternal unity, displaying the former as an emanation from the latter, but in no way reducing one to the other. One could almost say it is Teilhard's basic view of reality caught in a unique comprehensive glimpse.

It is one great glimpse of a total Reality that is itself reflected in myriad facets which we can view singly. Woodroffe remarks: "The picture of the constituent forces [of anything] is called the *Yantra* of that thing. And though . . . each particular object must have its own peculiar *Yantra*, . . . it is to be observed that its *Yantra* must only be a modification or particular form of the *Mahāyantra*, . . . which stands for the Cosmos as a Whole."[256] Teilhard, also, says that "we are obliged to admit that . . . the elementary cosmic centres can be partially themselves and partially one same thing upon which they impinge . . . the total centre, Omega."[257]

In both systems the "total center" can be seen as a personal agent who has a dual nature. It (or He or She) is comprehensive of the evolutionary scheme and also transcends the evolutionary scheme. It is a question, both in Teilhard and in Woodroffe's presentation of Śakti-vāda, of the "perfect experience." "Omega," says Teilhard, "appears to us fundamentally as the centre which is defined by the finite concentration upon itself of the noosphere—and indirectly, therefore, of all the isospheres that precede it. In Omega, then, a maximum complexity, cosmic in extent, coincides with a maximum cosmic centricity."[258] Perfect Experience, for the Śākta, is also the supreme, or the maximum, in all categories: supreme time, infinitely concentrated power, supreme energy, "an experience which subsumes all dual and imperfect experiences."[259] It, too, is an experience of the whole.

In Teilhard's view, because it is supreme in all orders, Omega is "supremely centred" and "possesses an ego proper to itself and distinct from ours."[260] Woodroffe is less categorical. If, he says, the Perfect Experience is regarded as a subjective experience, then it must be "possessed" by a Perfect Centre or Self. This "Supreme Centre or 'I' " is distinguished from "Finite Centres or the individual Egos."[261] "In other words, we must define Perfect Experience as the experience of the Lord [Īśvara]. Approximately, i.e., to the highest reach of our understanding and expression, it is so, of course."[262]

So conceived, "the [Śākta's] Lord is the 'Limit' or Ideal of local or rational experience. He is thus the Supreme Cause; the Supreme Agent."[263] Teilhard holds that Omega—which is, we must always recall, Christ the Lord—is not only the ideal image "which is destined to take shape in the future at the focus point of the convergent universe. It is . . . a source of light that . . . acts." Omega, he says, is "the only agent" that can exercise the supreme action in the universe.[264]

Yet Omega is also "partially transcendent . . . partially independent of the evolution that culminates in it. . . . Through one aspect of itself, different from that in which we see it take shape, . . . it has been emerging since all time above a world from which, seen from another angle, it is nevertheless in process of emerging."[265] The Śākta's Lord is seen with similar ambiguity. "The Lord's Supreme Experience presents to himself and to man's thought the poles of a Supreme Self and a Supreme Object [corresponds to Teilhard's "in process of emerging"]; but it has, and presents to the Lord, another and a 'greater' supreme aspect, *viz.* a Whole and alogical Experience or Fact. . . . He has an aspect of being and experience larger than and transcending what He presents to man's thought [corresponds to Teilhard's "above the world"]."[266] "In the meeting of these two halves of itself," says Teilhard, in "the emerged and the emergent," the "universal unification, in the form of a 'bi-polar' union, moves toward its completion."[267] And Woodroffe sums up by saying that "Perfect Experience is not in Time and in Space and yet it manifests itself as . . . cosmic flux and cosmic configuration; . . . it is not Cosmos, and yet myriads of worlds appear and disappear in it like bubbles on water; . . . it is the Whole and yet all aspects are Its aspects."[268]

Ignorant of these subtle, highly nuanced, and complex systems in the Śākta and other traditions, Teilhard was complaining as late as 1950 of "the Hindu mysticism of fusion"[269] and calling for a new mysticism of the West, because "it is still impossible . . . to find a single printed work which affirms the existence and describes the specific properties of . . . the *centric* cosmic sense."[270]

The "centric cosmic sense," of course, is what we have just set forth above as Śakti-vāda, or Tantrism. Another development of it appears in the Tantric teaching on the convertibility of the macrocosmic scheme and the microcosmic, or human self, scheme. Both "universes of energy" are figured as centers upon centers upon centers, with increasing tightness of organization, consciousness, and intensity of being.[271] The yantras, of which we have just been speaking, are images which represent equally well either the outward cosmos or the inward cosmos. The same Śakti which passes through the great transformations of outward Nature in the process we call evolution, passes through a similar unfolding in each individual human body.[272] In the latter case the Śakti, or energy, is called *Kuṇḍalinī,* the "coiled up," for in the beginning of the evolution the energy is latent and hidden, holding within itself the potentiality for "uncoiling" and manifesting itself in a series of successively higher levels of consciousness and activity.[273]

Kuṇḍalinī is visualized as resting in its latent state at the base of the spinal column of the human body. The spine can also be seen as a symbol of the axis of development of the evolutionary energy. The evolution of consciousness is imaged as Kuṇḍalinī rising from its base, passing through, or piercing, the *chakras,* or energy centers located on this vertical axis. Each chakra represents a level of consciousness, a degree of integration, of comprehensive control, of freedom. The lowest chakra represents matter, inertia, and the first vibrations of energy. The middle chakras symbolize gradually higher levels of life until the center between the eyebrows is reached in which are seated the cognitive faculties. The highest chakra, called *sahasrāra* (because it is pictured as a "thousand" petaled lotus), is at the top of the head; it represents the union of the dynamic energy with the motionless Transcendent.[274]

In the macrocosm the realms corresponding to those chakras are called *lokas* (places, or worlds). In Tantric cosmology the Earth is the lowest of the seven worlds, matching the lowest chakra in which all the energy of manifestation is potential, as all the evolutionary sequence is somehow potential in inanimate matter. Each succeeding world is paired with a human chakra, up to the supreme world, *Satyaloka,* the place of pure Being, corresponding to the transcendent sahasrāra.[275] A more personified image conceives the universe as the body of Devī (the Goddess) and identifies Her chakras as governing the cosmic elements earth, water, fire, air, ether, mind, and the union of the many with the One. The cosmic Śakti rises up through the centers in the Divine Body on the universal scale, just as the individual consciousness-energy rises in the individual body. At each level many rays are emitted, and it is this diversity of Devī's evolution which is represented in the yantra by the complex figures formed by the intersecting triangles.[276]

As the rays emanate from Devī, so this "world-process" is duplicated in the human organism as "emanations out of the soul," says Zimmer.[277] And as the human being is built around his soul, so Devī is seen as essentially "pure intelligence" which "shines in the minds of the sages." As such She is "the awakener of pure knowledge, the embodiment of all bliss, whose nature is pure Consciousness."[278] The "awakening" is the opening of the chakras, making available the energies, the consciousness, and the control appropriate to each level. As each chakra opens, it is a kind of "breakthrough"[279]—Eliade calls it a "rupture of plane"[280]—or what Teilhard might call a "change of state."

The details of this system are irrelevant for us here. All that we intend to see in this example is that there is a Hindu tradition in which there is an image of the world as a series of concentric and inclusive spheres, with corresponding levels of consciousness, reaching all the way from inanimate matter to the transcendent Divinity, ranged on an axis which gives a unique direction to their development. Furthermore, the human being is conceived as a kind of recapitulation of the whole cosmic movement up to his level of being. The rising of the consciousness-energy in him is seen as caused by its being "drawn upward,"[281]—much as Omega "draws" the evolving consciousness toward the highest center of universal union in the transcendent. These are the points which show a preparation and receptivity in this Hindu tradition for the kind of evolutionary theory Teilhard is proposing.

Teilhard says that we can see all of evolution within ourselves. In "the veil of determinism" which conceals "the repetition and disorganized multitude of our actions" we witness "a true birth of matter." Tracing our history through narrow but gradually widening potentialities of "perception and choice," we recognize "the dark roads that life climbed up to thought." And above our present condition, if we "join and exalt our individual powers," we "glimpse the grandeur towards which the phenomenon of man is progressing."[282] We ourselves are the most comprehensive instance of cosmic energy so far evolved; consequently, "by analyzing the conditions of our activity, we can hope to discover the fundamental conditions which govern the general functioning of the universe."[283] The conclusion of this analysis, for Teilhard, is that evolution is a process of spiritualization. "Life represents the goal of a *transformation* of great breadth, in the course of which what we call 'matter' . . . *interiorizes* the operation covering . . . the whole history of the Earth. The phenomenon of spirit . . . reveals a gradual and systematic passage from the unconscious to the conscious . . . to the self-conscious."[284]

This is very much the Tantric's point of view. He sees the human body as the microcosm of the universe, and in terms of its life and consciousness he expects to unite the cosmic Power with the cosmic Wisdom, passing from the determinisms of matter, through the various vital energies to self-consciousness and transcendent consciousness. It is for him a process of continuous interiorization. As Troy Organ says, "the outwardly directed behavior" must give way to "an inner-directed behavior" so that energy will be directed "to the strengthening of the inner life."[285] Tantrism takes over much of its philosophy from Sāṃkhya, and Sāṃkhya, as P. T. Raju points out, "is inherently a philosophy of inwardness," explaining "the world through man's inwardness": "From the standpoint of man, even the physical world is an evolution of man's inwardness."[286] This is a point of view, Raju notes, adopted by many Vedantic schools. And Troy Organ remarks that the Taittirīya Upanishad "conveys the supreme teaching that man, the being in whom the material, the vital, the mental, the intellectual, and the spiritual are harmonized, is one with the Absolute, not only in the highest element of his being, but also in each element of his being, and hence there is no element without its peculiar honor and there is no conflict among the elements."[287]

Man is the key to the universe, all these voices are saying. And this is Teilhard's great insight. It was when it occurred to him to "construct a physics whose starting-point is spirit" that, as he says, "it suddenly seemed to me that reality was vanquished and lay disarmed at my feet." Man, "the thinking animal," appeared to him as "the highest embryonic stage we know in the growth of spirit on earth." But, then, "if man is the key to the earth, surely the earth must, in turn, be the key to the world." And what truth does this key open for us? The truth that the "constant increase in *psyche* throughout time" is "the most general expression we can arrive at of universal evolution."[288] The Śākta would say that it is Kuṇḍalinī rising through the chakras of the human body or the chakras of the cosmic body of Devī. The individual's "essential function," in Teilhard's view, is "to advance this movement a little further; and the very multiplicity of the attempts made to force matter to give way to spontaneity, and to organize it in centers that can be charged with cosmic energies, even this multiplicity is absorbed in the unity of one and the same general direction . . . and this direction . . . leads towards freedom and light."[289]

The uniqueness of this direction of the evolutionary movement—ever toward light, freedom, and ultimately toward God—is Teilhard's primary thesis. He argues, on the one hand, that if God is to make a soul, He must make a world, and that means a progressive world. Starting from nothing, a system of participated being must be erected which is gradually more capable of sustaining the creative action.[290] And on the other hand, he urges that life cannot develop other than in the direction of the truth; therefore we can discover the direction of the truth by checking the life forms that have succeeded.[291] Both the a priori argument and the a posteriori argument lead him to the conclusion that our world is an evolution toward divinity.

Teilhard admits that while biological scientists agree that there is evolution, they do not agree that it is directed.[292] Nevertheless, he himself claims that a "privileged axis" is clearly discernible in the development of greater complexity, greater consciousness, and especially in the concentration of evolutionary energy on the nervous system, the brain, and finally on reflective thought and human culture.[293] The "demonstration" he offers of this thesis rests on points we have already covered or will cover in detail elsewhere in this study: 1) "Life is not an accident in the Material Universe, but the essence of the phenomenon." 2) "Reflection (that is to say, Man) is not an incident in the biological world, but is a higher form of Life." 3) "In the human world the social phenomenon is not a superficial arrangement, but denotes an essential advance of Reflection." He then adds "from the Christian point of view," 4) 'The Christian phylum is not an accessory or divergent shoot in the human social organism, but constitutes the axis itself of socialisation."[294] The last proposition may be translated for those who do not adopt a Christian point of view into an affirmation of the centrality of spiritual development in general. (However, it is to be noted that this is not what Teilhard meant; he meant very specifically that the axis of all evolution runs through his particular religion, the Roman Catholic Church.[295]) Altogether, it means that consciousness is the most general, essential, and fundamental being in the universe; it is *the* phenomenon, and its advance constitutes the axis of cosmogenesis.[296] It is an axis with an "ascent" that is "invincible."[297]

Śāktas also think of the world as being fundamentally consciousness engaged in an inevitable advance to higher and higher levels.[298] "The whole idea," Dasgupta says, is that "it is possible to control the dissipated forces of any center and pass on to a more concentrated point of manifestation of the energy, and this process is regarded as the upward process of ascension from one stage to another."[299] It is not necessarily a perfectly steady ascent, with no backsliding. Woodroffe describes the world process as being more like a "Cosmic Spiral." Our limited experience of only segments of the spiral could lead us to the misconception that the world allows for both progress and regress, and that on balance it is not going anywhere in particular. Teilhard, too, had warned against this tempting error when describing the "groping" movement of evolution and its occasional extinction in a "blind alley." But the Śākta denies this lack of orientation and insists that even though resisted by the formation of many eddies, the current of the world is always flowing "towards the highest end."[300]

Teilhard accepts this imagery: there are basic "drifts," he says, always in "the same direction," though hidden under "cyclic movements."[301] Under all periodic phenomena, there is "an ever-ascending curve, the points of transformation of which are never repeated."[302]

The human being, of course, is in the center of Teilhard's axis of evolution; further progress must be looked for in the growth of his spiritual nature.[303] The Śākta can add constructively to this idea, because he believes that by taking thought and disciplining the energies of which he is composed, the human being can multiply and amplify the progressive tides in his (and the world's) evolution and minimize or eliminate the regressive tides.[304] By "pursuing the appropriate method," the Śākta, "starting from ordinary pragmatic World-experience," can pass through "progressively higher and fuller 'universes,' coming at last to Pure and Perfect Experience which sums up all Existence."[305] And this is exactly Teilhard's aspiration:

> I believe that in virtue of all my experience and of all my thirst for greater happiness: There is indeed an *absolute* fuller-being and an *absolute* better-being, and they are rightly to be described as a progress in consciousness, in freedom, and in moral sense.[306]

Collective Consciousness

Evolving consciousness has reached its present height in the human being. But this is not the end, says Teilhard, and in one sense or another, almost every Hindu tradition would agree with him, for all seek some kind of advance over the present state of human experience. However, the most striking agreement on this phase of Teilhard's theory is to be found in Teilhard's contemporary, Śrī Aurobindo.

Śrī Aurobindo, for those who have not yet made his acquaintance, was born in Calcutta in 1872 and educated in England. On his return to India he became a zealous patriot and a leader of the independence movement before Gandhi. Taking up yoga as a means to strengthen his political efforts, he discovered—almost accidentally—the immense ranges of the spiritual energy spectrum. His eagerness to free India was dwarfed by the new aspiration to realize the whole of spiritual being and to free and transform the whole world. He retired to the French territory of Pondicherry to pursue this quest in seclusion, and there, between the years 1914-1918, he developed the basic positions of his philosophy of evolutionary integral nondualism. Curiously enough, it was during this same period, 1914-1918, that the foundations of Teilhard's own creative thought were laid in the midst of the battlefields of France.

The correlations between these two thinkers are so many and so close that a full-length study would not be too extensive for tracing them. We will mention only the main points necessary as background to our limited discussion of their development of the idea that the next level in the evolution of consciousness will be some kind of "collective" consciousness.

Increasing complexity of form and increasing intensity

of consciousness are the most general characteristics of Nature in both Śrī Aurobindo's and Teilhard's theories of evolution. In Aurobindo's words:

> There is in the scale of terrestrial existence . . . a progressively complex . . . organization of matter . . . of consciousness in living matter; . . . the better organized the form, the more it is capable of housing . . . a more developed . . . consciousness.[307]

Like Teilhard, Aurobindo attributes "consciousness" in a broad sense to the lowliest of beings: "There is . . . an obscure mind . . . of the very cells, molecules, corpuscles."[308] Consciousness exists in grades, each of which becomes dominant in turn.[309] Aurobindo describes this movement by images similar to Teilhard's "pressure," "change of state," and "doubling back" to attain a "new sphere"[310]:

> The action of evolutionary Nature in a type of being and consciousness is first to develop the type to its utmost capacity by . . . increasing complexity till it is ready for her bursting of the shell, the ripened decisive emergence, reversal, turning over of consciousness on itself that constitutes a new stage.[311]

This process involves a "heightening and widening of consciousness," a "taking up of the lower levels," and a "new formation of existence in the terms of the dominant being," says Aurobindo.[312]

Like Teilhard again, Aurobindo holds that both complexity and consciousness have evolved, but that at the level of humanity their relative importance shifted. "The balance is reversed," Teilhard says, as consciousness now "takes the initiative" in arranging the complexity of matter.[313] Previously, according to Aurobindo, Nature's "first care" had been "physical organization" for the sake of "change of consciousness." "But in man a reversal" occurs, for "it is through his consciousness . . . and no longer through a new bodily organism . . . that the evolution . . . must be effected. . . . The consciousness itself by its mutation will . . . operate whatever mutation is needed for the body."[314] As Teilhard holds that evolution is essentially an evolution of consciousness, so Aurobindo claims that "a change of consciousness was always the major fact"; it was only "the balance" of physical and psychic that needed to be "righted."[315]

Even these first introductory citations show how very similar Teilhard and Aurobindo are. They are so congenial that we can let them, as it were, talk to one another. In what follows we will take advantage of this opportunity, setting their words together in the same sentence, or alternating their utterances as if in conversation.

The tendency of both men to view evolution in terms of the collective is already evident in their organization of its levels into unified spheres: Matter, Life (biosphere), Mind (noosphere).[316] They see some *one great thing* forming through Nature's slow, groping processes. This one great thing is of the nature of consciousness, they agree, and the evolution is not yet complete. "Mankind is still embryonic," says Teilhard[317]; "he cannot be the last term of this evolution," demurs Aurobindo, "he is too imperfect an expression of the Spirit."[318]

May there not be another sphere beyond our present humanity's noosphere, merely mental consciousness? Perhaps man is "the *bud* from which something more complicated and more centred than man himself should emerge," Teilhard suggests.[319] Aurobindo is more sure: "The line" of evolution "cannot stop" where man now is, but must either go "beyond its present term in him or else beyond him if he himself has not the force to go forwards."[320] And there is the important question with which Aurobindo and Teilhard concern themselves: Will humanity survive to be transformed into the next level of consciousness, or will it fail (refuse?) to meet the conditions for this new mutation and break the chain of evolution which had momentarily climaxed in itself?

Both men feel that they can assume at least one of the characteristics of the next sphere from Nature's general pattern: each succeeding level is a *collection* and *union* of elements from the preceding level. As atoms form molecules, which form cells, which form organisms, so there should be "in formation ahead of us, humanity as the sum of organized persons," Teilhard projects.[321] Furthermore, it is Nature's custom, Aurobindo adds, while organizing "the body and mind of the individual being," to create also "collective powers of consciousness which are large subjective formations of cosmic Nature."[322]

The main thrust of evolution has already shifted from organic bodies to social bodies, Teilhard remarks,[323] pointing out instances of technological cooperation (we think of nuclear physics, the IGY, and space exploration) as early signs of the operation of collective intelligence.[324] Or take empire building, suggests Aurobindo, the appearance of would-be world-religions, economic and social ideologies which seek to convert all societies—these too are evidences of the as yet unenlightened instinct working to bring all into one totality.[325]

A more illumined drive toward totalization, Aurobindo predicts, will recognize its obligation to satisfy "the legitimate needs," including "ease, leisure, . . . opportunity," of all, "so that the whole of mankind and no longer only the favored . . . class . . . may be free to develop the emotional and intellectual being to its full capacity."[326] Teilhard concurs in this judgment, noting that by the laws of universal evolutionary process, "the gates of the future . . . are not thrown open to a few of the privileged nor to one chosen people to the exclusion of all others. They will open to an advance of *all together,* in a direction in which *all together* can join and find completion in a spiritual renovation of the earth."[327]

However, neither of them expects that this will be an evolutionary advance which will come upon us as passive recipients. Evolution is carried on now not only *in* man but *by* man: in Teilhard's words, *"we are evolution."* Up to now the world has created us, but now, promises Śrī Aurobindo, the time is approaching when "it is we who must create ourselves and our world."[329]

At this point both prophets warn carefully that the unification—or "totalization"—of mankind must be approached with the greatest circumspection, so as not to suppress the proper movements of the individuals and smaller community units involved.[330] Early efforts at totalization have not been particularly encouraging in this respect. Teilhard admits that "instead of the upsurge of consciousness which we expected, it is mechanisation that seems to emerge inevitably from totalisation."[331] Aurobindo thinks that the present drive toward unification has tried to accomplish its goal too quickly and too simply, by the institution of "a life of identity for the community in place of a life of difference," a "mechanized compression of the elements of life."[332]

The difficulty is that these first attempts at totalization have placed the primacy on "the pure totality" itself, as Teilhard says,[333] ranking the individual as secondary. "The communal ego is idealised as the psyche of the nation, the race, the community," Aurobindo writes and warns sternly that "this is a colossal and may turn out to be a fatal error."[334] It is the individual's development in his unique personhood which will enable the totality to be the "higher" level being we expect, and therefore our "first object," Teilhard says,[335] should be to assure the individual a "maximum of elementary solidity and 'efficiency,'" or in Aurobindo's words, "The human soul's individual liberty . . . must always be the first object of the Yoga."[336]

However, development of true personhood and real freedom demands transcendence of much that now passes for "individual liberty"–which usually boils down to the right to get ahead at one's neighbor's expense. The true *person*, or what Aurobindo calls the "psychic entity," must be distinguished from mere individuality, with its "desire-soul." Both Teilhard and Aurobindo make this distinction in the same way, showing that "the sense of individuality" gives a sense of "separateness from others" [Aurobindo],[337] "tries to separate itself as much as possible from others" [Teilhard].[338] It is "an ego striving against other egos," according to Aurobindo,[339] but "in so doing it becomes retrograde and seeks to drag the world backwards towards plurality and into matter," Teilhard comments.[340] The true person, on the other hand, recognizes that "unity, mutuality, and harmony" are "the inescapable law of . . . collective . . . life" [Aurobindo],[341] and that "the acme of our originality is not our individuality but our personality, and . . . we can only find our person by uniting together" [Teilhard].[342] But collective egoism, with its most destructive expression, war, must also be abolished. In a world community composed of true persons, "war . . . could have no ground for existence," says Aurobindo[343]; it would be "eliminated at its source in our hearts," Teilhard tells us.[344]

All of this sounds very idealistic, especially in view of the current scene, but our response to the contemporary inept attempts at totalization "should not be one of despair," Teilhard counsels. The "life-instinct," Aurobindo consoles us, is seeking a "new foundation" for life; like Teilhard, Aurobindo realizes that evolution works by groping and that considerable patience is required: "All evolution must proceed at first by a slow unfolding . . . a vague . . . tendency . . . . . . then half-suppressed hints . . . imperfect beginnings . . . afterwards . . . small or large formations, a more . . . recognizable quality . . . finally . . . the decisive emergence, a reversal of consciousness."[345] If we take a longer look, Teilhard feels confident, we can see that the forces needed to lift the process of collectivization to the level of higher consciousness are available and can be activated under certain conditions.[346]

The first of these conditions to be met is a certain elevation of mind. Our consciousness has been set in the forms of separate individuality, and this was not without a purpose in evolution's overall pattern. It is one phase of the differentiation within unity which always characterizes Nature's productions. On the level of reflexive, self-possessing consciousness, it took the form of self-identification by exclusion *within* and led to self-aggrandizement and defensiveness or even hostility in the tangential relations *without*. However, it achieved its end of establishing differentiated centers of reflexive consciousness. Teilhard relates this situation to his discussions of original sin, in which he recognizes the inevitable shadows following any world of multiplicity.[347] Aurobindo refers to the phenomenon as "mental" consciousness operating in the realm of "Ignorance" (Avidyā). Both Teilhard and Aurobindo believe that we have now reached the point in the evolution of consciousness at which this type of organization is sufficiently secure, and we may turn our attention to dissolving the unnecessary veils over our vision and walls around our concern which had corresponded to our previous need to establish ourselves as individuals, and may give ourselves without fear to the new level of collective consciousness. In Teilhard's scheme it is one of the "critical points."

The change in our mind involves first of all some insight into what Nature (God) is trying to do and a willingness to cooperate in it. It was to provide this insight and inspire this cooperation that both Teilhard and Aurobindo wrote at such length and with such ardor. "To the eye that has become adjusted to the perspectives of evolution," says Teilhard, the further evolution of our consciousness appears "as a continuation of the very lines of the universe amongst other realities as vast as itself."[348] "If an evolution of being is the law," replies Aurobindo, "then what we are seeking for is not only possible but part of the eventual necessity of things."[349]

In Teilhard's vision Humanity as a whole is the "powerful reality in which all the thoughts of individuals are steeped, and by which they are guided to form from their linked multiplicity a single spirit of the earth."[350] Aurobindo speaks from the same vision: "It is our spiritual destiny to manifest and become this supernature,—for it is the nature of our . . . unevolved, whole being."[351]

The moment has come, both Teilhard and Aurobindo preach urgently, when mankind must choose between faith and the refusal of faith in earth's spiritual progress toward unity and the higher consciousness. This vision itself, says Teilhard, will "play an essential part in the building of the future, if only by creating the atmosphere, the psychic *field of attraction*" within which humanity can unite.[352] "What is necessary," Aurobindo affirms, "is that there should be a turn in humanity felt by some or many towards the vision of this change, a feeling of its imperative need, the sense of its possibility, the will to make it possible in ourselves and to find the way."[353] Teilhard would persuade us that

> . . . the more we allow ourselves to believe in this possible super-organization of the world, the more shall we find reasons to believe in it, and the more numerous will become the believers. It seems that already a collective intuition in this sense, which nothing will be able to arrest, is on the move.[354]

"This trend is not absent," Aurobindo assents, "and it must increase with the tension of the crisis in human world-destiny; . . . the feeling that there is no other solution than the spiritual cannot but grow and become more imperative."[355]

The second condition for the possibility of our evolving to a higher state of consciousness is that we learn to love. "Love," like "consciousness," is a general term in Teilhard's vocabulary, where it means "the affinity of being for being."[356] One way of telling the story of Teilhard's theory of evolution is to tell it in terms of the evolution of love-energy. Expressed that way, evolution becomes a matter of "amorization," in which the "affinity of being for being" takes different forms as the power and clarity of consciousness increases until it becomes the highly unique experience we call personal love.[357]

Aurobindo has a very similar way of speaking of love, and he and Teilhard have a high agreement on its role in the collective consciousness. Love, says Aurobindo, is "the desire to give oneself to others and to receive others in exchange; it is a commerce between being and being."[358] In the ideal collective, according to Teilhard, "since it is a question of achieving a synthesis of centres [persons], it is centre to centre that they must make contact. . . . Intercentric energies are wanted, and that means love."[359] Aurobindo elaborates this theme by describing the new powers of consciousness in the collective as having "the character . . . of a breaking down of the barriers between soul and soul, mind and mind, life and life . . . a greater identity of being and consciousness between individual and individual unified in their spiritual substance."[360]

Aurobindo expects ideal collective living to "include not only the individual life of the being but the life of others made one with the individual in a *common uniting consciousness*."[361] And Teilhard rejoices that this is the direction in which we already are moving. "The organization of human energy, taken as a whole . . . pushes us towards the ultimate formation, over and above each personal element, of a *common soul of humanity*,"[362] "a harmonised collectivity of consciousnesses equivalent to a sort of super-consciousness."[363]

But such a common consciousness can be built up only by what Aurobindo calls a "type of mutual giving . . . an increasingly joyous sacrifice of interchange. . . . The All in the individual gives itself to the All in the universe and receives its realised universality as a divine recompense."[364] Teilhard calls it "the cosmic sense"[365] or the sense of the Whole. We must strive, he says, to integrate all the diverse contents of our consciousness—efforts, desires, passions, actions—in the "exuberant simplicity" of a single aspiration, "love of the whole."[366] Aurobindo joins him in urging that every aspect of the complex instrumentation of the force of being in us should be used in "its widest and richest powers for the one object: . . . to arrive at the divine universality."[367]

As we awaken to "the vast and extreme organicity of the universe as a whole," Teilhard believes, we shall experience "the emergence of a powerful field of internal attraction, in which we shall find ourselves caught *from within.*"[368] This "indispensable inner factor," which Aurobindo also mentions, requires "the clear recognition by man in all his thought and life of a single soul in humanity of which each man and each people is an incarnation."[369] The recognition of a single soul in humanity is what Teilhard calls a "rebirth of the Sense of Species."[370] Each of us realizes that our own person is insufficient for us and that the most important portion of our being is what we are "still expecting from the unrealized part of the universe. . . . Man must believe in humanity more than in himself."[371] And the more we believe in humanity and in life, the more the universe can build itself around us and we can build the perfect society.

To attain collective consciousness, then, we must see it as the logical next step for evolving Nature and we must love our neighbors unselfishly in the realization that somehow we and our neighbors together constitute a greater "ourself." But it is a fact of our psychology that the whole, simply as totality, cannot actually move us affectively, stimulate and unify us. To be perfectly gathered together within ourselves in the integral consciousness which alone has the security to open itself to others, we must have all our faculties focused on a single, supreme object. But any such supreme object of contemplation and delight would necessarily transcend the whole cosmic order. Paradoxically, in order to be free to love our neighbors and unite with them in a "common consciousness," we require a center of love which transcends even this level of shared consciousness.[372] It is the usual relation of radial to tangential energy. The presence of the "inner factor" in the "vertical" order is the condition for the emergence of the lateral relations.

The supreme focus of energy which generates that "powerful field of internal attraction" is for Teilhard, of course, Omega.[373] For Aurobindo it is something he calls "Supermind." In his system it is the link between the Absolute Being, Consciousness, and Bliss and the present world of Matter, Life, and Mind. It is a principle of unity which grounds all the multiplicity of the world, the supreme consciousness transcending all particular forms which can be objects of consciousness. It is, further, the animating principle of all the particular beings inferior to it yet contained within it, vitalizing by its reciprocal presence within them the whole evolutionary movement. And finally, it—i.e., its full expression in the completely evolved world—is also the goal of Nature's restless seeking and striving, the ultimate perfection of the recurrent pattern of diversification and union.[374]

Teilhard holds that in order to fulfill its function, Omega must be "real and present," "diffusing its presence within each smallest advance of evolution."[375] Aurobindo agrees that "this Supermind . . . pervades . . . all the forms . . . as an indwelling Presence."[376] But Teilhard goes further: Omega must be personal if it is to be the energy focus for human beings. This can be seen from the nature of *persons*. Persons have their whole being as dynamic interchanges of conscious-energy with other persons. Therefore the soul opens its door and comes out only in response to the call of another *person*. *A*nd it comes out from its most remote chamber only in response to the summons of the Supreme Person. For Teilhard, Omega is the Supreme Person, for it is Christ. But Aurobindo has something functionally similar. "The Divine Being," he says, "is . . . the one transcendent Conscious Being and the All-Person of whom all conscious beings are the selves and personalities; for He is the highest Self and the universal indwelling Presence."[377] And the Supreme Person manifests Himself on the human level as the Avatar, "comes as the divine personality which shall fill the consciousness of the human being . . . so that it shall be liberated out of ego into . . . universality . . . comes as the divine power and love which calls men to itself."[378]

As every level of evolution has its own kind of governing "center," in Teilhard's view, so the next level of collective consciousness will also have a center. But since its function now is to unify what are already personal centers themselves, it must maintain its own distinction as a personal center while acting as "Center of centers." Aurobindo, too, sees Nature as following "in building up her human aggregates . . . the same law that she observes in her physical aggregates": a natural body, a common life for the constituents of the body, a common mind, and a "center or governing organ" through which the unified being "can realise itself and act."[379]

But the "governing center" of the personal collective must realize itself and act in terms of love, for love is the strongest centralizing power we know and therefore the one best able to save us from diffusion of our energy in mechanical, tangential relations, such as characterize those totalitarian societies which both Teilhard and Aurobindo reject. What is missing in those societies is the personal element, and now we see that it must be a superpersonal element. The superpersonal focus is the third condition for our rising to the next level of consciousness.

It is remarkable how parallel are some passages from these two authors on this topic:

Teilhard:

> Only a veritable *super-love,* the attractive power of a veritable 'super-being,' can of psychological necessity dominate, possess and synthesise the host of earthly loves. Failing such a centre . . . there can be no true union among totalised Mankind. . . . A world culminating in the Impersonal can

> bring us neither the warmth of attraction nor the hope of . . . immortality without which individual egoism will always have the last word.[380]

Aurobindo:

> A first condition of the soul's complete emergence is a direct contact . . . with the spiritual Reality . . . through a love and adoration of the All-beautiful . . . the all-Good, the True. . . . The soul, the life, the whole nature [is offered] to that which they worship. This approach through adoration can get its full power and impetus only when the mind goes beyond impersonality to the awareness of a supreme Personal Being. . . .
>
> It is . . . through . . . this uplifting of our personal nature by love and adoration to . . . the supreme Person . . . that the soul of man fulfills itself most completely . . . and possesses by that fulfilment the foundation of immortality.[381]

Union with the Supreme Person is the key to totalized, or universalized, consciousness among human persons, according to both Teilhard and Aurobindo. Teilhard sees it objectively: "The world's history bears the form of a vast cosmogenesis, in the course of which all the threads of reality converge without fusing in a Christ who is at the same time personal and universal."[382] Describing the same union with the Supreme Person in terms of the subjective experience of the person, Aurobindo says, "The formations of our larger true individuality . . . are . . . that concealed part of our being in which our individuality is close to our universality. . . . The soul of man then feels itself to be one . . . with the Puruṣottama [Supreme Person] and in its universalised personality a manifest power of the Godhead."[383] This realization comes, Aurobindo tells us, through "a supreme delight in God and an illimitable adoration."[384] But "the appearance in man of the love of God, understood in the fullness that we give it here," points out Teilhard, "is not a simple sporadic accident, but appears as the regular product of a long evolution."[385]

These are the conditions which Aurobindo and Teilhard identify as essential to the mutation of consciousness which will enable a future society to enter into the conscious human fellowship of the ideal collective. The question is whether they will be met. We will have more to say about our responsibility in this respect and about the relation of freedom and determinism in conscious evolution in the next chapter. Here we will notice instead the urgency with which both Teilhard and Aurobindo press the consideration of our situation upon our attention and the attitude with which they recommend that we approach the problem of the evolution of our own consciousness.

There is no question but that both Aurobindo and Teilhard felt that the pressure to superorganize ourselves into a collectivity of individual consciousnesses had already reached crisis proportions fifty years ago. "The transition from the individual to the collective is the present *crucial problem* confronting human energy," says Teilhard.[386] And Aurobindo warns, "At present mankind is undergoing an evolutionary *crisis* in which is concealed a choice of its destiny. . . . The problem is fundamental and in putting it evolutionary Nature in man is confronting herself with a critical choice which must one day be solved in the true sense if the race is to arrive or even to survive."[387] Teilhard calls this our "hour of choice":

> In this momentous hour we cannot continue physically to exist (to act) without deciding here and now which of the two attitudes we shall adopt: that of defiance or that of faith in the unification of mankind.[388]

We continue to move "towards a super-state of psychic tension," according to Teilhard's analysis.[389] At this moment we are passing from a long period of divergence, in the development of our species and our consciousness, to a new period of convergence.[390] The two symptoms we are displaying, mass-formation (overpopulation and compression of populations in urban areas) and the liberation of unused powers (the increase in leisure time and even the climb of unemployment), are the two *regular* symptoms of a leap in radial energy to a new stage in consciousness.[391]

"If it be supposed," Aurobindo continues the thought, "that her next step is the spiritual and supramental being, the stress of spirituality in the race may be taken as a sign that that is Nature's intention, the sign too of the capacity of man to operate in himself or aid her to operate the transition."[392]

It is vitally important to believe in that capacity, Teilhard feels: "At this decisive moment . . . what [man] needs before anything else . . . is to be quite certain . . . that the sort of temporal-spatial . . . cone into which his destiny is leading him is not a blind alley."[393] Failure to take evolution seriously at this point would result, Aurobindo thinks, in "an unnerving of the life-impulse . . . a missing of our natural response to the Divine Being's larger joy in cosmic existence and a failure of the great progressive human idealism by which we are spurred to a collective self-development."[394]

"Faith in the future," as Teilhard says, is what "must save us."[395] And fortunately we are encouraged to believe in the universe because it "has hitherto been successful in the unlikely task of bringing human thought to birth in what seems to us an unimaginable tangle of chances and mishaps."[396] Our own appearance certainly would have seemed impossible, if viewed from the original state of the universe; yet here we are. Shall we not believe that Nature will continue her program with comparable success? "Inconscience is the beginning, an evolution in the Ignorance is the middle," Aurobindo recounts, "but the end is the liberation of the spirit into its true consciousness and an evolution in the Knowledge."[397] He goes on:

> This is actually what we find to be the law and method of the process which has hitherto been followed and by all signs is likely to be followed in her future working by evolutionary Nature.[398]

So, asks Teilhard, why should we not have confidence in still another radical transformation of the universe, beyond its present state?

> Some hundreds of thousands of years ago, upon the first emergence of reflective consciousness, the Universe was surely and beyond question transformed in the very laws of its internal development. Why then, should we suppose that nothing new will appear under the sun of tomorrow, when the rebounding of Evolution is in full flood?[399]

Trust Evolution, our authors are saying. "The world . . . has from the beginning juggled miraculously with too many improbables," Teilhard concludes, "for there to be any risk whatever in committing ourselves further and following it right to the end."[400] Aurobindo also makes his act of faith: "It is this evolution which has enabled man to appear in Matter and it is this evolution which will enable him progressively to manifest God."[401]

Collective consciousness is something we must usher in with our own free choices and actions, and yet collective consciousness may be confidently expected to appear as the next phase in the universal evolution. Aurobindo speaks of it as a "gnostic" consciousness because it will come about in a "knowledge" which liberates us from the isolation of selfish individualism on the merely "mental" plane.

> As there has been established on earth a mental Consciousness and Power which shapes a race of mental beings and takes up into them all of earthly nature that is ready for the change, so now there will be established on earth a gnostic Consciousness and Power which will shape a race of gnostic spiritual beings and take up into itself all of earth-nature that is ready for this new transformation.[402]

For Teilhard it will be a triumph of the love which, immanent in all, will eventually reach its perfect convergence around Omega:

> Despite all checks and all improbabilities, we are inevitably approaching a new age, in which the world will throw off its chains and at last give itself up to the power of its inner affinities. Either we must doubt the value of everything around us, or we must utterly believe in . . . the inevitable consequences of universal love.[403]

REFERENCES

[1] Cf. Chittenjoor Kunhan Raja, *Some Fundamental Problems in Indian Philosophy* (Delhi: Motilal Banarsidass, 1960), p. 126.

[2] Pierre Teilhard de Chardin, *Human Energy,* tr. J. M. Cohen (New York: Harcourt Brace Jovanovich, 1969), p. 168.

[3] Teilhard, *The Phenomenon of Man* (New York: Harper Torchbook, 1961), p. 216.

[4] Teilhard, *The Vision of the Past,* tr. J. M. Cohen (New York: Harper & Row, 1966), p. 130.

[5] Teilhard, *Christianity and Evolution* (New York: Harcourt Brace Jovanovich, 1971), p. 207.

[6] Ainslie T. Embree, ed., *The Hindu Tradition* (New York: Modern Library, 1966), p. 220.

[7] *Ibid.*

[8] Bhagavad Gītā VIII. 17 (Edgerton).

[9] See Embree, pp. 220-21.

[10] Kunhan Raja, p. 158.

[11] Rig Veda VIII. 70. 5.

[12] Mircea Eliade, *Yoga:* Immortality and Freedom, tr. W. R. Trask (New York: Pantheon, 1958), p. 172.

[13] Teilhard, *The Phenomenon of Man,* p. 296.

[14] Cf. S. Chatterjee and D. Datta, *An Introduction to Indian Philosophy* (University of Calcutta, 1968), p. 227.

[15] *Ibid.,* p. 244.

[16] Cf. Teilhard, *Activation of Energy,* tr. René Hague (New York: Harcourt Brace Jovanovich, 1970), pp. 273-74, 324; Teilhard, *The Appearance of Man,* tr. J. M. Cohen (New York: Harper & Row, 1965), p. 219.

[17] Troy Wilson Organ, *The Hindu Quest for the Perfection of Man* (Athens: Ohio University, 1970), p. 305; cf. Surendranath Dasgupta, A *History of Indian Philosophy* (Cambridge University Press, 1968), I. 211-12 and M. Hiriyanna, *Outlines of Indian Philosophy* (London: Allen & Unwin, 1932), pp. 268-69. The earliest document we have is the *Sāṃkhya-kārikā* of the fifth century A.D., but Indian thought systems characteristically carry for long periods before being codified. There are traces of *Sāṃkhya* thought in much earlier material.

[18] Cf. Organ, p. 307, who suggests "cosmic energy."

[19] Cf. Chatterjee and Datta, pp. 261-62.

[20] Teilhard, *The Phenomenon of Man,* pp. 40-41.

[21] Cf. Dasgupta, I. 245.

[22] Teilhard, *The Phenomenon of Man,* p. 42.

[23] B. N. Seal, *Positive Sciences of the Ancient Hindus* (New York: Longmans Green, 1915), p. 7.

[24] Cf. Teilhard, *Human Energy,* p. 95.

[25] Teilhard, *The Phenomenon of Man,* p. 165.

[26] Dasgupta, I. 246-47.

[27] Teilhard, *The Phenomenon of Man,* p. 151 (translation corrected).

[28] Cf. *ibid.,* pp. 78, 168.

[29] Cf. *ibid.,* pp. 169, 86; also, Teilhard, *The Vision of the Past,* p. 148.

[30] Dasgupta, I. 247.

[31] Cf. Teilhard, *The Phenomenon of Man,* pp. 110, 268; *The Vision of the Past,* p. 97.

[32] Teilhard, *The Vision of the Past,* p. 109.

[33] Teilhard, *Letters from a Traveller* (New York: Harper & Row, 1962), p. 88.

[34] Cf. Teilhard, *The Divine Milieu* (New York: Harper & Row, 1960), pp. 108-9; *The Phenomenon of Man,* pp. 54, 84.

[35] Teilhard, *The Phenomenon of Man,* pp. 112-13.

[36] Teilhard, *The Vision of the Past,* p. 121.

[37] Cf. Teilhard, *Christianity and Evolution,* p. 98; *The Vision of the Past,* p. 148; also Teilhard, *The Future of Man,* tr. Norman Denny (New York:

Harper & Row, 1964), p. 23.

[38] Teilhard. *Christianity and Evolution,* p. 16.

[39] Teilhard, *The Phenomenon of Man,* p. 71.

[40] Eliade, p. 22.

[41] Teilhard, *The Making of a Mind,* tr. René Hague (New York: Harper & Row, 1965), p. 126.

[42] Teilhard, *The Appearance of Man,* p. 214 n.2; *The Future of Man,* p. 290.

[43] Teilhard, *The Future of Man,* pp. 129-30.

[44] Teilhard, *The Phenomenon of Man,* p. 71.

[45] Cf. Teilhard, *Activation of Energy,* p. 274, and *Human Energy,* p. 98.

[46] Teilhard, *Human Energy,* p. 97; *The Appearance of Man,* p. 161.

[47] Teilhard, *The Phenomenon of Man,* p. 56.

[48] *Ibid.,* pp. 58-59, 54 ff.

[49] Teilhard, *The Future of Man,* p. 130; *The Phenomenon of Man,* p. 60.

[50] Teilhard, *The Future of Man,* p. 174.

[51] Teilhard, *The Appearance of Man,* p. 139.

[52] Teilhard, *The Phenomenon of Man,* pp. 60-61.

[53] Teilhard, *Human Energy,* p. 11.

[54] Teilhard, *The Phenomenon of Man,* p. 300

[55] *Ibid.,* p. 89.

[56] Teilhard, *The Future of Man,* p. 66.

[57] Teilhard, *Christianity and Evolution,* p. 238. Cf. *Activation of Energy,* p. 324.

[58] Chatterjee and Datta, pp. 268-69.

[59] Eliade, p. 20.

[60] *Ibid.,* p. 21; cf. Chatterjee and Datta, pp. 270-73.

[61] Eliade, p. 21.

[62] Kunhan Raja, p. 126.

[63] Organ, p. 105.

[64] Alain Danielou, *Hindu Polytheism* (New York: Pantheon, 1964), p. 42.

[65] Vijayananda Tripathi, "Devata tattva," *Sanmarga* III (1942), 682.

[66] Cf. Teilhard, *The Vision of the Past,* pp. 249, 269.

[67] Teilhard, *The Future of Man,* pp. 65-66; *The Vision of the Past,* p. 21.

[68] Teilhard, *The Vision of the Past,* p. 158.

[69] *Ibid.,* p. 99.

[70] Teilhard, *The Future of Man,* p. 292.

[71] Teilhard, *The Vision of the Past,* p. 72.

[72] *Ibid.,* p. 150.

[73] Teilhard, *The Phenomenon of Man,* p. 258.

[74] Kunhan Raja, p. 126.

[75] Chatterjee and Datta, pp. 267, 273.

[76] Organ, p. 308.

[77] *Sāṃkhya-kārikā* 21 (Jha).

[78] Dasgupta, I. 248; cf. Organ, p. 308, and Chatterjee and Datta, p. 363.

[79] Cf. Organ, p. 305.

[80] Teilhard, *The Phenomenon of Man,* p. 66.

[81] Teilhard, *Man's Place in Nature,* tr. René Hague (New York: Harper & Row, 1966), p. 32.

[82] Teilhard, *The Phenomenon of Man,* p. 51.

[83] Teilhard, *Human Energy,* p. 23.

[84] Cf. Teilhard. *The Future of Man,* pp. 48-49.

[85] Teilhard, *Science and Christ,* tr. René Hague (New York: Harper & Row, 1968), p. 40.

[86] Teilhard, *The Future of Man,* p. 78.

[87] Cf. Teilhard, *The Appearance of Man,* pp. 265-66, and *Letters from a Traveller,* p. 151.

[88] Alain Danielou, *Hindu Polytheism* (New York: Pantheon, 1964), p. 253.

[89] Heinrich Zimmer, *Myths and Symbols in Indian Art and Civilization,* ed. J. Campbell (New York: Pantheon, 1946), p. 212.

[90] Cf. Danielou, pp. 268-84.

[91] Cf. Arthur and Ellen Avalon, *Hymns to the Goddess,* tr. from the Sanskrit, 3rd ed, (Madras: Ganesh, 1964), p. 9.

[92] Teilhard, *The Phenomenon of Man,* pp. 86, 188, 301.

[93] Cf. *ibid.,* pp. 110, 280, 301; Teilhard, *The Vision of the Past,* pp. 147-48, 273.

[94] Cf. Teilhard, *The Vision of the Past,* p. 91; *The Appearance of Man,* p. 136; *The Making of a Mind,* p. 205.

[95] Teilhard, *The Vision of the Past,* p. 72.

[96] Teilhard, *The Phenomenon of Man,* pp. 116, 223.

[97] *Ibid.,* p. 110.

[98] Cf. Teilhard, *Human Energy,* pp. 97-98.

[99] Teilhard, *The Vision of the Past,* p. 181.

[100] *Ibid.,* p. 159.

[101] Teilhard, *The Phenomenon of Man,* pp. 146, 167.

[102] Teilhard, *Writings in Time of War,* tr. René Hague (New York: Harper & Row, 1968), p. 79, italics omitted.

[103] Cf. Teilhard, *The Making of a Mind,* p. 166.

[104] Teilhard, *The Vision of the Past,* p. 186.

[105] Sir John Woodroffe and Pramatha Natha Mukhyopādhyāya, *Mahāmāyā: The World as Power: Power as Consciousness (Chit-Shakti)* (Madras: Ganesh, 1964), p. 35.

[106] Cf. *ibid.,* pp. xxiv-xxvi.

[107] *Ibid.,* pp. xxxiii-xliv.

[108] *Ibid.,* pp. 217-19.

[109] *Ibid.,* pp. 218-19.

[110] *Ibid.,* pp. 220-22.

[111] *Ibid.,* p. 222.

[112] *Ibid.,* pp. 226-27.

[113] Cf. *ibid.,* p. 228.

[114] Teilhard, *The Phenomenon of Man,* p. 178.

[115] Cf. *ibid.,* pp. 150-51; *The Future of Man,* p. 15.

[116] Teilhard, *Writings in Time of War,* p. 41; *The Phenomenon of Man,* p. 178.

[117] Teilhard, *The Phenomenon of Man,* p. 230.

[118] *Ibid.,* p. 42.

[119] *Ibid.,* p. 63; cf. p. 16.

[120] *Ibid.,* p. 64.

[121] Teilhard, *Letters from a Traveller,* p. 159; *Writings in Time of War,* p. 41.

[122] Cf. Teilhard, *The Vision of the Past,* p. 180; *The Future of Man,* pp. 201-2.

[123] Teilhard, *The Phenomenon of Man,* p. 64; cf. pp. 30, 219-20.

[124] Zimmer, *Myths,* p. 25, apparently quoting a lexicon.

[125] Śvetāśvatara Upanishad I. 3.

[126] *Ibid.,* II. 16-17.

[127] *Ibid.,* III. 15.

[128] *Ibid.,* III. 20-21.

[129] *Ibid.,* VI. 5-13.

[130] *Ibid.,* IV. 1.
[131] *Ibid.,* IV. 5.
[132] Dasgupta, V. 170.
[133] *Ibid.,* V. 184-85.
[134] *Ibid.,* V. 68.
[135] *Ibid.,* V. 90.
[136] *Ibid.,* V. 81-82.
[137] *Ibid.,* V. 99, 112.
[138] *Ibid.,* V. 48.
[139] R. C. Zaehner, *Hinduism* (Oxford University Press, 1966), p. 89.
[140] *Ibid.*
[141] Dasgupta, V. 169.
[142] Zimmer, *Myths,* pp. 202-3.
[143] Dasgupta, V. 29-30.
[144] *Ibid.,* V. 100.
[145] Zimmer, *Myths,* pp. 202-3.
[146] Avalon, *Hymns,* pp. 3-4.
[147] Heinrich Zimmer, "The Indian World Mother" [1938], in *The Mystic Vision,* Papers from the Eranos Yearbooks VI, ed. Joseph Campbell (Princeton University Press, 1968), pp. 77-78.
[148] Cf. Rig Veda III. 55.
[149] Avalon, *Hymns, passim.*
[150] Cf. S. Radhakrishnan, *The Principal Upanishads* (London: Allen & Unwin, 1953), p. 83 n.1.
[151] Eliade, p. 15.
[152] Avalon, *Hymns,* p. 69.
[153] Danielou, p. 32.
[154] Cf. H. V. Glasenapp, "Tantrismus und Schaktismus," *Ostasiatische Zeitschrift* VI. 22 (1936) 120.
[155] Cf. Woodroffe and Mukhyopādhyāya, *Mahāmāyā,* pp. 219, 229.
[156] Dasgupta, V. 172.
[157] Chintaharan Chakravarti, *The Tantras: Studies on Their Religion and Literature* (Calcutta: Punthi Pustak, 1963), p. 39.
[158] *Mahānirvāna Tantra* IV. 11.
[159] Avalon, *Hymns,* p. 9.
[160] Rig Veda X. 125. 1-8. Comments in brackets added.
[161] Teilhard, *The Phenomenon of Man,* pp. 30, 219-20, 153.
[162] Teilhard, *The Future of Man,* p. 208 n.1.
[163] Dasgupta, V. 31.
[164] Teilhard, *Letters from a Traveller,* p. 142.
[165] Teilhard, *Writings in Time of War,* p. 129.
[166] Cf. Teilhard, *The Phenomenon of Man,* p. 250.
[167] Teilhard, *Writings in Time of War,* p. 128.
[168] Cf. Teilhard, *Hymn of the Universe* (New York: Harper & Row, 1965), p. 23.
[169] *Ibid.,* p. 150.
[170] *Ibid.,* p. 21; cf. p. 78.
[171] *Ibid.,* pp. 79, 118.
[172] Teilhard, *The Future of Man,* p. 260.
[173] *Ibid.,* pp. 222, 172.
[174] *Ibid.,* p. 204.
[175] Teilhard, *Letters from a Traveller,* p. 364.
[176] Teilhard, *Hymn of the Universe,* p. 22.

[177] *Ibid.*, p. 29.
[178] Ananda K. Coomaraswamy, *The Dance of Shiva* (New York: Noonday, 1957), p. 70.
[179] Rig Veda X. 88. 2.
[180] *Ibid.*, I. 68. 2.
[181] *Ibid.* VII. 4. 3-4.
[182] *Ibid.* VII. 4. 6.
[183] *Ibid.* VI. 8. 1-2.
[184] Embree, pp. 20-21; cf. Rig Veda I. 1.
[185] Abinash Chandra Bose, *Hymns from the Vedas* (New York: Asia Publishing House, 1966), p. 30.
[186] Rig Veda VI. 9. 5.
[187] *Ibid.* VI. 14. 2.
[188] *Ibid.* VII. 3. 1.
[189] Teilhard, *The Phenomenon of Man*, pp. 64-65.
[190] *Ibid.*, pp. 63-64; *The Appearance of Man*, p. 265 n.1.
[191] Cf. Teilhard, *The Phenomenon of Man*, p. 65; *The Appearance of Man*, p. 393.
[192] Cf. Teilhard, *Activation of Energy*, p. 393.
[193] Teilhard, *The Appearance of Man*, p. 265.
[194] Teilhard, *Activation of Energy*, p. 121 n.10.
[195] *Ibid.*, p. 102.
[196] *Ibid.*, pp. 10-13.
[197] Teilhard, *Christianity and Evolution*, p. 137.
[198] Woodroffe and Mukhyopādhyāya, *Mahāmāyā*, p. 201.
[199] *Ibid.*, p. 147.
[200] *Ibid.*, pp. 218-19. Cf. Sir John Woodroffe, *The World as Power* (Madras: Ganesh, 1966), p. 265.
[201] Cf. Woodroffe and Mukhyopādhyāya, *Mahāmāyā*, p. 29.
[202] *Ibid.*, pp. 24-27.
[203] *Ibid.*, pp. 199-200; cf. p. 158.
[204] Teilhard, *Activation of Energy*, p. 104.
[205] Woodroffe and Mukhyopādhyāya, *Mahāmāyā*, p. 71 n.4.
[206] *Ibid.*, p. 63.
[207] Cf. *ibid.*, p. 71.
[208] *Ibid.*, pp. 64-65.
[209] *Ibid.*, pp. 29, 25, 27.
[210] *Ibid.*, p. 32.
[211] *Ibid.*, p. 220.
[212] *Ibid.*, p. 219.
[213] Teilhard, *Activation of Energy*, pp. 102-3.
[214] Woodroffe and Mukhyopādhyāya, *Mahāmāyā*, p. 221.
[215] Teilhard, *Activation of Energy*, p. 105.
[216] Cf. Teilhard, *The Phenomenon of Man*, p. 45; *The Vision of the Past*, p. 223; *Man's Place in Nature*, p. 109.
[217] Teilhard, *The Phenomenon of Man*, p. 89.
[218] Teilhard, *The Vision of the Past*, p. 225.
[219] Cf. *ibid.*, pp. 89, 82; Teilhard, *The Appearance of Man*, pp. 128-31, 122, 30, 52, 147.
[220] Woodroffe, *The World as Power*, p. 263.
[221] *Ibid.*, p. 267.
[222] Woodroffe and Mukhyopādhyāya, *Mahāmāyā*, p. 175.
[223] Woodroffe, *The World as Power*, p. 254.

[224] Cf. Chāndogya Upanishad III. 14. 3.
[225] Woodroffe, *The World as Power,* p. 268.
[226] *Ibid.,* 299.
[227] *Ibid.,* 279.
[228] Teilhard, *Activation of Energy,* p. 377.
[229] Cf. Teilhard, "The Spiritual Share of the Far East."
[230] Cf. Teilhard, *The Vision of the Past,* p. 96.
[231] Cf. *ibid.,* p. 197; Teilhard, *The Appearance of Man,* pp. 140-41; *The Phenomenon of Man,* pp. 165-66; *Activation of Energy,* p. 323.
[232] Teilhard, *The Vision of the Past,* p. 180.
[233] *Ibid.,* p. 158.
[234] Teilhard, *The Phenomenon of Man,* p. 180.
[235] Teilhard, *The Appearance of Man,* p. 53.
[236] *Ibid.,* p. 49; cf. Teilhard, *The Phenomenon of Man,* p. 170.
[237] Teilhard, *The Vision of the Past,* p. 73.
[238] Teilhard, *The Appearance of Man,* p. 137; *The Phenomenon of Man,* p. 163.
[239] Teilhard, *The Phenomenon of Man,* p. 171; cf. *The Appearance of Man,* pp. 226-27.
[240] Teilhard, *The Appearance of Man,* p. 138.
[241] Teilhard, *The Phenomenon of Man,* p. 171.
[242] Teilhard, *The Vision of the Past,* p. 262; *The Appearance of Man,* pp. 224-25.
[243] Cf. Teilhard, *The Future of Man,* p. 14; *The Vision of the Past,* pp. 207-8; *The Phenomenon of Man,* p. 302.
[244] Cf. Teilhard, *The Vision of the Past,* pp. 260, 262, 64-66, 136; *The Phenomenon of Man,* pp. 34, 181.
[245] Woodroffe and Mukhyopādhyāya, *Mahāmāyā,* p. 241.
[246] *Ibid.*
[247] Cf. Teilhard, *The Vision of the Past,* p. 64. Cf. *The Appearance of Man,* p. 232.
[248] Teilhard, *Activation of Energy,* p. 100.
[249] Cf. Zimmer, *Myths,* pp. 140-42.
[250] Woodroffe and Mukhyopādhyāya, *Mahāmāyā,* p. 61.
[251] *Ibid.,* p. 215.
[252] Woodroffe and Mukhyopādhyāya, *Mahāmāyā,* p. 69 n.1. Cf. M. P. Pandit, *Studies in the Tantras and the Veda* (Madras: Ganesh, 1964), p. 38.
[253] *Ibid.,* p. 72.
[254] Teilhard, *Human Energy,* pp. 147-48.
[255] Cf. Eliade, p. 265.
[256] Woodroffe and Mukhyopādhyāya, *Mahāmāyā,* p. 206.
[257] Teilhard, *Activation of Energy,* pp. 104-5.
[258] *Ibid.,* p. 111.
[259] Woodroffe and Mukhyopādhyāya, *Mahāmāyā,* p. 90.
[260] Teilhard, *Activation of Energy,* p. 112.
[261] Woodroffe and Mukhyopādhyāya, *Mahāmāyā,* p. 89.
[262] *Ibid.,* p. 92.
[263] *Ibid.,* p. 93.
[264] Teilhard, *Activation of Energy,* p. 112.
[265] *Ibid.,* p. 113.
[266] Woodroffe and Mukhyopādhyāya, *Mahāmāyā,* pp. 93-94.
[267] Teilhard, *Activation of Energy,* p. 113.
[268] Woodroffe and Mukhyopādhyāya, *Mahāmāyā,* p. 96.

[269] Teilhard, *Activation of Energy,* p. 226.

[270] *Ibid.,* pp. 226-27.

[271] According to the Tantrics, the universe consists of a "grand cosmos," *Mahābrahmānda,* and of numerous macrocosms evolved from it, which in turn contain microcosms. Each derivative level, the *Nirvāna Tantra* teaches, reflects faithfully all that was contained in the greater form above it. The Hermetic maxim, "As above, so below," is expressed in the *Vishvasāra Tantra* as "What is here is elsewhere; what is not here is nowhere." Sir John Woodroffe, *Introduction to Tantra Shastra* (Madras: Ganesh, 1969), p. 35.

[272] Woodroffe and Muckhyopādhyāya, *Mahāmāyā,* p. 239.

[273] Cf. Eliade, p. 245.

[274] Cf. Eliade, pp. 241-43.

[275] Cf. Woodroffe, *Introduction,* pp. 25-26, 35; Pandit, pp. 63-64.

[276] Cf. *The Saundaryalahari,* tr. W. Norman Brown (Cambridge: Harvard University Press, 1958), vss. 9-11.

[277] Zimmer, *Myths,* p. 143.

[278] *Satcakranirupa,* 2-3 (Woodroffe).

[279] Cf. Pandit, p. 84.

[280] Eliade, p. 82; cf. p. 94.

[281] *Goraksha Shataka,* 49 (Briggs).

[282] Teilhard, *The Vision of the Past,* p. 171.

[283] Teilhard, *Human Energy,* p. 121.

[284] *Ibid.,* pp. 96-97.

[285] Organ, p. 325.

[286] P. T. Raju, *Introduction to Comparative Philosophy* (Lincoln: University of Nebraska Press, 1962), pp. 231-32.

[287] Organ, pp. 105-6.

[288] Teilhard, *Christianity and Evolution,* pp. 106-7.

[289] Teilhard, *Writings in Time of War,* p. 24.

[290] Teilhard, *Christianity and Evolution,* p. 32 and n.4.

[291] Teilhard, *The Making of a Mind,* p. 96.

[292] Teilhard, *The Phenomenon of Man,* p. 141.

[293] Cf. *ibid.,* pp. 142, 146, 148, 180; Teilhard, *The Future of Man,* p. 64; *The Vision of the Past,* p. 246; *The Appearance of Man,* pp. 151, 215, 218, 220, 222.

[294] Teilhard, *The Future of Man,* pp. 214-15.

[295] Cf. *The Future of Man,* p. 223f; *The Phenomenon of Man,* pp. 210, 297-98; *Letters from a Traveller,* pp. 299, 300.

[296] Teilhard, *The Vision of the Past,* pp. 227-28.

[297] Teilhard, *The Phenomenon of Man,* p. 109.

[298] Woodroffe and Mukhyopādhyāya, *Mahāmāyā,* pp. 33-34.

[299] Dasgupta, V. 60.

[300] Woodroffe and Mukhyopādhyāya, *Mahāmāyā,* pp. 223-24.

[301] Teilhard, *The Appearance of Man,* p. 168.

[302] Teilhard, *The Phenomenon of Man,* p. 101; cf. *The Appearance of Man,* p. 45.

[303] Teilhard, *Christianity and Evolution,* p. 106 and n.2; *The Vision of the Past,* p. 206.

[304] Woodroffe and Mukhyopādhyāya, *Mahāmāyā,* p. 225.

[305] *Ibid.,* p. 33.

[306] Teilhard, *Writings in Time of War.* p. 32.

[307] Śrī Aurobindo, *The Life Divine,* Vol. III of the Śrī Aurobindo Center

of Education Collection (Pondicherry: Śrī Aurobindo Ashram Press, 1960), p. 996.

[308] Śrī Aurobindo, *On Yoga* Volume II Tome I (Pondicherry: Śrī Aurobindo Ashram Press, 1958), p. 346; cf. *The Life Divine,* pp. 102, 665.

[309] Aurobindo, *The Life Divine,* pp. 838, 792-93.

[310] Teilhard, *The Phenomenon of Man,* p. 165.

[311] Aurobindo, *The Life Divine,* p. 1003.

[312] *Ibid.,* p. 1112.

[313] Teilhard, *Man's Place in Nature,* p. 121 n.1.

[314] Aurobindo, *The Life Divine,* pp. 1005-6.

[315] *Ibid.,* p. 1006.

[316] *Ibid.,* p. 26 and *passim.*

[317] Teilhard, *The Future of Man,* p. 280.

[318] Aurobindo, *The Life Divine,* p. 1009.

[319] Teilhard, *The Vision of the Past,* p. 229.

[320] Aurobindo, *The Life Divine,* pp. 249-50.

[321] Teilhard, *The Vision of the Past,* p. 229.

[322] Aurobindo, *The Life Divine,* p. 825.

[323] Teilhard, *The Vision of the Past,* p. 253.

[324] Teilhard, *The Appearance of Man,* p. 163; *The Future of Man,* pp. 143-44, 171-72.

[325] Aurobindo, *The Ideal of Human Unity* (New York, Dutton, 1950), p. 161; *The Synthesis of Yoga* (Pondicherry: Śrī Aurobindo Ashram Press, 1957), p. 14.

[326] Aurobindo, *The Synthesis of Yoga,* p. 15.

[327] Teilhard, *The Phenomenon of Man,* p. 244.

[328] "Le Coeur de la Matière" (unpublished).

[329] Aurobindo, *The Life Divine,* p. 1213.

[330] Cf. Teilhard, *Building the Earth* (Wilkes-Barre: Dimension Books, 1965), p. 54; *The Phenomenon of Man,* p. 262; *Human Energy,* p. 144; Aurobindo, *The Ideal of Human Unity,* pp. 162-63.

[331] Teilhard, *The Phenomenon of Man,* p. 257.

[332] Aurobindo, *The Life Divine,* p. 1255; cf. *The Ideal of Human Unity,* p. 163.

[333] Teilhard, *Human Energy,* p. 151.

[334] Aurobindo, *The Life Divine,* p. 1256.

[335] Teilhard, *Human Energy,* pp. 126-27.

[336] Aurobindo, The *Synthesis of Yoga,* p. 700.

[337] Aurobindo, *The Life Divine,* p. 617.

[338] Teilhard, *The Phenomenon of Man,* p. 263.

[339] Aurobindo, *The Life Divine,* p. 1228.

[340] Teilhard, *The Phenomenon of Man,* p. 263; cf. *Human Energy,* pp. 64-65.

[341] Aurobindo, *The Life Divine,* p. 1228.

[342] Teilhard, *The Phenomenon of Man,* p. 263.

[343] Aurobindo, *The Life Divine,* p. 1267.

[344] Teilhard, *The Future of Man,* p. 146.

[345] Aurobindo, *The Life Divine,* pp. 1255, 1027.

[346] Cf. Teilhard, *Man's Place in Nature,* pp. 100-102; *Human Energy,* pp. 64, 123; *The Future of Man,* pp. 46, 118-19.

[347] Cf. Teilhard, *Science and Christ,* pp. 80, 16.

[348] Teilhard, *The Phenomenon of Man,* pp. 246-47.

[349] Aurobindo, *The Life Divine,* p. 1231.

[350] Teilhard, *Human Energy,* p. 118.
[351] Aurobindo, The *Life Divine,* p. 1231.
[352] Teilhard, *The Future of Man,* pp. 256-57; cf. *Science and Christ,* p. 144.
[353] Aurobindo, *The Life Divine,* p. 1260.
[354] Teilhard, *The Future of Man,* pp. 258-59.
[355] Aurobindo, *The Life Divine,* p. 1260.
[356] Teilhard, *The Phenomenon of Man,* p. 264.
[357] See my "Teilhard de Chardin: The Amorization of the World," *World Union* XI (1972), 2, pp. 18 ff.
[358] Aurobindo, *The Life Divine,* p. 244.
[359] Teilhard, *The Phenomenon of Man,* p. 263.
[360] Aurobindo, *The Life Divine,* p. 1236.
[361] *Ibid.*
[362] Teilhard, *Human Energy,* p. 137.
[363] Teilhard, *The Phenomenon of Man,* p. 251.
[364] Aurobindo, *The Life Divine,* p. 233.
[365] Teilhard, *Human Energy,* p. 82.
[366] Teilhard, *Building the Earth,* p. 89.
[367] Aurobindo, *The Life Divine,* p. 818.
[368] Teilhard, *The Future of Man,* pp. 285, 287.
[369] Aurobindo, *The Ideal of Human Unity,* p. 308.
[370] Teilhard, *The Future of Man,* p. 287.
[371] Teilhard, *Human Energy,* p. 31; cf. *The Making of a Mind,* p. 236.
[372] Cf. Teilhard, *The Phenomenon of Man,* pp. 266-67, and Aurobindo, *The Life Divine*. p. 1219.
[373] Teilhard, *The Phenomenon of Man,* pp. 270-71; *Human Energy,* pp. 147-48; *Science and Christ,* pp. 49-50, 52-53.
[374] Aurobindo, *The Life Divine,* pp. 170-71, 255, 281, 209, 840, 160-61, 341, 207, 143-45.
[375] Teilhard, *The Phenomenon of Man,* p. 269; *Human Energy,* pp. 147-48.
[376] Aurobindo, *The Life Divine,* p. 160.
[377] *Ibid.,* p. 789.
[378] Aurobindo, *Essays on the Gita* (Pondicherry: Śrī Aurobindo Ashram Press, 1950), p. 157.
[379] Aurobindo, *The Ideal of Human Unity,* p. 66.
[380] Teilhard, *The Future of Man,* pp. 286-87.
[381] Aurobindo, *The Life Divine,* pp. 1073, 1075; *Essays on the Gita,* pp. 394-95.
[382] Teilhard, *Human Energy,* p. 155.
[383] Aurobindo, *Essays on the Gita,* p. 478.
[384] *Ibid.*
[385] Teilhard, *Human Energy,* p. 156.
[386] *Ibid.,* p. 150.
[387] Aurobindo, *The Life Divine,* pp. 1252, 1255.
[388] Teilhard, *The Future of Man,* p. 255.
[389] *Ibid.,* p. 295.
[390] Teilhard, *Man's Place in Nature,* p. 102.
[391] Teilhard, *The Phenomenon of Man,* p. 252.
[392] Aurobindo, *The Life Divine,* p. 1003.
[393] Teilhard, *Man's Place in Nature,* pp. 103-4.
[394] Aurobindo, *The Life Divine,* pp. 805-6.
[395] Teilhard, *The Future of Man,* p. 81.
[396] Teilhard, *Science and Christ,* p. 41.
[397] Aurobindo, *The Life Divine,* p. 839.

[398] *Ibid.*
[399] Teilhard, *The Future of Man,* p. 212.
[400] Teilhard, *The Phenomenon of Man,* p. 232.
[401] Aurobindo, *The Life Divine,* p. 70.
[402] *Ibid.,* p. 1151.
[403] Teilhard, *Human Energy,* p. 153.

4

EVOLUTION TOWARD DIVINITY

Man's Responsibility To Act

We saw in the last chapter the vehemence with which Teilhard urged that humanity is presently facing a grave crisis in its own evolution and must take thoughtful and dedicated action in order to survive into the next era of cosmogenesis. This stress on action is a large concern—even the paramount concern—in the Teilhardian outlook on life, and is at the bottom of all his negative judgments of Hinduism. The Hindu tradition, he felt, is passive, it gives up in the face of difficulties, it encourages people to forsake earthly life and to interest themselves only in some kind of Nirvana—a nothingness in which all that evolution had struggled for in the way of individuality, freedom, and consciousness would melt away in a vast, faceless, nameless non-being. And it is not hard to understand why, given everything else that he stood for, Teilhard should feel this way about any culture that encouraged such attitudes in its people. But is it correct to so characterize the Hindu traditions in general, to write them off the list of truthful and useful formulations of humanity's position in the universe?

It is not as though Teilhard had not a leg to stand on in taking this position. Aurobindo also complained bitterly of the apathy of his people and attributed it to certain religious and philosophical doctrines then current and even deeply entrenched.[1] These doctrines come down basically to a set of ideas which may be grouped under the head "Māyāvāda" and which were given their momentum in India by Śaṅkara. However, in defense of Śaṅkara it must be said that the popularization of his doctrine which led to the attitude of disregard for this world is an oversimplification which misses the subtlety of Śaṅkara's logic and the elevation of his whole point of view. Furthermore, as we have already said, even Śaṅkara's own doctrine in its purity cannot maintain itself as an *orthodox*—i.e. Vedic—Hindu position. So it is hardly correct to identify "Hinduism" in terms of his teachings, much less in terms of popular corruptions of them.[2]

Another point that has to be taken into consideration is the fact that India, at the time at which the world-renouncing mood was strongly upon it, had been for a very long time under foreign domination. The humiliations and deprivations imposed by foreign rulers, combined with the poverty and enforced ignorance of the majority of the citizens, could hardly provide the best field in which to cultivate faith in the progressive tendency of the world and aspirations to enlarge the city of man.[3] Such situations, on the contrary, rather open men's eyes to the reality of the transcendent realm—something that is also true, no matter how enamored we may become of building the earth. Teilhard himself admitted to such moods on occasions of personal tragedy—"wouldn't it be better to abandon to its own sort of suicide this absurd world which destroys its own best productions, and preoccupy oneself with the supernatural alone . . ."[4] . . . "what an absurd thing life is . . . so absurd that . . . if there were no such thing as spirit . . . we should have to be idiots not to call off the whole human effort"[5]—and in the end he made a strange peace with this view, as we shall see in his treatment of death.

Nevertheless, the Hindu traditions arising from happier periods of Indian history have always put a good deal of emphasis on action in the world and on man's responsibility in his own realm and for the lower kingdoms over which he has some control. The great word *Dharma,* which runs through all traditions, expresses precisely this sense of obligation, responsibility, commitment, devotion to one's proper role in the context of community life and of the whole cosmos. It is to these traditions that the great activist leaders of India have turned and in which they have found plentiful inspiration for their exhortations to the Indian people and the people of the world to dedicate themselves to strength, to skill, to compassion, to intelligence, service, perseverance, and all the other virtues of the active life. As K. M. Sen says, "It is often said that the Hindu ideal is inactivity, but in fact a considerable part of the Hindu scriptures discuss the value of an active life."[6]

For instance, in the Rig Veda we find hymns to Ushas, the dawn goddess, who is worshiped as the patroness of daily life, the one who leads people "not only from darkness to light, but . . . from inaction to action."[7] She calls equally to all classes of human activity:

> One to rulership, one to high fame,
> One to a desired pursuit, one to gainful labor, . . .
> All to look after their different vocations
> All living creatures has Ushas awakened.[8]

And the Vedic people responded with alacrity and confidence:

> Arise! The breath, the life has reached us,
> Darkness has passed away, light is coming.
> She has left a path for the sun to travel,
> And we have come where men extend their lives.[9]

The actions now undertaken are not just for sport; they are for achievement. The limitations of the human condition must be recognized and the most effective use made of one's time:

> As a mist dims a form, age diminishes us;
> Before this hurt falls upon us, arrive.[10]

The same advice is repeated in the *Kulārnava Tantra*: "Before the adversities arrive, before the limbs decay, achieve thy weal."[11]

The Śakti-Vādins, as might be expected, are particularly strong on the importance of action. They see no point in worshiping pure inactivity. Pure contemplation without action is dead contemplation, they say.[12] It is impossible, in any case, to give up all action, says the *Kulārnava Tantra,* following the Bhagavad Gītā. What one must give up, if he would be free, is egoistic attachment to the fruits of his action.[13] This does not mean that one should not enjoy his life in this world. When one does not identify with the success or failure of one's own conscientious efforts, but feels instead an identification with the whole creative action of the Divine Mother, then one is truly liberated from egoism and free to enjoy all that the Mother does in the world.[14]

The great Hindu epics, the *Rāmāyana* and the *Mahābhārata,* glorify the active lives led by their heroes. Poets sing of the beauty of life on earth and sometimes even contrast it with the lesser life of the gods in heaven.[15] Summing up Sanskrit literary production in the words of Chittenjoor Kunhan Raja, we may say that

> there is no literary work, small poems or longer epics or dramas in Sanskrit literature, in which Samnyāsa, or renunciation, and the Vedantic [Māyāvāda] ideals are glorified. Practically no ascetic comes on the stage, and if any ascetics are introduced, it is only to engage them in helping active life in the world. . . . Home and married life, duty of the citizens, the aspirations and the activities and the disappointments and successes of the individuals, are the main themes worked out in all the literary works.[16]

If he had known of this enthusiasm for the active life and the high regard with which the Hindu views the human being's place in the general scheme of things, Teilhard might have revised his judgment on the universal passivity of the oriental religions. The position of man as the active factor in the evolutionary process was an important part of his theory, and in Hinduism he could have found a parallel to his ideas as close as in his own religious tradition. The Judaeo-Christian culture had certainly accentuated the significance of man with respect to God's relation to the world and the latter's destiny. In fact, it had so concentrated on man that the rest of the cosmos was seen only in terms of its support of man and service to him. Teilhard himself is not free of this exploitative attitude, speaking of mastering, dominating Nature, conquering the world, exercising humanity's rights as the chosen elite over all other creatures[17]—but at other times he seems to have some attraction to a broader view which he might have developed, had his theology encouraged it.

More ready to criticize the scientific than the religious outlook here, Teilhard complains that man suffers in the modern scientific view from being almost lost amidst the cosmic energies.[18] Morphologically he may not be very different from the other higher animals, but the way in which he is different makes all the difference, and science, says Teilhard, has failed to fit human intelligence into its general theory of the universe, neglecting an entire dimension of reality.[19] But man alone, Teilhard insists, is the key to explain all of Nature. Therefore science must replace man in Nature.[20] He must be seen in the context of the whole of Nature, not as separated. Humanity forms an independent zone of the universe, but it was produced by the whole earth.[21] Man was born from the earth in his entirety: not only in his body, but in his thought.[22] He is, in fact, the objective of all of Nature's evolution, the one fruit the universe was concerned to produce.[23]

> By the simple fact of his presence in Nature, man imposes on the cosmos, first a *certain stuff* and then a *certain structure;* and the result of this dual operation is to make him, man, *the most significant and the most valuable portion of the universe* in the field of our experience.[24] . . . He is of unique value . . . because he is . . . the most mobile in the course of transformation. To decipher man is to find out how the world was made and how it ought to go on making itself.[25]

In these last views Teilhard could clasp hands with the Hindus on several points. Man is, with them also, "the most significant and the most valuable portion of the universe" —and this is in comparison, in their case, not only with animals, vegetables, and minerals, but also in comparison with those ideal beings, the devas. Man is greater than the devas, as Troy Organ says, because "his becoming-being is rich with real possibilities, whereas [a] god's fixed-being is complete in its ideality."[26] Teilhard says that "humanity" is "wholly unique in its destiny and structural potentialities."[27] And Organ, representing the Hindu view, continues, "Man is the possible. This is why the Purāṇas say that the life of man is desirable even by the gods of heaven, since it is only through a human incarnation that final liberation can be achieved." And he adds an image that reminds us of Teilhard's "axis" of evolution: "Man is on the main line to the Self."[28]

M. P. Pandit explains the value that Hindus place on man in a way that brings out another Teilhardian theme when he says, "Birth in the human body is rightly considered to be an event of crucial importance in the evolution of the soul. It is only the human being who gets the chance to exercise his faculties consciously and choose his destiny. He alone, among created beings, can evolve in the direction he prefers."[29] As Teilhard puts it, man progresses not by the acquisition of any particular material organs, but by the development of the very source of all action: he has "kept his liberty . . . at the maximum."[30]

The reason given in the Hindu scheme of things for this unique superiority is the same reason Teilhard offers: man's reflexive consciousness. Professor Organ says, "The primal ignorance can become identified, and hence overcome, only in the creature for whom Self-consciousness is a possibility. Man is that creature. Only he can know that he knows. Only in him can objectification and plurification turn back upon Itself."[31] We may notice also in this last remark the Teilhardian ideas of man being the point at which the manyness of the world begins to draw into unity, and of its doing this by a process of "turning back on itself." It is for this reason that Teilhard proclaims that man has "the possibility and power of forming in the heart of space and time, *a single point of universalisation* for the very stuff of the world."[32]

Consequently, Teilhard feels, and the Hindu traditions we are citing agree, man's responsibility in the world is critical and inescapable, both for his own evolution and for all other creatures. "If man is to come up to his full measure," says Teilhard, *"he must become conscious of his infinite capacity for carrying himself still further;* he must realize the duties it involves, and he must feel its intoxicating wonder. He must abandon all the illusions of narrow individualism and extend himself, intellectually and emotionally, to the dimensions of the universe: and this even though, his mind reeling at the prospect of his new greatness, he should think that he is already in possession of the divine, is God himself, or is himself the artisan of Godhead."[33] An amazing statement from the man who dismissed the Hindu outlook on man, world, and God so quickly. It is almost a perfect summary of precisely what the Hindu is trying to do. Compare these words from Professor Organ, who presents an extremely convincing case for "Hindu humanism":

> Man is the being that includes the potentiality of becoming more than his status as man. . . . If man's potentialities are infinite and eternal, then perfection cannot be defined within any limits. . . . Hinduism is a pursuit, . . . a striving. . . . This continuous endeavor toward fulfilment is a promise, and, like all ideals, a forever falling short of the goal. . . . While it is correct to say that for Hinduism man is the being who must come to know his own being, it is incorrect to construe this "knowing" in either a discursive or an intuitive fashion. Self-realization is a process, not a cognitive state. . . . His ultimate *dharma* lies in the service of ideals he cannot possibly achieve. His salvation is in losing himself in quest of a Perfection beyond realization. Man's "being" is a becoming. His is-ness is in process such that he never *is* with the finality of God or beast. In process he *creates* his being.[34]

One of Teilhard's most quoted sayings is "God makes us make ourselves."[35] He has also said, "Created beings must work if they would be yet further created."[36] As for man, his function is to build and direct the whole of the Earth,[37] to complete cosmic evolution by making the energies at the heart of matter work until all their potencies are realized.[38] Teilhard says that the man who understands evolution finds in his heart

> . . . the fearful task of conserving, increasing and transmitting the fortunes of a whole world. His life, in a true sense, has ceased to be private to him. Body and soul, he is the product of a huge creative work with which the totality of things has collaborated from the beginning; if he refuses the task assigned to him, some part of that effort will be lost for ever. . . . The success of the whole affair, of this huge universal childbirth, actually rests in the hands of the least among us. These are the holy words which everyone must try to say, but which the evolutionist, most of all, has the true right to repeat.[39]

This, then, is the meaning and value of action: the completion of creation.[40] Ultimately nothing else can mean anything to man, Teilhard says[41]; the human vocation is to create an eternal work which cannot exist without us.[42] And to do this we must concentrate our energies on perfecting man.[43] We are to save the great work which is the world by saving ourselves.[44] If we quit, all evolution will come to a halt, because *"we are evolution."*[45]

Here we come again to the problem we have touched on several times already, the problem of determinism and freedom in Teilhard's conception of evolution. The universe is governed by a general plan of development to which each advancing level conforms, under the law of "recurrence of pattern." If it is not to be utterly absurd, it must eventually fulfill and complete the totalized form toward which it is tending. Yet, at the critical stage of hominization, when evolving Nature produces the self-conscious being, the very process of evolution itself passes into the freedom of man. It is not just that under the rule of his freedom the world will continue to evolve, but that his *freedom itself*—the self-possession of freedom, the reflexive consciousness of being free, the way in which freedom is exercised—must now evolve. This is what Teilhard means when he says "we are evolution," and this is the crisis of action at the human level. Let us see it in a little more detail.

As we have noted a number of times, Teilhard considers that the law of irreversibility of living forms is invariable.[46] Complexity and consciousness *always* advance with advancing time. But how can we reconcile this persistent growth with the chemical determinism of molecules, with the blind play of gene combinations in chromosomes, with the now established failure of acquired characters to be transmitted to offspring?[47] A movement toward the improbable, which is what evolution is, must clearly be a movement toward the indeterminate. But since all of the world stuff seems to be possessed of such an impulse toward arrangement, it must be a fact of Nature that there is a "center of indeterminacy at the very heart of every element of matter."[48] If the cosmic matter itself were entirely passive, indifferent to the process of complexification, or opposed to it, the organized universe could never have arisen by the sheer play of chance.[49] As for mutations, how could they be so successful if they are completely blind and mechanical, or purely random? These external changes, Teilhard believes, must be only facades for some secret development of instinct, or life-tendency. Such a suggestion immediately raises the specter of vitalism, he acknowledges, but what is unscientific about vitalism, he argues, is making it directly responsible for physico-chemical effects. In his own conception, life is a way of synthesizing the physico-chemical determinisms which already exist in their own right, and this synthesizing ability is exercised on a higher level, a "meta-level" with respect to the physico-chemical effects themselves.[50]

The synthesizing tendency, which is the essence of life, is itself the continuum of freedom, Teilhard claims. On the higher reaches of the scale, in human consciousness, we recognize it as deliberate choice, but it is really the same kind of ability, more and more restricted as we descend the scale, which accounts for the building of all improbable structures.[51] That what is free can be analyzed into a set of determinisms does not prove that the living world is not based on freedom, Teilhard asserts.[52] "Spirit always will, as it always has, make sport of every sort of determinism and chance. It represents the indestructible portion of the universe."[53]

Śaktism, and other Hindu traditions, have a similar view of the situation. The evolving world, they say, is fundamentally an expression of free play, or sport, *līlā*. It is spontaneous activity which, when it takes upon itself the limitations of the various types of being, appears in the form of a series of more or less determined individuals. As Woodroffe says, "The world shows centres in different stages of growth: they appear to constitute an hierarchy from 'dead' matter to the highest Spirit. It both means and requires that their positions in the cosmic dynamic system are different, and . . . [that the] more or less spontaneous activities by which those positions are sought to be altered, are different." Nevertheless, "at the root, we can have nothing but *Chit* 'elaborating' its Bliss by Play; no particular Centre can, therefore, have its action absolutely determined."[54] This "Play" takes the form of a synthesizing activity, as is shown in the *Rudra-saṃhita* of the *Śiva-Mahāpurāṇa,* where the creation of the world is described. In "the beginning," there was only a state which was neither being nor nonbeing; it was beyond all name and form—that is, it had no structure at all. It was pure consciousness and pure bliss, devoid of all qualities.[55] Then there arose within this consciousness the will to produce form by spontaneous activity. The production of form from the relatively formless is, of course, precisely what synthesis is. And the form that this creative energy produced was its own body, even as Teilhard suggests that Life builds its own bodies of increasing complexity and freedom.[56]

Life, says Teilhard, builds up *"machines for accumulating and multiplying indeterminacy,"* thus gradually "escaping from chance."[57] It may be through strokes of chance that life proceeds, but it is strokes of chance which are recognized and grasped, which are psychically selected.[58] The root of life, Teilhard suggests, in unknown sympathy with the Śāktas and other Hindus, is an energy which is desire.[59] He says:

> To wake and nourish human energy, there must have been at the very outset an inner attraction towards a desired object. Things cannot have happened otherwise.[60]

And the Hindu scriptures say:

> In the beginning there was desire,
> Which was the primal germ of the mind.[61]
>
> It [Being alone, one only, without a second] thought,
> May I be many, may I grow forth.[62]
>
> He, the Ātman, desired: May I become many; let me procreate myself. He performed Tapas. Having performed Tapas he created all this.[63]

Compare, too, the hymn of creation in Rig Veda X. 190. 1: "Universal Order and Truth were born of blazing Tapas." *Tapas* is concentrated energy of will-consciousness, sometimes translated "austerity." It refers to the effort that is made to attain some goal, usually a spiritual ideal, and is associated with heat. I think that we may fairly call it "an energy which is desire."[64]

Material determinism, Teilhard concludes, is really only

an epiphenomenon to the advance of conscious freedom.[65] It is something like the relation of Māyā to the manifesting Spirit, in the Hindu conception. The Supreme Spirit, or Self, is free and blissful, and the world is Her play. As Mahāmāyā, She controls Māyā, the principle of measurement, definition, limitation, specific form. But the individual selves, produced by the finite manifestation of the Supreme Spirit, are subject to the conditioning effect of Māyā. They can be only such and do only so, according to the limited forms and functions assigned them. The heart of their reality is pure Spirit, no doubt, but this freedom is variously restricted and veiled by the material determinisms in which they are clothed.[66]

The appearance of determinism being the ground of existence, in contrast with which freedom is an aberration, is accounted for, says Teilhard, by the statistical pattern thrown over a large number of elementary spontaneous freedoms.[67] Each of them exercising its own spontaneity in and through the conditions of its given stage in the evolution, makes the total picture look as though the behavior was rigorously fixed. Woodroffe says something rather similar in the course of explaining the Śākta view of the complex relations of spontaneity (play, *līlā*) and conditioning due to past action (*adṛṣṭa*). Every being is a combination of both factors, but one or the other may predominate according to the observer of the given being. The appearance of "the so-called causal chain of necessity" is therefore due to looking only at the adṛṣṭa factor, "an outcome of abstract analysis of physical . . . science." Actually, every being possesses also the play factor as a "dynamic power" that "tends to make things depart from any line that may have been predetermined for them by the total assemblage of conditions. It implies . . . freedom . . . transcending the causal chain of necessity. . . . The result, accordingly, is that the world does not move in an absolutely fixed line."[68] As Teilhard says, "Organic life under cover of the determinisms analysed by . . . science is . . . an infinite fumbling and perpetual discovery."[69]

Teilhard is sure that the impetus of the world, seen in the great drive of consciousness, can only have its source in an inner principle, which alone can explain its advance toward higher psychisms.[70] "Bones and tissues," he says, "are only the shells in which psychic tendencies have successively clothed themselves; and these tendencies were the product always of the same fundamental aspiration to know and act."[71] The Śākta would say that the Power of Consciousness, Bliss, and Play has "chosen to subject itself to varying limitations, or as it has been often put, clothed itself with 'sheaths' [*kośas*] of varying density." This is a precondition of the evolution of a world of various forms, all seeking "self-determination," "freedom to act," and a "readiness to create."[72]

Both Teilhard and the Hindus—particularly the Śakti-vādins—see the pilgrimage of life forms, and especially of man, through this world in terms of a certain balance of the forces of determinism and freedom. Freedom, Teilhard says, emerges from Nature by gaining control of the determinisms.[73] We advance toward freedom by making choices within the world of determinism.[74] In Śakti-vāda, one can speak of a "ratio of determination and freedom," or of adṛṣṭa and līlā, the extent to which the Cosmic Power is either latent in the being or patently exhibited. Adṛṣṭa represents the set of conditions imposed upon the being, the determinisms to which it is subject. These are constituted by its latent relations with other beings and can be traced to earlier conditions in the history of the being. The Cosmic Power, which is itself pure freedom, is static, or latent; in this case, we may note a resemblance to Teilhard's "tangential energy." Līlā, on the other hand, is the spontaneity of the being, its ability to place its own actions (*karma*), to be "self-determined" rather than "other-determined." In this case the Cosmic Power is patent and operative, and corresponds to Teilhard's "radial energy," because its function is to advance the being to higher evolutionary stages.

According as the ratio of līlā, or karma, to adṛṣṭa is higher, so the being ranks above those having lower ratios. Adṛṣṭa predominates in matter. In mind karma (free action) rules. Life represents a balance midway between. "The greater its coefficient of *Karma,* involving control of *Adṛṣṭa,* and the greater therefore its manifestation of Joy and Play, the higher is the place of a Centre or group of centres in the Scheme of Beings," Woodroffe tells us.[75] This measure of the position of a form in the evolutionary procession is precisely the same as that pointed out by Teilhard: "This *coefficient of centro-complexity* (or, which comes to the same thing, of consciousness) is the true absolute measure of being in the beings that surround us."[76]

But a being can move within the system by virtue of its exercise of karma. From the lowest forms of spontaneous action in the atoms, through the different functions of the life-energy, to the deliberate actions of the self-conscious human being, karma (exercise of freedom) is the source of progress through the grades. "Shastra [the revealed Scriptures], therefore, holds," says Woodroffe, "that any Centre, by appropriate *Karma,* can raise itself to the level of the Highest Centre."[77] There is also collective as well as individual *karma,* and so the world-process moves "on the whole towards betterment or 'progress.' "[78]

To appreciate the irony, let us call to mind once more Teilhard's words, from *The Phenomenon of Man*:

> The primitive soul of India arose in its hour like a great wind but, like a great wind also, again in its hour, it passed away. How indeed could it have been otherwise? Phenomena regarded as an illusion (Maya) and their connections as a chain (Karma), what was left in these doctrines to animate and direct human evolution?[79]

The misunderstanding is so glaring now that no comment is necessary. We may content ourselves with an apt quotation from Professor Organ's thoroughly documented book, *The Hindu Quest for the Perfection of Man,* showing just how "otherwise" things in fact are, and what *is* "left in these doctrines to animate and direct human evolution":

> To regard Hinduism as fatalism is a serious error, since the cause and effect relationship in human affairs is the presupposition of any theory of meaningful freedom. Man's coming-to-be, which is his self-realization, is not a playing with the self, not an introvertive activity having little or no relation to the world of external phenomena, for man must realize himself in relations to other men, to nature, and to God.[80]

Now, let us go back and pick up the problem of determinism and freedom from a somewhat different point of view. Recognizing that evolution is now concentrating on the human level, that this means that another "change of state" is in the offing as the next advance in the world's development, and that this change of state will involve a collective union of human individuals in which love of one's fellows must supersede our customary selfishness, we see this problem: How can the evolving universe insist that its free products, human persons, *spontaneously* create the conscious union that *must* appear if Nature's pattern of development is to remain consistent? Teilhard (and Aurobindo, representing a Hindu response to the same problem) had answered that the human elements will unite in a new and higher level of consciousness because they sufficiently *desire* to do so.

It is desire that is the resolution of the determinism/freedom dilemma. When a being moves under the influence of desire, the origin of the movement is in itself; the movement is not an *effect*. Yet the movement is not altogether original with the desiring being, for it is essentially a *response*. It presupposes another being which "beckons," so to speak, and which therefore must be imaged as "up ahead" or "above." This is why Teilhard says that the persistent rise of the world toward ever more improbable states of complexity is a process not supported by a base in the past but suspended from a point of aspiration in the future. It is this, he says, which renders the movement of the world not only irreversible but irresistible.[81]

Desire, then, or love or self-donation or dedication—any positive movement of the will—is the reconciliation of determinism and spontaneity. If the "beckoning being" is so adjusted to the incomplete nature of the "desiring being" that it unquestionably represents the fulfillment of that creature's nature, then the creature cannot avoid desiring it without contradicting its own being. The urgency of "determinism" thus is at its ultimate degree for that kind of being, namely a being capable of desire. But at the same time, because his movement, properly considered, begins only when he himself responds to the attraction, his freedom is intact. He is not acted upon by the other. The only thing the "beckoning being" has to do initially is to *be* sufficiently desirable and to be *present.*

But is there such a "beckoning being" in the consciousness of the persons who are called upon to advance the progress of evolution by their free action? Is there really something to desire, to believe in, to hope for, to expect with confidence? One of Teilhard's constantly repeated themes is that human action is paralyzed by realization of futility.[82] We cannot give ourselves to action without some rational justification, he says; the object of our labors must be worth the effort expended.[83] As he becomes more conscious, man sees the problem of action. He is obliged to act if he is to live. But are life and Nature only playing with him? Is he being seduced by drives programmed into him to play a role in a game ultimately meaningless? Satisfaction of instincts or even the fulfillment of economic needs is not really enough to make his work worthwhile.[84] He needs a future that includes the most valuable elements in his life in order to be encouraged to go forward.[85] Only the evolution of life itself can be his motive. And only the intrinsic value of man himself can justify this struggle to advance.

We move forward, then, drawn by hope. But we have several very stringent conditions. First, the object of our hope must be of *universal* dimensions. We must have faith in the "final completion of *everything* around us."[86] Second, we refuse to work unless the effort has some chance of success.[87] Everything that diminishes faith in the result of the action diminishes our power to act.[88] Third, we will not move except toward that which is endlessly new.[89] Fourth, we insist that we and the fruit of our labors should escape destruction.[90] We demand not only personal immortality in order to have the heart to exert ourselves, but collective immortality.[91] And as workers, we see our dilemma, says Teilhard. Why should we work if our product is not immortal? Why should anyone submit to evolution if he is not traveling toward something that is forever? A vast stretch of time is not acceptable. Mere positivist "progress" does not finally eliminate death. That on which we set all our hopes, and which at bottom motivates us to act, must be independent of all the forces on which things in this world are dependent.[92] In fine, what we require for even the simplest deliberate action is the implicit presence of an absolute.[93] Humanity needs an infinite objective to which it can wholly dedicate itself.[94]

Such must be the Being which "beckons" to us from the future and from above. Teilhard is arguing that belief in God is a necessity for survival and for the further progress of evolution. "Biologically," he says, humanity "is faced with a choice between suicide and adoration."[95] But if believing in God is a condition for our successful action in life, then God must be true and more real than ourselves. Otherwise the condition for life would be less real than the life itself.[96]

We said earlier that all the "beckoning being" had to do initially in order to motivate human action was to be present and to be desirable. Now, in order to complete the Teilhardian—and Hindu—argument for the reconciliation of freedom and determinism, we must explore one further dimension. When this divine Being *is desired* and *is sought,* a new question arises. If the God we seek is a Supreme Person, as we have concluded in earlier sections, then the mere response of desire or even of striving on the part of the desiring being is not the end of the story. For the Beckoner is also free and must freely give Himself to His lover. When He does so, this is what we call *grace,* and it is a clear Hindu concept as well as a Christian one, as we documented in the section on the personal God.

Divine grace, in the end, is revealed as the real guarantee of evolution and consequently the sure ground of our hope and the liberator of our energy of action. The Bhagavad Gītā says, "In [the Lord] alone take refuge with all your being, all your love; and by his grace you will attain an eternal state, the highest peace."[97] And strangely enough, this attainment, achieved beyond our own efforts, is more sure than is our own work. In Teilhard's words:

> Hitherto, in our anticipation of fuller-being we had proceeded entirely by way of reason, our successive intuitions remaining within the scientific framework of "hypothesis." As soon, however, as we admit the reality of a *reply* coming from on high, we in some way enter the order of certainty.[98]

The Gītā, too, holds that certainty comes through the grace of God: if one rejects it and relies only on his own powers, he will perish.[99]

But humanity must not perish. It must go on to form the next level of evolving consciousness, the collective consciousness of the community of mutually loving persons. And this is what divine grace guarantees, because it is itself the "binding energy" of this collective being, the common life of this new being. It is through grace, says Teilhard, as a "single and identical life" that we are to become "much more than kinsmen, much more, even, than brothers: we become identified with one and the same higher Reality."[100] Here Śrī Aurobindo, who shares so much of Teilhard's vision of the coming collective life, agrees very strongly with him. There is such a Reality, Aurobindo confirms, and "the community is a formation of the Reality" in which each member recognizes "the Divine which is in him and in all."[101] As this Divine Spirit grows within, "oneness with our fellowmen will become the leading principle of all our life . . . a deeper brotherhood, a real and an inner sense of unity . . . and a common life."[102]

This will be the perfection of our freedom, Teilhard holds, and Śrī Aurobindo supports his view. "A single freedom, taken in isolation," says Teilhard, "is weak and uncertain and may easily lose itself in mere groping. But a totality of freedom, freely operating, will always end by finding its road."[103] Freedom does not mean, Aurobindo agrees, "an independent will acting on its own isolated account . . . [a] single unrelated movement."[104] In any case, "the will of the individual, even when completely free, could not act in an isolated independence, because the individual being and nature are included in the universal being and Nature and depend on the all-overruling Transcendence."[105] This is really the point, and now the hiatus between our conceptions of determinism and of freedom closes in the presence of the Transcendent, that is, in the action of the Absolute Being. Teilhard sees it thus:

> No doubt it is true that up to a point we are free *as individuals* to resist the trends and demands of Life. But does

> this mean (it is a very different matter) that we can escape collectively from the fundamental set of the tide? I do not think so. . . . Nothing . . . can prevent the universe from succeeding—nothing, not even our human liberties, whose essential tendency to union may fail in detail but cannot (without "cosmic" contradiction) err "statistically."[106]

The conclusion is that our action, which is necessary, but which is possible only when we are properly motivated, finds its true freedom when it unites itself with the action of God. In Aurobindo's words, it is only "when it becomes an instrumentation of a higher instead of a lower Power that the will of the being becomes free."[107] And Teilhard summarizes the whole argument by focusing on the apparent paradox:

> Determinism appears at either end of the process of cosmic evolution, but in antithetically opposed forms: at the lower end it is forced along the line of the most probable *for lack of freedom;* at the upper end it is an ascent into the improbable through *the triumph of freedom.*[108]

The reconciliation of determinism and freedom in a transcendent Absolute who is also an active Person is a great vision and is the most profound insight of either Teilhard or the Hindu tradition into the significance of action. The thesis of God's action as the matrix within which all finite actions are situated is essential to the teaching of the great Hindu scripture, the Bhagavad Gītā. Maryse Choisy points this out in a little book on Teilhard and India, which puts the finger so well on many of the sensitive spots in this area. According to the Bhagavad Gītā, as Choisy rightly says, to the dynamic of our personal nature is added all the force of the will of God. Our actions are integrated into the plan of the Cosmos itself. By this continuous relation with God, not only does the multiple become the One, but, says the Gītā, the One becomes also eternally the multiple in a communion without cessation. Choisy boldly concludes that "the Gītā here completes the design of Father Teilhard."[109]

This is the final working out in the Bhagavad Gītā of a train of thought which began in the Upanishads with the doctrine that Brahman is identical with Ātman. It is the dynamic interpretation of that union, its application to actuation. As K. M. Sen says, "Once the Upanishads reveal their doctrine of the all-pervading God, the ideal of selfless work preached by the Bhagavad Gītā is difficult to avoid."[110] In the Gītā the Brahman-Ātman identity is elevated still higher to the Puruṣottama, as we have seen earlier, and this Supreme Person becomes incarnate as the Lord Kṛṣṇa. He appears as the Divine Worker, the one whose constant activity upholds the world. Just as Jesus is seen by Teilhard as the animator of human action,[111] so Kṛṣṇa is represented as the model of holy work:

> Whatever the noblest does, that too will others do: the standard that he sets all the world will follow.
>
> In the three worlds there is nothing that I need do, nor anything unattained that I need to gain, yet work [is the element] in which I move.
>
> For if I were not tirelessly to busy Myself with works, then would men everywhere follow in my footsteps.
>
> If I were not to do my work, these worlds would fall to ruin.[112]

Teilhard says that the duty of serving the world is hard to bear, like a cross—and that is why Christ chose it, so that every man could recognize himself there[113]—but he never suspected, Choisy tells us, that his thesis of the collaboration of man with God for the achievement of the world actually forms the backbone of the Bhagavad Gītā.[114] Teilhard thought that "Eastern religions logically lead to passive renunciation,"[115] not realizing that in the Gītā there is continuous and consistent advocacy of the active life and open rejection of passive renunciation of action.[116]

> Not by leaving works undone does a man win freedom from [the bond of] works, not by renunciation alone can he win perfection's prize.[117]

This passage is one of many in which Kṛṣṇa addresses Himself directly to the problem of action, which is the central problem of the Gītā. Here we have another rather curious instance of Teilhard's presumption that something which only now comes to consciousness in the West is appearing on the human scene absolutely for the first time. Prior to the passage we are about to quote, Teilhard has noted that as human beings we must act, whether we will or not, for it is our nature. He then raises the question of whether we should resist the current of evolution or passively submit to it or cooperate with it. He concludes, "Hence it is that, *for the first time* since the awakening of life on earth, the fundamental problem of action has finally emerged into our human consciousness in the twentieth century. Up to now man has acted principally out of instinct, from day to day, without much knowledge of why or for whom he was working."[118]

But compare the Gītā. First, Śrī Kṛṣṇa points out that "not for a moment can a man stand still and do no work, for every man is powerless and made to work by the constituents born of Nature [the guṇas of Prakṛti]."[119] He then attacks the problem of action: Does one attain the highest end by engaging in action or by renouncing action? And He answers that one must neither resist the current nor submit passively, but act wholeheartedly in cooperation with the divine action. He even distinguishes between acting "out of instinct . . . without . . . knowledge of why or for whom" one is working and acting with wisdom:

> As witless [fools] perform their works attached to the work [they do], so, unattached, should the wise man do, longing to bring about the welfare [and coherence] of the world.[120]

It is essentially the same problem that Teilhard poses, and even the same solution chosen from among the same alternatives. Teilhard is asking, To what does our action lead? does it lead to salvation? And the Gītā asks, How shall we gain salvation? is it by action? So "the fundamental problem of action" emerged into human consciousness quite some time before the twentieth century.

The famous answer of the Bhagavad Gītā to the action problem is: "Act without attachment to the fruits of the action."[121] The worker is not to make devotion to his task depend on his private satisfaction in it, on whether he is praised or blamed.

> Winning some pleasant thing [the sage] will not rejoice, nor shrink disquietened when the unpleasant comes his way.[122]

If he acts with a selfish motive—"cooks for his sake"—he does evil.[123] He should rather offer his work, whatever it is, to the Lord of work as a sacrifice.[124] *Sacrifice* is the Vedic image of the cosmic work which maintains the order of the universe. By recommending work done as sacrifice, comments Mircea Eliade, Kṛṣṇa is teaching that men should transform all their actions into "transpersonal dynamisms contributing to the maintenance of cosmic order."[125] It is the same attitude which Teilhard recommends:

> Why, before I act, should I be concerned to know whether my effort will be noticed or appreciated? Why should I feed my appetite for action with the empty hope of prestige or popularity? The only reward for my labour I now covet is to be able to think that it is being used for the essential and lasting progress of the universe.[126]

Action with such a motive is what the Hindus call *karma yoga,* union with God in action. Teilhard himself describes it very well, saying, "Every action, as soon as it is oriented towards [Christ], takes on, without any change in itself, the psychic character . . . of an act of love. . . . [One] can unite oneself directly to the divine Centre through action itself, no matter what form such action takes."[127] In the Bhagavad Gītā, action offered to God is an act of love, is received by the Lord as such, and returned. Śrī Kṛṣṇa says, "It is I who of all sacrifices am recipient and Lord,"[128] and He encourages the devotee to "cast all your works on Me."[129] Whatever action is offered, the Lord says, He willingly accepts, "for it was love that made the offering."[130]

> In whatsoever way [devoted] men approach Me, in that same way do I return their love.[131]

It does not matter, says Teilhard, what the work is. "Never, at any time," he advises, " 'whether eating or drinking,' consent to do anything without first of all raising its significance . . . *in Christo Jesu.* . . . This is . . . the very path to sanctity for each man according to his state and calling . . . be it lowly or eminent, to which [he] is destined both by natural endowment and by supernatural gift."[132] He could hardly have defined karma yoga more precisely. In the Gītā, the Blessed Lord says:

> Whatever you do, whatever you eat, whatever you offer in sacrifice or give away in alms, whatever penance you may perform, offer it up to Me.[133]

And again,

> By doing the work that is proper to him . . . prescribed by his own nature . . . [and] rejoicing [in the doing], a man succeeds, perfects himself. . . . By dedicating the work . . . to Him who is the source of the activity of all beings, by whom this whole universe was spun, a man attains perfection and success.[134]

Henri de Lubac, discussing Teilhard's view of detachment, says that it is not minimized in comparison with earlier Christian attitudes of forsaking "the world," but that "it will be renunciation of personal satisfaction, not of use . . ."; it must take primarily the form of an "emergence" or a "passing beyond." It must derive, he says, now quoting Teilhard, "from 'a sort of higher indifference (impassioned indifference) which is born of attachment, in all things, to what is above all.' "[135] This is very much the view of the Gītā, in which desireless action is done by raising one's consciousness to the level of the Divine[136]:

> Therefore, detached, perform unceasingly the works that must be done, for the man detached who labors on to the highest must win through.[137]

The movement of the will, which in the unenlightened, is directed toward the specific fruits of particular actions which benefit the agent and those with whom he identifies himself, is replaced in the enlightened person by a pure love of God, who is the Supreme Agent, the one who reigns over the world.[138] Therefore our concern in our actions can only be to identify ourselves with the Lord's action, surrender all to Him, and loving and trusting Him, find our fulfillment. Teilhard says, "This concern . . . to make God reign over all things must be . . . an *habitual guiding force* behind all our actions (even the most trifling), which are then made as perfectly as possible in order that God may dwell more intensely in our souls and, through them, in everything else too."[139] And Śrī Kṛṣṇa, in the Gītā, says:

> Let him then do all manner of works continually, putting his trust in Me; for by my grace he will attain.
>
> Give up in thought to Me all that you do, make Me your goal; relying on the integration of the soul, think on Me constantly.
>
> Bear Me in mind, love Me and worship Me . . . so will you come to Me.
>
> . . . he comes to know Me as I really am, how great I am and who; and once he knows Me as I am, he enters [Me] forthwith.[140]

The Problem of Death and the Taste for Life

Teilhard's quest for the Holy Grail, a single cup to hold the mingled wine of all his loves, had led him into conflict with a number of giants. Most of these he had conquered, at least according to his standards of conquest. Creation *by* God but *by means of* evolution was relatively easily handled. The directionality of evolution itself, progressing always toward the higher regions of increased complexity, consciousness, and freedom, he had argued to his own satisfaction, if not to that of the modern biologist. The integration of all substances and all forces in some highly generalized "psychic energy" was a much more daring exploit, a challenge to the towering guardians of conservative conceptions of the physical and psychological worlds. But the integrity of his own system held fast in the conflict, and he proceeded to the projection of the next level of evolution, which took the form of a superorganization of the individual grains of thought into a single earth-covering envelope of unanimity.

With all these conquests behind him, Teilhard now comes to confront what his mentor, St. Paul, had aptly called "The Last Enemy": the two-headed dragon of death and despair. Reality is evolution, evolution is progress toward greater freedom under the impulse of the freedom already achieved, and therefore evolution will only go forward if the free elements in it choose to go forward. The next step is precisely an organization of these free units *as free*; it is an organization of their free relations to one another, an organic network of loves. But love is inescapably an orientation to the future; it is a will that all be well and be ever better with the beloved. How can it coexist with a conviction that things *cannot* be well with the beloved? What can it do in face of the possible nonexistence of the beloved? Persuaded of the finality of total death, how could we go on? We could not, says Teilhard; the only response to total death is total despair and the cessation of all action.

> We must strive for ever more greatness; but we cannot do so if we are faced by the prospect of an eventual decline, a disaster at the end. With the germ of consciousness hatched upon its surface, the Earth, our perishable earth that contemplates the final, absolute zero, has brought into the Universe a demand, henceforth irrepressible, not only that all things shall not die, but that what is best in the world, that which has become most complex, most highly centrated, shall be saved. . . . Evolution proclaims its challenge: either it must be irreversible, or it need not go on at all![141]

Taking comfort in our immediate and temporary progress does not answer the challenge. Our material acquisitions, our political organizations, our artistic creations, our whole civilization—these are enormous entities, perduring over long stretches of time, but they do not escape destruction. To console ourselves with these is only to push back the problem, Teilhard says. However great our achievements, "however large the radius traced [by them] within time and space, does the circle ever embrace anything but the perishable?"[142] On this level it does not, he admits. "Ultimately we find ourselves thoroughly uprooted . . . from everything perceptible on earth."[143] Nevertheless, the human spirit boldly issues its own ultimatum. The only conditions under which men will continue to act are: 1) that consciousness survive the final death of the earth; and 2) that this immortality apply to all the deepest parts of our consciousness, that is to our *person*.[144]

The problem of death is an especially difficult problem for Teilhard, not only because it is characterized by ultimacy and finality, but because it is two-pronged. It is a question not only of the death of the individual but of the death of the universe. Teilhard accepts the scientific opinion according to which the entire material universe, under pressure of increasing entropy, will eventually degenerate into a homogeneous mass of particles reduced to the same energy level. All organizations broken down, no action will be possible. If this is to be the case, what becomes of that whole beautiful picture of a cosmogenesis? Was there not an opposed current, a trend *toward* organization, toward the unification of the multiple? How reconcile this with the inescapable "heat death" of the stellar universe? There will be an ingenious way out of this quandry, but first let us state the companion problem, that of individual death.

A person lives in the midst of the cosmogenetic process, being himself an element in it. He dies, still in the midst of that process. On the cosmic scale, the process is still going on, but he is no longer an element in it. If he—or we—conceive his reality in terms of his contribution to the cosmogenesis, what meaning do we attach to what is frequently his abrupt removal before his work is finished? If he does indeed survive in spirit, what is his relation to the cosmogenesis that is still going on among those from whom he has been removed? Teilhard himself does not frame this last question, but surely it is implicit in his own schema.

The Teilhardian solution to the problem of death is based on the thesis that the evolutionary process exists to produce and conserve, not material energies, but persons.[145] Not only does all material being exist *for the sake of* human souls,[146] but there is a "*general 'drift' of matter* towards spirit. This movement must have its term: one day the whole divisible substance of matter will have passed into the souls of men."[147] The world " 'tumbles' . . . forward and upward upon the spiritual . . . giving a cosmic consistency to the centres of consciousness . . .: that personal treasure, the centre within every soul, is imperishable, and the supreme Centre must be both lovable and loving."[148] The goal, as we already know, is the formation of an "organism" of persons centered on the Supreme Person, Christ-Omega.[149] This organism is constantly growing, gradually accumulating its constituent elements from humanity as each person freely chooses to order his perspectives, his loves, and his actions so as to take his place in the whole.[150] When it has matured, Mankind will detach itself from its base on the planet Earth, on which it no longer depends, and find its whole support in its point of spiritual concentration, Omega.[151]

The Earth may die of excessive entropy, but the free persons will live beyond this death in the highest achievement of the unification of the multiple, the cosmic body of Christ. Nor is this merely a rescue or an escape; it is a natural and inevitable culmination of the very processes inherent in cosmogenesis itself, Teilhard claims. Because Mankind is convergent and concentrated upon itself, through "very excess of unification and co-reflexion" it will achieve "a new break-through . . . outside Time and Space."[152] The last "critical threshold" will be the one crossed from planetary life to life purely in "the one true . . . essence of things, the Omega point."[153] This is "the hominisation of death itself" in which the universe continues to organize itself "above our heads in the inverse direction of matter which vanishes."[154] Without surprise we should expect to pass by "dematerialisation to another sphere of the universe."[155] It is the "ultimate break-up of the partnership complexity/consciousness, to release, in the free state, a thinking without brain."[156] Death, therefore, in the sense of the separation of the soul, or the personal consciousness, from dependence on the body, or space-time-matter vehicle, far from being a problem for evolution, is a *requirement* for the last stage of evolution as envisioned by Teilhard.

As for the individuals who die along the way of the advancing trajectory of the cosmogenesis, Teilhard seems to believe that they are doing on the individual level the same thing that the personalized universe will do as a whole at the Omega point of its evolution:

> All around us, 'souls' break away, carrying upwards their incommunicable load of consciousness.[157]
>
> The 'gathering together' of the Spirit gradually accomplished in the course of the 'coiling' of the Universe, occurs in two tempos and by two stages—*a* by slow 'evaporation' (individual deaths); and simultaneously *b* by incorporation in the collective human organism ('the mystical body') whose maturation will only be complete at the end of Time.[158]

It is a brilliant solution, no doubt, especially when we consider that Teilhard had to work it out in terms of his evolutionary schema in general, but also with one eye on the theological position of his Church. Nevertheless, there are difficulties with it, one or two of them serious.

The first difficulty is the status of the individual who separates from the cosmogenetic process in mid-course. Since the evolution is an evolution of individuals, each individual is himself only as far advanced as the evolution as a whole is at the time of his death (even if we define the degree of progress of the whole by its most advanced member). The evolution was supposed to reach gradually the point at which persons could detach themselves from the space-time-matter matrix; that was the solution of the problem of cosmic death. But the universe has not reached this point at the time our individual dies. Teilhard himself had said that the world has not yet "reached a stage of development so advanced that its 'soul' can be detached . . . as something wholly formed. . . . Any immediate withdrawal . . . would certainly be premature."[159] Then, is not this "harvesting" of individual souls[160] likewise premature?

What is the position of this individual? Does he go on evolving "alongside" the material universe, keeping abreast of its development so that he will be ready to join in that great spiritual concentration around Omega at the end? But he is by definition outside space and even outside time. Without time there can be no evolution. Is he then fixed forever at whatever stage of evolution he had attained at the time of his death? If so, how can he enter into the Ultra-Humanity of the last days? Participation in that unity requires that one have attained that level of development; in fact, entrance into it is identically the evolutionary advance itself. Perhaps the individual is abruptly and supernaturally transformed at the moment of his death into a person developed to that stage necessary for entrance into the Supreme Noosphere. But this would contradict two of Teilhard's cherished principles: that everything happens by gradual evolution, not arbitrary leaps, and that the Divine does not intervene in the regular progress of the universe. It is difficult to see what solution is possible within the limitations of Teilhard's presuppositions, scientific and theological.

Would the Hindu traditions have anything useful to offer at this point? The first thing we think of is, of course, the theory of reincarnation. It seems at first glance an easy way out of the difficulty. If the individual cannot "keep up" with the rest of the cosmogenesis on the "outside," then let him re-enter the temporal world and so continue in the total stream of development. Remembering the usual accompanying doctrine, that the conditions of the succeeding life are determined by the actions of the preceding life, we may think that Teilhard's word, "God makes us make ourselves," even finds an echo in the Brahmana's "Every man is born in the world fashioned by himself."[161]

It should be noted, in passing, that the doctrine of reincarnation does not characterize the entire body of Hindu tradition. It was unknown to the Aryan authors of the Rig Veda and appears as a new doctrine in the Upanishads. We should be aware, also, that the hypothesis of reincarnation was not introduced among the Hindus in the context of our evolutionary problem, but rather as an answer to the question of whether the heavenly life after death does not also end in a death of its own which projects the subject again into earthly life.[162] This consideration gave rise, in the Upanishadic period, not so much to an optimistic pursuit of the journey of life as to a search for a way to transcend both life and death. However, the Brihad-Āraṇyaka Upanishad does indicate that the transmigrating soul aims to make the new body better than its predecessor, and in the later Tantric development, the succession of lives is seen as a means of improving one's life from level to level, together with the general progress of the whole world. We will say more about that in the following section.

In such an adaptation to the evolutionary framework, the reincarnation hypothesis does seem a rather tidy way of solving the problem on the theoretical level, because it handles both the individual and the universe under one structural scheme. If individuals separate from the general cosmic process at random points, it would seem that two distinct theoretical constructs are required to account for their respective destinies, and in order to hold true to Teilhard's basic vision of the intrinsic relations of matter and spirit, world and person, we would then be obliged to seek a further generalization which would reduce these two to one. The reincarnation proposal would seem, if not to obviate, at least to minimize this difficulty.

However, the rebirth doctrine brings problems of its own, chief of which is the lack of empirical evidence. And even on the theoretical level there are many questions. How do we account for expanding populations? Does this process of rebirth apply to all living things? If so, what defines individuality at the lower levels of life? What are the implications for the law of complexity/consciousness if the non-material "portion" of a living being can detach itself from this material vehicle and install itself in another? How, precisely, is the "transfer" effected? And what exactly is it that "transfers"?

The Brihad-Āraṇyaka Upanishad attempts to answer the last two questions in the case of the human being by saying that the essence of the life-forces survives the particular body, together with intelligence, knowledge, and the work that one has done. These constitute the link to the next embodiment. The soul, consisting of these principles of continuity, reaches out for the new body even before it has quite departed from its present one. Here there is some vague resemblance to Teilhard's description of an advance in evolution being made by an overlapping leaf in the sheaf of species, that is, a new start being made even before the old pattern has been abandoned. But over-all, the problems with the reincarnation hypothesis are numerous, subtle, complicated in themselves, and attempts to resolve them are severely hampered by the unavailability of what our present scientific method demands in the way of testing and evidence.

Teilhard himself felt that reincarnation was of no help to him because the reincarnated person cannot remember and recognize himself as being the same as in the previous life.[163] But this is just what reflexive consciousness—human being—requires. Without reflexive, self-possessing consciousness, one is not human. And not to remember or recognize oneself would argue that one is not reflexively conscious—or at least, that the reflexivity as such did not bind over from one life to the next. Somewhere in the interval or the transfer, reflexivity was interrupted. There is no way in Teilhard's theory to account for such an interruption.

On the other hand, Teilhard admits that "everything, in some extremely attenuated extension of itself, has existed from the very first."[164] Erik Erikson comments, in *Gandhi's Truth*: "Let us face it: 'deep down' nobody in his right mind *can* visualize his own existence without assuming that he has always lived and will live hereafter; and the religious world-views of old only endowed this psychological given with images and ideas which could be shared, transmitted, and ritualized."[165] Perhaps this is the significant thread of unity in this case between Teilhard and this Hindu image of the greater life, and perhaps we should leave the problem of the departing individual's relation to the continuing cosmogenesis unresolved while we turn our attention to the Hindu attitude toward the general question of individual death.

The most important note in the Hindu attitude toward life and death, and that with which Teilhard is in full agreement, is the affirmation that the most truly "I" part of the human being must be saved and that when life reaches its perfection nothing of value will be lost.[166] Closely allied with this thought is the conception of body, life, and mind as "conditions or instruments for the life of spirit in man." As Radhakrishnan says, "They are not ends in themselves, but are means or opportunities for the expression of the Universal Spirit in us."[167] How much this sounds like Teilhard's assertion that in "alliance" with matter we "draw nearer to the Spirit."[168] The universe which began from a single giant atom concentrating all matter in itself, will end, says Teilhard, in a single "idea-emotion," the Christ-centered Noosphere, all spirit. It is a "spindle-shaped universe, closed at each end . . . by two peaks of diametrically opposite character."[169] In the *Sāṃkhya Kārikā* it is written: "As a dancer desists from dancing, having exhibited herself to the audience, so does Primal Matter desist, having exhibited herself to the spirit."[170]

Death, in the Yoga tradition, is really a new birth into

life, because through its enforced reversal of attention from the external to the internal, the spirit is liberated. A Rig Vedic poet says that not only the immortality of the spirit but the mortality of the body is the shadow of God,[171] and a Yajur Vedic sage pronounces a benediction on death: "May a blessing rest on the Lord of Death, a blessing on the Ender, a blessing on death."[172] The practice of yoga is the effort to free oneself from the round of births and deaths—that is, from the space-time matrix subject to so many painful conditions. Such liberation from the conditioned world is a "death," and conversely the meaning of death may be understood as that kind of liberation: On the other side of the last death is *"rebirth to a nonconditioned mode of being."*[173] This is accomplished, in the Yoga tradition, by the yoking, or unifying, of all the potencies and faculties of the person, a profound centering of his being on the spirit, even on God. And this is not far from Teilhard's notion of the spirit detaching itself from its base on this planet, freed by the perfection of its centration on the Point Omega, a "dematerialisation" by which one passes to "another sphere of the universe."[174]

In general, the Hindu traditions, on the problem of death, are in very much the same position as all other traditions. Obliged by the facts to seek some consolation for the human being who desires to live, they have devised doctrines, mythologies, and spiritual practices to open what Teilhard would call "a way out" of the trap in which men otherwise find themselves.

But now let us see another difficulty with Teilhard's hypothesis, this time with regard to the cosmic aspect. He has described an evolution of the material world in which interiority is gradually increased to the point where it evolves completely out of the material matrix, escaping as it does, from space and time as well, joining an eternal being, Christ-Omega. This is what Teilhard has in mind when he calls the world "an irreversible medium of personalisation,"[175] and says that its essential vocation is "to attain to its completion, through a chosen part of itself [i.e., human persons], in the plenitude of the Incarnate Word."[176] The difficulty is this, and it applies to the individual as well as to the world as a whole: Such an "attainment" in such a "completion" as the projected union with the eternal Omega constitutes an attempt to bridge this temporal world, in the space-time matrix, to a "surviving" world which escapes time, is eternal. Each individual soul is obliged to accomplish this leap on the occasion of his bodily death, and humanity as a whole—representing that "chosen portion of the world"—must perform the same feat before the cosmic heat death closes down the life-support-system of the Earth. There is logical and metaphysical inconsistency in proposing a development from the temporal condition to the eternal condition. Nothing can *become* eternal; that which is eternal is precisely that which has no traffic with *becoming*.

The same anomaly characterizes Teilhard's conception of the Omega Point. It is described on the one hand as something that will be *reached* in time, and on the other hand as something eternal and ever-present. In *Man's Place in Nature* Teilhard says:

> Unless it is to be powerless to form the keystone of the noosphere, 'Omega' . . . can only be conceived as the *meeting-point* between a universe that has reached the limit of centration, and another, even deeper, centre—that being the self-subsistent centre and absolutely final principle of irreversibility and personalisation: the one and only true Omega.[177]

There is a clear gap here between the evolving world and the Omega which is somehow to be the intrinsic completion of this world when the world (of persons) is separated from space, time, and matter.

> It seems that the mind cannot free itself except by some clean break, some escape, *of a completely different order* from the slow organization of matter that led up to the elaboration of the brain. In this sense there is indeed a discontinuity between heaven and earth. (That's where death comes in.)[178]

And for Teilhard himself, "It is the Other that I now seek, the Thing across the gap, the Thing on the other side."[179] But such gaps cannot be closed. A philosophic system which desires to unite the temporal and the eternal, the finite and the infinite, the relative and the absolute, must simply begin with them already united. It is not a union which can be achieved.

Now this is where the Hindu traditions have something very useful to suggest to Teilhard. They have not attempted to secure a passage for an essentially temporal being into eternity. They have announced that whatever claim he has on the eternal he has always had; it is his reality. For some Vedāntins this is simplified to the point of saying that the only truth that can be said of one is that he is the Ātman and the Ātman transcends all becoming. It is only a covering of ignorance that has misled us into conceiving ourselves as temporal beings. For others the situation is more complex. For instance, S. S. Suryanarayana Sastri, a contemporary Advaitin, says, "*For* the real there is no progress; but *in* the real there is progress."[180]

Śrī Aurobindo claims that the Upanishads support his thesis that the Absolute Being has three distinct poises: Transcendent, Cosmic, and Individual. The human person also participates in these three poises, being therefore both eternal and temporal in different aspects of his being. The Chāndogya Upanishad, for instance, teaches that one is free who understands that as Ātman he is identical with the whole world, that he has come from Being and that he is Being.[181] The Brihad-Āraṇyaka Upanishad describes the various states of the soul—in dream, in dreamless sleep beyond fear or desire, as realizing immortality through liberation from desire, and as seated in its own impassibility:

> The Ātman is unseizable, for it cannot be seized.
> It is indestructible, for it cannot be destroyed.
> It is unattached, for it does not attach itself.
> It is unbound. It does not tremble. It is not
> injured. . . . One sees the Ātman just in the Ātman.
> One sees everything as the Ātman.[182]

Rabindranath Tagore, also, was persuaded that the reality in which we participate is characterized by both immanence and transcendence, and was as fond as was Aurobindo of quoting the Īsā Upanishad on the Ultimate Reality:

It moves. It moves not.
It is far, and It is near.
It is within all this.
And It is outside of all this.[183]

This mysterious Being is also the Source of all finite beings. According to the Maitrī Upanishad, "From Him, indeed, who is in the soul (Ātman) come forth all breathing creatures, all worlds, all the Vedas, all gods, all beings. The mystic meaning . . . thereof is: The Real of the real."[184]

When one is perfectly centered on the Most Real, then one has freedom, and this freedom transcends time although it also is found within the frame of time. Troy Organ comments that "This state of freedom is to be experienced here and now; it is not located in a post-death time, for it is not subject to time. . . . Liberation is now, the eternal now. *Mokṣa* [liberation] is now, for it cannot be at any other time. It is always *now* when *mokṣa* is. Time does not limit or contain *mokṣa*. . . . It is an eternal condition which may be or may not be in time. . . . It *is* whenever man is ready for it. . . . Nothing happens, nothing needs to happen, and yet there is a new orientation. He now *sees* what before he merely was. He awakens to who he is. *Ātman* is Brahman."[185]

The effect of this view is to make physical death, although symbolic of the realization of freedom, literally irrelevant with respect to the attainment of the goal. It undercuts the whole problem of death as Teilhard's system presents it. Could an amendment have been made, based on these Hindu doctrines, which would have been advantageous to Teilhard? It may be so, but it would be a complex task to work it out. Meanwhile, we may examine what has become of the other head of Teilhard's dragon, the danger of despair.

The greatest danger to humanity is the loss of the appetite for living, says Teilhard.[186] Lack of faith in the future is the greatest threat that confronts us.[187] Even ill will and ill fortune are not so much to be feared.

> Once the evolutive movement has been launched and is underway nothing, it would appear, can then prevent life on our earth from attaining the maximum possible degree of its development: nothing—except, indeed, the general

> instantaneous slackening-off that could be brought about by the fatal shock of a great disillusionment.[188]

Before man appeared on the earth, Teilhard explains, evolution was fueled primarily by thermodynamic energies. But with the onset of hominization a further power was required. Evolution coiled on itself to become self-evolution and a new complexity of the energy structure was formed: a psychic energy in which the evolutionary pressure took the form of a self-conscious zest for life.[189] The drive to live had always been there, of course, but a hominized drive to live is a realized savor of life, a directed desire.

In the Brihad-Āraṇyaka Upanishad desire is also recognized—though pejoratively—as the energy that binds from one life to another, through the continuity of action.

> . . . The self is identified with desire alone. As is its desire, so is its resolution; and as its resolution, so is its deed; and whatever deed it does that it reaps. . . . Having exhausted [in the other world] the results of whatever work it did in this life, it returns from that world to this world for [fresh work]. Thus does the man who desires [transmigrate].[190]

The Upanishad would even agree with Teilhard that if this desire should ever cease, all action would stop, and the cosmic order would be undermined. But, unlike the Upanishad, Teilhard regards this possibility as a catastrophe and sees it arising from men failing to do their duty: ". . . the universe threatened by failure because its most noble elements, surrendering to anarchy, shirk the common tasks. . . ."[191]

Teilhard's attitude is much more like the older Vedic sense of the goodness of the desire for life, with its affirmation of Ṛta, right order in the world, and the responsibility of men to protect the cosmic order by their own works. In the Rig Veda it is written:

> In the beginning there was desire,
> Which was the primal germ of the mind;
> The sages searching in their hearts with wisdom
> found in non-existence the kin of existence. . . .
> There was the seed-bearer, there were mighty forces;
> impulse from below and forward movement beyond.[192]

The "impulse from below" had been evolution's power from the beginning, but with thinking beings, "the sages," the importance of "non-existence"—the future—first became apparent. The "forward movement beyond," now depends on these peculiarly human experiences, faith and hope, in which, by the wisdom of the heart, the nonexistent future is seen as kin to existence already known.

Hope, that is what we need, says Teilhard, "a great hope."

> This must be born spontaneously in every generous soul in face of the anticipated work, and it also represents the essential impetus without which nothing will be done. A passionate love of growth, of being, that is what we need.[193]

One of the characters of the *Mahābhārata* strikes a consonant note in this speech:

> When . . . does Hope arise? . . . Hope is the sheet-anchor of every man. When Hope is destroyed, great grief follows which . . . is almost equal to death itself. . . . Hope . . . is really immeasurable . . . highly difficult of being understood and equally difficult of being conquered. Seeing this last attribute of Hope, I ask, what else is so unconquerable as this?[194]

Hope, or what Teilhard more often calls the "taste for life," is the "within" aspect of the continuity of the life-force itself. This is why he calls our attention to those nagging questions we harbor in the backs of our minds ("Have we ever moved? Are we still moving? And if so, are we going forward or back or simply in a circle?") and why he issues this warning which sounds on first hearing so excessive:

> This is an attitude of doubt that will prove fatal if we do not take care, because in destroying the love of life it also destroyed the life-force of Mankind.[195]

The Tantras point out this same vital connection between desire and delight in life and the formation of the world. In their view, any particular center of being has its persistence in existence assured only by the fact that the Absolute Being-Consciousness-Bliss Power (with which it is identical) wills to evolve as this particular form. "This 'will' is the 'seed' and 'root' of this particular centre's manifestation; and this seed also is (conditionally) imperishable, that is, as long as the Basic Will lasts. . . . When the Basic Will of *Chit* to be and become *this* particular centre goes, . . . the root of this particular manifestation 'dies.' "[196]

From the Tantric point of view, this is no misfortune, for the particular center in "dying" has also realized its identity with the Whole. But for Teilhard, it is a disaster, for the evolutionary vigor of man would be lost if men should lose interest in life.[197] We worry now about our reserves of natural resources, he says. But what would happen if we lost our passion for life and growth?[198] That would be far worse. All the resources of the earth would be of no avail in that case.[199]

Cultures evolve, says Teilhard, just as species do. They have their waxing and waning in terms of the vitality or lassitude of their attitude toward life.[200] The downfall of a civilization first shows in the negative elements in its psychic life—cynicism, anomie, apathy, despair. The remedy for this is not necessarily some violent motivation, such as starting another war to rouse and unify people with fear, anger, and hatred. Even the instinct of self-preservation is not our deepest motive, Teilhard claims. Rather, it is the ambition to live: to be and to be more. To stimulate and unite mankind we do not need a common enemy but a common aspiration.[201]

The common hope and aspiration, however, must be something tangible, not an abstraction, or some vague conclusion to a speculative metaphysical system.[202] As Rāmānuja remarked, in a disdainful critique of Śaṅkara, "No sensible person exerts himself under the influence of the idea that after he himself has perished there will remain some entity termed 'pure light'!"[203] The aspiration has to be toward something humanly conceivable and humanly desirable. It has to be a human future. Without it, people will stop building and give up inventing, Teilhard says.[204] But this savor for life can be evoked, in Teilhard's view, by the sense of evolution itself and by what we may so far see of Omega, ahead and above.[205]

> Whatever appetite we may experience . . . we must have within us a much more fundamental appetite: that for feeling God grow within us through the universal and domi-

> nating action of his providence. And I really do believe that this appetite can ultimately replace all others, by which I mean that it can make us find life passionately interesting even in the most commonplace and tedious setting. The real substance of even such circumstances is divine.[206]

The echo is faint, the voice having sounded a long time ago in a different state of knowledge, but we can hear it in the Rig Veda:

> As each successor fails not his foregoer, so form the lives of these, O great Ordainer. Live your full lives and find old age delightful, all of you striving one behind the other.[207]

This is typical of the Vedic view, in which every type of well-being, virtue, knowledge, progress, and spiritual advance, in friendship with all beings, was ardently desired.[208] As Alain Danielou says, "All the verses of the Veda can be said to be directly or indirectly but the praise of life." In the Hymn to the Earth of the Atharva Veda these blessings are implored of the great Goddess, Earth, from whom they may be confidently expected, for She is the "all-sustaining, treasure-bearing, firm staying-place," who "bears in many forms the breathing and moving life" and is "the Mother of the people, the fulfiller of wishes, far-extending." She has "opted for Indra [the power of Light] and not Vitra [the power of Darkness]" and has protected and promoted right order. Did the ṛiṣhi who composed this Hymn have any concept of the earth's astronomical position? its geological history? its evolution?

> Earth, which at first was in the water of the ocean,
> and which sages sought with wondrous powers,
> Earth, whose heart was in Eternal Heaven,
> wrapped in Truth, immortal . . .
> A vast abode art Thou, and mighty,
> and mighty is Thy speed, Thy moving and Thy shaking . . .
> As a horse scatters dust, so did Earth, since She was born,
> scatter the people who dwelt on the land,
> And She joyously sped on, the world's protectress. . . .
> When, O Goddess, proceeding forward,
> and extolled by Devas, Thou hadst spread Thy renown,

Then a great glory entered into Thee, . . .
who had entered the light in the mid-air's ocean,
And the delicious vessel hidden in mystery
became manifest for the nurture of those
who found her their Mother. . . .
I call to Earth, the purifier,
the patient Earth, growing strong through
spiritual might.[209]

Teilhard says that the courage and joy of action of those who wish to touch the depths of things depends on their possessing a vision of the whole of Nature in which human being is included with all other levels of being in a coherent picture of the world.[210] Would he not have appreciated these verses describing "the sacred fire" in the Earth?

There lies the fire within the Earth,
and in plants,
and waters carry it;
the fire is in stone.
There is a fire deep within men,
a fire in the kine,
and a fire in horses.

The same fire that burns in the heavens;
the mid-air belongs to that Fire Divine. . . .

May Earth, clad in her fiery mantle, . . .
make me aflame.[211]

Certainly this poem reveals a profound savor for life and a sense of a universal order, including man; perhaps, also, there is a concept of the forward movement of life, always in touch with the tangible goodness of earthly and divine living. Against such a background it should not be difficult to construct the metaphysics that Teilhard wants, in which we and our world are not just contingent and gratuitous, as we appear to be in the Scholastic system Teilhard had been taught as a young Jesuit.[212] Somehow, he felt, we must have a view of ourselves which gives us our own meaning. We must believe that it all amounts to *something* in its own terms. If we do find this ultimate value, we can dedicate ourselves to it and continue to act. If we do not, we are truly lost. Eventually it is "a choice between suicide and adoration."[213]

"The more we believe in life," says Teilhard, "the more the universe is able to build itself around us in its *mystical reality* —of which all that has already taken shape makes itself manifest . . . to our *vision in faith* (inseparable from our *action in faith*)."[214] Perhaps Teilhard's thoughts are not so distant from those of the ṛiṣhi who found the source of all meaning in that "vessel hidden in mystery" but "become manifest for the nurture of those who found in her their Mother."[215] Teilhard would also find support among those heirs of the Vedic love of life, the Tantrics, for according to them, the Divine manifests out of its own Bliss, and the universe is a great play of delight in which man is intended to participate with freedom and joy.[216]

But is not all this emphasis on our need to take pleasure in life and our right to savor it merely a self-serving subjective interest? By what argument can we project our desires onto reality? By the argument that we, and especially our desires, *are* the reality, in fact, the most crucial portion of reality for purposes of this affirmation. "Every consciousness as it becomes more cerebralised," says Teilhard, inevitably inclines "rather toward being than not-being."[217] The preference for life over death is the obvious condition *sine qua non* for all evolution. And now *we are evolution,* and "we" means our *consciousness,* and our "consciousness" means our *thoughts,* our *beliefs,* our *desires.* Therefore, "our desires" are the surest indication of which way evolution must go, if it goes at all. A scandalous argument, but it repays close attention, for it is perfectly consistent with all that Teilhard has carefully shown up to this point.

Finally, since he has convincingly argued that there is no total death, Teilhard feels confident in assuring us that the universe can nourish in us forever an appetite for life, growing always more critical, more exacting, and more refined.[218] The zest for life, so necessary for evolution, so fundamental to our sense of worth, meaning, and happiness, the source of all passion and all insight, can only be called divine.[219] We live in it and by it, yet we ought always to pray for it: "May the Lord only preserve in me a passionate taste for the world. . . ."[220]

> O God, whose call precedes the very first of our movements, grant me the desire to desire being—that, by means of this divine thirst which is your gift, the access to the great waters may open wide within me. Do not deprive me of the sacred taste for being, that primordial energy. . . .[221]

Christogenesis and the Yoga of Transformation

In his effort to prove that real Christianity and real human life are identical, Teilhard had spoken of "a blessed desire to go on advancing, discovering, fashioning and experiencing the world so as to penetrate ever further and further" into God.[222] We have to go to heaven, he insists, "with all our zest for the Earth."[223] Unfortunately, he did not find this attitude in his contemporaries—they did not really expect the Kingdom of Heaven, he notes sadly—perhaps because it was not clear to them how the Parousia, the coming of the Lord, was connected with the outcome of our own human efforts.[224]

To Teilhard the connection is quite clear. Is it not better to be than not to be? If we choose nonbeing, we go nowhere, obviously. But if we choose being, we must eventually go to God.[225] All being is a going, a becoming, a transformation; all effort is directed toward the perfection of that being which is a continual becoming; and all effort toward perfection must have God as its goal. Life is yoga, Teilhard might have said, if he had been disposed to use the word: it is the effort to unite, it is the process of unification, and it is the reality of the union. Through this yoga—the gigantic yoga of the cosmos, as Aurobindo termed it[226]—the multiple are being transformed into one, and the expressed and incarnate Godhead, the Christ, is being generated. So simple is the Teilhardian thesis.

If people could only see this, Teilhard felt, they would no longer regard life as a burden; this insight into the goal of life would give them inspiration and courage.[227] Logically, he argued, there is no alternative to determination to reach the divine; at least, the alternative is too terrible to contemplate. For the option is a choice between faith in Supreme Unity, together with the will to attain it by our actions, and despair in the face of death, reduction to the nonbeing of total disorganization.[228] Organization, the building up of more and more complex forms, once begun, cannot stop halfway. It must go on to totality. Otherwise, it will fall down the stair by which it climbed, disintegrating from step to step toward the homogeneity of maximal entropy. Confronted thus by God, the psychic summit of the evolutionary pyramid, humanity must realize that what is required of it is a total effort in the presence of a total risk.

This is why the demands and threats of Christ, as represented in Christianity, are so extravagant, so uncompromising. It is not a matter of personal whimsy on the part of the Deity, or of arbitrary and inordinate pride and willfulness. It is a matter of *fact,* of the *structure* of the universe. The Christ is that psychic union which is in process of formation, necessarily through the free choices of the persons of which it is composed, and which alone can be the structural climax of the real and observed process of evolution in which we find ourselves. It is a scientific proposition, Teilhard would say, not just a religious one, that each person must either elect to enter into this union, or be relegated to the exterior darkness of cosmic death. Read in terms of the forces of entropy (disorganization) and of anti-entropy (organization), the familiar text takes on a new meaning: "He who does not gather with me, scatters."

Now, perhaps, in our generation, we are beginning to understand this, Teilhard thinks. Now that we know about evolution in scientific terms and are more familiar with the method of projection or extrapolation, now perhaps we can receive the religious pronouncements of old into a new framework.

> Not only does the idea of a possible raising of our consciousness to a state of super-consciousness show itself daily, in the light of scientific experience, to be better founded and psychologically more necessary for preserving in Man his will to act; but furthermore this idea, carried to its logical extreme, appears to be the only one capable of paving the way for the great event we look for—the manifestation of a unified impulse of worship in which will be joined and mutually exalted both a passionate desire to conquer the World and a passionate longing to be united with God: the

> vital act, specifically new, corresponding to a new age in the history of the Earth.[229]

Once we have seen this goal of the world, Teilhard believes, everything will appear valuable to us.[230] Human beings will recognize that we are the arrow pointing the way to the final unification of the world: we compose that species which is "the last-born, the freshest, the most complicated, the most subtle of all the successive layers of life."[231] Our daily lives *are* the process of hominization, the elaboration into reflexive consciousness of the essence of the universe, the "progressive phyletic spiritualisation in human civilisation of all the forces [of the] world." [232]

An important part of this new vision will lie in an appreciation of the fact that no developing being can be understood from its embryonic form but only from its adult stage. Therefore to know what we ourselves are, and what the world is, we must try to look ahead.[233] Contrary to all the foolish fears of the religionists, what evolution teaches is that human nature is to be evaluated not by reference to its origin—whether from apes, tadpoles, or the original single-celled living being—but by reference to its consummation.[234] Since this consummation, our adulthood, remains to be achieved, and can only be achieved through our freely directed action, the meaning of human life is evident. All our efforts to master energy and to perfect psychic life are efforts to produce types of perfection which would otherwise not exist.[235] Therefore it becomes a matter of conscience with us that we "strive to extract from the world all that this world can hold of truth and energy. . . . *There must be nothing* in the direction of more-being that remains *unattempted*."[236] Through our work we will complete in ourselves the subject of the intended divine union.[237]

Teilhard confides to us that at one point he was disappointed with Catholicism because of "its failure to understand the part played by matter." But continued meditation on "the incarnate God whom Christianity revealed to me" led him to see that the entire universe is necessarily involved in the process of salvation, that the whole world is divine—or better, divinizing, through "an arduous process of differentiation." Thus, for each being to be most truly and deeply itself, means to be most thoroughly committed to the process of transformation into the ultimate union in God, and conversely, "the total Christ is consummated and may be attained, only at the term of universal evolution."[238]

Consequently, love for God may be mediated through love for the evolving world. Love is thus pantheized and the charity of the Gospel becomes love for cosmogenesis.[239] But cosmogenesis has now transcended itself and been transformed into *Christogenesis.*

> With cosmogenesis being transformed . . . into Christogenesis, . . . we now find that it is becoming not only possible but *imperative* literally to *love* evolution.[240]

It is Christ "who invests Himself with the whole reality of the Universe."[241] Therefore, says Teilhard, *"through all nature I* [*am*] *immersed in God."*[242] But the universe is still being created, and it is Christ who is reaching fulfillment in it. Even Christ awaits His completion by having His incarnation extended to the whole world.[243] He is slowly and carefully saying to the world, "This is My Body."[244]

By the Incarnation, the divine immensity has transformed itself into the omnipresence of Christification and guaranteed the final success of hominization.[245] It is Christ who is the organizing soul of the universe, the principle of unity, gradually drawing and focusing all the highly differentiated elements onto and through Himself as Center.[246] The Man of Nazareth is only the germ of the total Christ-Omega.[247] Everything is still in motion because the Christ has not yet reached the peak of His growth.[248] He is being formed slowly, for the building up of His Body is being carried out as a natural evolution.[249] In fact, this is all that evolution is, ever was, or ever was intended to be. It is one great Feast of the Nativity.[250] Through all the transposing forms of Nature, it is one Christ who is being born. Christ alone is the beginning, the middle, and the end of evolution, and *evolution is holy.*[251]

Here we have at last, says Teilhard, the truth that makes us free. There is a single "mysterious Divinity" moving in the world, forming novel complex organizations, liberating unsuspected powers, rousing the latent consciousness. calling for deliberate exertions, promising and delivering more and more being, more and more unity, more and more freedom. Its attributes are so recognizable by now, its presence so unmistakable, that whenever we find ourselves at a critical turn in our history we know who is the secret Mover: "It is once again *that same Divinity, it is Evolution.*[252] . . . [It is] CHRIST-THE-EVOLVER."[253]

Christ-the-Evolver is God active in creation, engaged in *creative union,* embodied in the universe. The object of all this divine activity is that God should become manifest in the world and that the world should attain its final unification in God.[254] It is an evolution toward divinity. Christ is the organic image of the universe thus deified, the one who collects in Himself all the forces of unity diffused through creation.[255] Under the impulse of His "amorization," the once merely potentially conscious elements of the cosmos have become reflexive, are presently gathering themselves into co-reflexion, and may confidently be expected to become pan-reflexive on the "Christic" level of cosmic organization and centering, in the Parousia of superconsciousness and divine union.[256]

The world expects to be united with the divine, Teilhard says, but it can do so only if it is united according to that which it is at its peak, a reflexive psychism. Divinization for such a being can only consist in being centered in some ultimate pan-reflexive Psyche whose own self-unity is so intense that it gathers all other psyches about itself like a giant magnet. But here is the paradox: the magnetism cannot be mechanical or coercive; it must be the personal magnetism of love.[257] Our natural human unity is but a preparation for evolution into this Christic unity.[258] It means a physical incorporation of mankind into Christ and therefore into God. This is the sanctifying work of evolution.[259]

> If a Christian really understands the inexpressibly wonderful work that is being carried out around him and by him, in *the whole of nature,* he cannot fail to see that the excitement and delight aroused in him by 'awakening to the cosmos' can be preserved by him not only in the form they take when transposed to a divine Ideal, but also in the

> substance of their most material and most earthly objects: to do so, he has only to learn to appreciate the value of *sacred evolution* as an instrument of beatification.[260]

Thanks to evolution, the same evolution which introduced individualistic consciousness, humankind is not imprisoned in phenomenalism or egocentrism.[261] Reflexive consciousness of the element unavoidably brought solitude, and too often selfishness. But the gradual growth of co-reflexion is dissolving these barriers, and the promise of the Christic pan-reflexion will restore balance and unity. Morality and self-forgetful holiness are not interesting and admirable curiosities or luxuries for this universe, but biological necessities. They are prerequisites for the cosmic unification, the psychic compression of the advancing life-force. And Christ, by being the Center of the convergence of love-energy, is the Savior of the world from scatteredness.[262] The "salvation" of the old dogmatics is the scientific "Christogenesis."[263] This yoga of transformation, or transforming union, "totalises itself into 'something' in which all differences vanish on the borderline between universe and person."[264]

There is no denying that this is a highly original synthesis of the materials with which Teilhard was dealing. He has contrived, with that combination of brilliance and simplicity which is the mark of genius, to so relate the thesis of religious revelation and the antithesis of scientific discovery as to present each of them as implying the propositions of the other. It might have seemed, before Teilhard began to open up their hidden meanings, that the dogmatic tenets of Christianity were quite inhospitable to the suggestions of modern evolutionary theory. Our question in this study has been, would the Hindu traditions have been any better? Is there a preparation there in the basic concepts and attitudes toward life for the kind of development Teilhard brought to the Christian world view?

Life—both in the stricter biological sense and in the broader philosophical sense—is an evolution toward divinity, Teilhard is saying. I think we may safely say, despite their great diversity, that most of the Hindu systems would agree that from the point of view of the questing phenomenal consciousness, this is precisely what life is. Some of them come closer to Teilhard's ideas than do others. The Tantrics, for instance, emphasize the gradual unfolding and working out of the world's play. They understand the physical world as related to the expressive and evolutionary tendencies of the psychic world, in which certain things must for a time be undeveloped or unmanifest, in order that there may be a moving world at all. They call this the veiling or involution (as opposed to evolution) of Nature. The empirical consciousness, identifying itself with its condition in space and time, is limited to those forms which are so far unveiled. Its relative ignorance at any given stage of development is unavoidable.[265] Teilhard agrees, saying that when we look ahead to the next level of consciousness, "it is inevitable that we should not see anything at all. . . . We have no idea of what each man, united with all other men . . . will become *capable of doing* . . . [or] what . . . *he will begin to see.*"[266]

But just as each succeeding level of development is superior to its predecessors, so are the previous levels inferior to the present. Ignorance, darkness, failure, and evil characterize all of them to various degrees. However, neither Teilhard nor the Hindus are scandalized by this. In a temporal world it can hardly be otherwise. Teilhard speaks of evil as "statistical":[267]

> For inexorable statistical reasons, it is physically impossible for some lack of arrangement, or some faulty arrangement, not to appear within a multitude which is *still undergoing the process of arrangement*—and this applies to every level of the universe, pre-living, living, and reflective. . . . Evil is thus a *secondary* effect, an inevitable *by*-product of the progress of a universe in evolution.[268]

Eliade, in his book on *Yoga,* notes that the Indians recognized that "pain is a cosmic necessity, an ontological modality to which every 'form' that manifests itself as such is condemned. . . . The mere fact of existing in time . . . implies pain." But:

> No Indian philosophy or gnosis falls into despair. On the contrary, the revelation of 'pain' as the law of existence can be regarded as the *conditio sine qua non* for emancipa-

> tion. Intrinsically, then, this universal suffering has a positive, stimulating value.[269]

It reminds us that a way out exists, the way of withdrawing from false identifications with entropic tendencies, of detachment from narrow personal possessions and ambitions, of devotion to the greater self and to the goal of psychic union. The way requires effort, struggle, perseverance, and confidence. It is the way of yoga, a yoga that transforms. Teilhard's words are complementary:

> Suffering . . . can be transformed into an expression of love and a principle of union: suffering that is first treated as an enemy who has to be defeated; then suffering vigorously fought against to the bitter end; and yet at the same time suffering rationally accepted and cordially welcomed inasmuch as by forcing us out of our egocentrism and compensating for our errors it can super-centre us upon God.[270]

Both the yogins and Teilhard would affirm that our sufferings are not a punishment for some sin of personal offense, but are an outgrowth of our ignorance of the true nature of spirit, an ignorance which is a necessary concomitant of evolution but which makes us identify ourselves too exclusively with our private psychomental experience. This is the solitude of individual reflexive consciousness of which Teilhard spoke, out of which we are evolving toward the greater unanimity and harmony of co-reflexion and pan-reflexion under the influence of the cosmic Christ. The yogin would say that we may expect to be released from ignorance and its accompanying suffering when we have seen the truth and united ourselves with the All and the One.[271]

For neither Teilhard nor the yogin is evil the last word. Cosmic bliss underlies all experience. Woodroffe and Mukhyopādyāya points out that the Hindu sacred teachings forbid the writing and enacting of tragic dramas: "Union and joy must be the last word, even in a play, instead of death and sorrow. . . . The Hindu . . . ancient drama, . . . though it admits evil and pain as a subsidiary element, has refused to admit it as the fundamental, essential, primary and final theme."[272]

For Teilhard, evil is only that portion of the universe which falls back into the entropic discard heap. The *real* is the chosen part of the universe which is taking on body and form in Christ.[273] The Sāṃkhya system adopts a similar attitude. It does not regard evil as a truly *human* experience, but merely a fact without genuine significance to the real self. Evil is not an attribute of the Puruṣa, the principle of consciousness and the subject of salvation, but characterizes Prakṛti, whose internal relations are partially governed by what Teilhard would call entropy. The yoga of Patañjali takes up and repeats this position of the Sāṃkhya.[274] In these schools the beings of nature are seen as composed of energies which develop in whatever direction is unobstructed. However, it is necessary that obstructions exist to establish definition in the cosmos. Dasgupta explains: "Had there been no such obstruction or if all obstructions were removed, then every thing could have become every other thing. There would be no definite order of evolution."[275]

In the Śaiva modification of this view, there is a presentation of a cosmic evolution for the sake of uniting human persons with the divinity which is not too unlike Teilhard's basic position.

> The natural obstructions of individuals are . . . due to the existence of impurities, and it is held that by the all-pervading nature of God the souls can be emancipated . . . when the natural obstructions are washed off. For this purpose the individual persons have to exert themselves . . . [and] through the near proximity of God [there develops a] cosmic process for the good of all . . . Souls . . . who are in bondage may also be in different conditions of progress and may have accordingly different kinds of knowledge and power. . . . But even though all souls are associated with *malas,* or impurities, they are pervaded in and through by Śiva; and as the *malas* are purged, the proximity of Śiva becomes more manifest, and the individual becomes more and more pure, until he becomes like Śiva.[276]

Overcoming evil by the transforming power of yoga, the spiritual aspirant, or the soul in the universe, gradually increases his freedom, just as Teilhard describes in the images of his context. Some Hindus have speculated that progress is made by a kind of trial and error, almost like Teilhard's "groping," which they call *krama-mukti,* or gradual liberation. The soul returns again and again to life in the cosmic process, but the drawing toward the higher levels works surreptitiously within him, little by little removing his bondage.[277] Others feel that the pursuit and the progress are more important than the attaining. Mysore Hiriyanna says frankly that "the question whether the highest value is attainable is not of much consequence. . . . What really matters is the deliberate choosing of it as the ideal to be pursued, and thereafter making a persistent and continued advance toward it."[278] But probably the most usual position is that expressed in the Paiṅgala Upanishad: "The desire for liberation arises in human beings at the end of many births through the ripening of their past virtuous conduct."[279]

This, we may suggest, is the significance of the image of reincarnation. It represents a long period of involvement with the cosmic process during which a gradual and sometimes hidden growth is taking place.

For each time it reincarnates the soul intends to improve its estate:

> As a goldsmith, taking a piece of gold, turns it into another, newer and more beautiful shape, even so does this soul, after having thrown away this body and dispelled its ignorance, make unto itself another, newer and more beautiful shape.[280]

According to the Muṇḍaka Upanishad, one continues to be reborn as long as one has desires. When the desires are fully satisfied, the perfected soul (consisting of the highest consciousness and deeds) is united with the Supreme Immutable Being.[281] In Teilhard's idiom this might be translated as saying that when the radial energies—the desires which have been driving evolution—are completely discharged, all the elementary consciousnesses will be unified in the Supreme Immutable Omega. In general, reincarnation means, as Radhakrishnan explains, that "the soul has chances of acquiring merit and advancing to life eternal. Until the union with the timeless Reality is attained, there will be some form of life or other, which will give scope to the individual soul to acquire enlightenment and attain life eternal."[282]

Perhaps the clearest statement of the concept of evolution toward divinity is to be found in the teaching of the Śakti-vāda, the worship of the Divine Mother. In this system spiritual progress is most intimately related to life in the world and to the entire cosmic process.

> The sadhaka [one who practises this discipline] cultivates, develops and progressively realises in himself the vision of the Divine Mother, the Supreme Shakti, as embodied in all things that are manifest for the varied delight of Her Lila [unmotivated activity]. She manifests Herself multitudinously and sports in the richness of Her creation from a million centres of enjoyment. By a progressive identification of his own consciousness with this larger Consciousness of the World-Mother, the sadhaka participates in the Lila, has the joy of things and in this very process of self-identification and merger grows into the nature of the Divine Mother.[283]

This tradition also emphasizes the usefulness of every type of activity for the attainment of the goal.

> Life in the world is turned into a means of approach to and of expression of the Divine. . . . Every part of life is taken up, purified and offered to the Cosmic Enjoyer in oneself. The individual . . . in the manner in which he enables the Divine to draw and receive the delight of life through him, . . . grows in consciousness towards identity with the Divine. All things in life serve as occasions for this.[284]

Teilhard should have approved this thoroughly. He urged so strongly that we must not drift with the current but fight our way toward a term still to be achieved.[285] We need to define and to organize the total natural human effort, combining all science, aesthetics, morality.[286] For him, all work, whether industrial, artistic, scientific, or humanistic, contributes to building up the Body of Christ.[287] He should satisfy, therefore, Troy Organ's conception of a European who can appreciate the Hindu's notion of spiritual life:

> If Western man is to understand *sādhana* in its integrative aspects he must think of religion, science, philosophy, art,

> education, politics, marriage, vocation, recreation, economics, literature, drama, and dance not as separate activities with varying aims and methods but as the manifest ways in which the function of being human expresses itself.[288]

But the integration of human activities, says Teilhard, must be for the sake of the whole universe, not just for some selfish interest.[289] There must be a precise result desired by God, he is persuaded; it is paradoxical, but in some sense the world must contribute to the self-sufficient God something vitally necessary to Him.[290] To discover this we must devote ourselves to scientific work to study the convergence of the universe, and to religious work to realize the universal nature of the Christ in process of formation through time and history.[291] From the Tantric point of view it is expressed this way:

> Each faculty of the being, the mind, the life, the body, all the energies are cultivated, purified and surrendered to the Divine Shakti as channels of Her manifestation and delight. . . . Nothing is excluded . . . the Tantra is thus a great movement for the uplift of human existence, for the recovery of the whole of man to God.[292]

Nor, continues Teilhard, should we neglect work toward the establishment of more harmonious social groups. They, too, are "an indispensable link in the series by which the universe moves towards its perfection."[293] Classical Indian sādhanas seem to emphasize individual effort, though this seeming may be due in part to their presumption of the community context in which they operate. Group life in the family, in the village, in the sense of caste has always been of tremendous importance as the background for any Indian quest after the divine—even when that quest took the form of rejecting one's membership in these groups. But there have also been some sādhanas proposed which explicitly stress the group aspect, the *collective* so dear to Teilhard. Śrī Aurobindo's sādhana is one of these, as we have seen. Another is that inspired by Keshub Chender Sen, one of the great figures of the Indian Renaissance movement of the late nineteenth century. His theory was that liberation, mokṣa, could be attained only collectively, and he actually established in 1872 a community which embodied this ideal, the Bharat Ashram, near Calcutta. One of its members, Bijay Krishna Goswami, wrote of its governing philosophy:

> There is no salvation through individual spiritual culture. All together in quest of salvation and bound by ties of family must advance towards the Kingdom of Heaven. It is selfishness to tread the solitary way to righteousness.[294]

Another great figure of a slightly later period, Rabindranath Tagore, added, "We have our greatest delight when we realize ourselves in others."[295]

But long before either Rabindranath or Keshub, all these thoughts had been summarized by one of the inspired contributors to the Yajur Veda:

> Blessed be effort, blessed strenuous effort;
> blessed be collective endeavor, blessed individual
> endeavor, blessed be enterprise.[296]

For Teilhard, this holy enterprise is the evolution of the world into the total Christ. He says that the world is placed in our hands "like a Host, ready to be charged with divine influence," on condition that we believe that it has the will and the power to become for us "the prolongation of the Body of Christ."[297] In a highly dramatic style, in *Hymn of the Universe,* Teilhard describes a vision of an expanding Host, which grows to include the entire world, then enters into each being in the world and draws all into Itself.[298] In a true sense, he says elsewhere, "the sacramental Species are formed by the totality of the world, and the duration of the creation is the time needed for its consecration."[299]

> As our humanity assimilates the material world, and as the Host assimilates our humanity, the eucharistic transformation goes beyond and completes the transubstantiation of the bread on the altar. Step by step it irresistibly invades the universe. . . . Christ reveals Himself in each reality around us, and shines like an ultimate determinant, like a centre, . . . like a universal element. . . . Christ—for whom and in whom we are formed, each with his own individuality and his own vocation— . . . our divine *milieu.*[300]

Radhakrishnan, commenting on the Brihad-Āraṇyaka Upanishad's account of the self becoming one with the Supreme Person, sounds several of the same chords:

> He who knows 'I am *Brahman,*' becomes the universe . . . for he is its soul. Man has potential universality which he actualizes in the state of liberation. We are one with the indeterminate pure silence in essence and with the personal Lord in the liberation of cosmic manifestation. . . . Essential unity with God is unity with one another through God.[301]

An even stronger statement is made by Śrī Barada Kanta Majumdar in his Introduction to the *Principles of Tantra*:

> The Divine Mother . . . is in every molecule, in every atom, in all things which constitute the world. In fact, She is the causeless Cause of whatever is. . . . The Tantric sadhaka . . . is led from the outset to feel, and then by a higher process of self-culture to realise, the All-blissful Mother in the universe . . . to regard the universe as the Mother Herself. . . . Every man and woman—nay, all living things—are glowing with Divinity. This state of mind not only quenches the thirst of his lower nature, but spiritualises its animal tendencies; not only does it buoy him up with fresh energy to pursue the Path but he attains liberation. . . . The man of the world who professes Tantrism has every faith in the reality of the world. To him it is not an illusion nor an evil, and therefore he exerts his utmost to make it the happy lap of the Mother, which it really is.[302]

The believer in Heaven, Teilhard would say, can now look back over all our arguments and see that the laboratory of human progress was necessary, that mankind had to grow through evolution. The sense of the Earth and the sense of God are mutually nourishing.[303] The spiritual success of the universe depends on the correct functioning of every zone of reality and the release of every energy.[304] For it is God and God alone whom the evolving consciousness pursues through the multitude of created things. The world is on the road to Christification.[305] We cannot see what it will be like to reach it, because we will have a different consciousness then. But it will be a united consciousness and it will be inspired by a single mysticism.[306] The one thing we do know is that it will be centered on the Supreme Psychic Reality, Christ-Omega, and that it will open onto "limitless psychic spaces."[307]

REFERENCES

[1] Beatrice Bruteau, *Worthy Is the World:* The Hindu Philosophy of Sri Aurobindo (Teaneck: Fairleigh Dickinson University Press, 1972), pp. 210 ff.

[2] Nevertheless, this is still a very popular way of summarizing Hinduism. Robert L. Faricy [*Teilhard de Chardin's Theology of the Christian in the World* (New York: Sheed & Ward, 1967), p. 80], defending Teilhard's evaluation of oriental religions, quotes E. Tomlin, *The Oriental Philosophers* (New York, 1963) as saying, "Characteristics such as reality and value are precisely those which Eastern thought, with certain exceptions, refuses to ascribe to the natural world."

[3] Cf. Gunnar Myrdal's Introduction to Kusum Nair, *Blossoms in the Dust* (London: Duckworth, 1961), p. xiv: Discussing the situation in the villages of India where "people's attitudes to work and life" are "hardened by stagnation, isolation, ignorance, and poverty," he says, "People, even and not least, the poorest people, often set their sights, not upon individual progress, but upon mere survival, and then they can still less be expected to have the inclination, and the daring, to aim at an intentional, concerted, cooperative effort to remake society."

[4] Pierre Teilhard de Chardin, *The Making of a Mind,* tr. René Hague (New York: Harper & Row, 1965), p. 123.

[5] Teilhard, *Letters from a Traveller* (New York: Harper & Row, 1962), p. 202.

[6] K. M. Sen, *Hinduism* (Baltimore: Penguin, 1961), p. 23.

[7] Abinash Chandra Bose, *Hymns from the Vedas* (New York: Asia Publishing House, 1966), p. 28.

[8] Rig Veda I. 113. 6.

[9] *Ibid.,* I. 113. 16.

[10] *Ibid.,* I. 71. 10.

[11] *Kulārnava Tantra,* 1. 27.

[12] Alain Danielou, *Hindu Polytheism* (New York: Pantheon, 1964), pp. 254-55.

[13] *Kulārnava Tantra,* 9. 125.

[14] Cf. M. P. Pandit, *Studies in the Tantras and the Veda* (Madras: Ganesh, 1964), p. 28.

[15] Cf. Chittenjoor Kunhan Raja, *Some Fundamental Problems in Indian Philosophy* (Delhi: Motilal Banarsidass, 1960), p. 249.

[16] *Ibid.*

[17] Teilhard, *Writings in Time of War,* tr. René Hague (New York: Harper & Row, 1968), p. 34.

[18] *Ibid.,* p. 14.

[19] Teilhard, *Christianity and Evolution* (Harcourt Brace Jovanovich, 1971), p. 105; Teilhard, *The Phenomenon of Man* (New York: Harper Torchbook, 1961), p. 163; Teilhard, *The Vision of the Past,* tr. J. M. Cohen (New York: Harper & Row, 1966), p. 166.

[20] Teilhard, *Human Energy,* tr. J. M. Cohen (New York: Harcourt Brace Jovanovich, 1969), p. 20.

[21] Teilhard, *The Vision of the Past,* pp. 51-52; cf. p. 162.

[22] Teilhard, *Human Energy,* p. 20.

[23] Teilhard, *The Appearance of Man,* tr. J. M. Cohen (New York: Harper & Row, 1965), p. 34; *Writings in Time of War,* pp. 34-35; cf. *Human Energy,* p. 115.

[24] Teilhard, *Human Energy,* p. 119.

[25] Teilhard, *The Phenomenon of Man,* p. 281.

[26] Troy Wilson Organ, *The Hindu Quest for the Perfection of Man* (Athens: Ohio University, 1970), p. 164.

[27] Teilhard, *The Future of Man,* tr. Norman Denny (New York: Harper & Row, 1964), p. 246.

[28] Organ, p. 164.

[29] Pandit, p. 8.

[30] Teilhard, *The Vision of the Past,* p. 73. See *The Appearance of Man,* p. 159: He is "the most actually adaptable cosmic substance we know."

[31] Organ, p. 204; cf. p. 115.

[32] Teilhard, *The Appearance of Man,* p. 269.

[33] Teilhard, *Writings in Time of War,* p. 16.

[34] Organ, pp. 166, 167, 172, 173, 336, 337.

[35] Teilhard, *The Divine Milieu* (New York: Harper & Row, 1960), p. 70.

[36] Teilhard, *Writings in Time of War,* p. 134.

[37] Teilhard, *Building the Earth* (Wilkes-Barre: Dimension Books, 1965), p. 35.

[38] Teilhard, *Writings in Time of War,* p. 33.

[39] Teilhard, *The Vision of the Past,* p. 137.

[40] Teilhard, *The Divine Milieu,* p. 62.

[41] Teilhard, *Christianity and Evolution,* p. 111.

[42] Teilhard, *Hymn of the Universe* (New York: Harper & Row, 1965), p. 114. Cf. *The Making of a Mind,* p. 126, where he says that it would be tempting God to simply let the world go its own way. We are not excused from the work of creation.

[43] Teilhard, *Writings in Time of War,* p. 35.

[44] Teilhard, *Christianity and Evolution,* p. 92.

[45] Teilhard, *The Phenomenon of Man,* p. 231.

[46] Teilhard, *The Appearance of Man,* p. 45.

[47] Teilhard, *The Phenomenon of Man,* p. 139. At this writing this is again somewhat in question inasmuch as the offspring of maze-trained rats take less time to learn the maze on which their ancestors were trained than do control individuals.

[48] Teilhard, *The Future of Man,* p. 251.

[49] Cf. *ibid.,* p. 296, and Teilhard, *The Appearance of Man,* p. 163n.

[50] Teilhard, *The Vision of the Past,* pp. 95-96.

[51] Cf. *ibid.*

[52] Teilhard, *The Phenomenon of Man,* p. 110.

[53] Teilhard, *Letters from a Traveller,* pp. 357-58.

[54] Sir John Woodroffe and Pramatha Natha Mukhyopādhyāya, *Mayāmāyā: The World as Power: Power as Consciousness* (Madras: Ganesh, 1964), p. 220.

[55] *Śiva-Mahāpurāṇa,* II. 1. 6, 11c, d-12.

[56] Cf. Surendranath Dasgupta, *A History of Indian Philosophy* (Cambridge University Press, 1968), V. 98-99.

[57] Teilhard, *The Appearance of Man,* p. 253; cf. p. 140. Also see *The Vision of the Past,* p. 235, and *The Future of Man,* pp. 227 ff and pp. 232 ff.

[58] Teilhard, *The Phenomenon of Man,* p. 149. n.1.

[59] Teilhard, *The Vision of the Past,* p. 97.

[60] Teilhard, *Human Energy,* p. 139.

[61] Rig Veda X. 129. 4 (Bose)

[62] Chāndogya Upanishad VI. 2. 3 (Radhakrishnan).

[63] Taittiriya Upanishad II. 6 (Bose); cf. Maitrī Upanishad VI. 17.

[64] Cf. S. Radhakrishnan, *The Principal Upanishads* (London: Allen & Unwin, 1953), p. 548.

[65] Teilhard, *Human Energy,* p. 102.

[66] Cf. Woodroffe and Mukhyopādhyāya, *Mahāmāyā,* pp, 152-53.

[67] Teilhard, *Human Energy,* pp. 119-20.

[68] Woodroffe and Mukhyopādhyāya, *Mahāmāyā,* pp. 200-201; cf. p. 26.

[69] Teilhard, *The Vision of the Past,* p. 72.

[70] Teilhard, *The Phenomenon of Man,* p. 149.

[71] Teilhard, *The Vision of the Past,* pp. 72-73.

[72] Woodroffe and Mukhyopādhyāya, *Mahāmāyā,* pp. 201-2.

[73] Teilhard, *Christianity and Evolution,* p. 98.

[74] Teilhard, *Activation of Energy,* tr. René Hague (New York: Harcourt Brace Jovanovich, 1970), p. 107.

[75] Woodroffe and Mukhyopādhyāya, *Mahāmāyā,* p. 221; cf. pp. 201-2, 220.

[76] Teilhard, *Activation of Energy,* p. 102.

[77] Woodroffe and Mukhyopādhyāya, *Mahāmāyā,* pp. 221-22.

[78] *Ibid.,* p. 223.

[79] Teilhard, *The Phenomenon of Man,* pp. 209-10.

[80] Organ, p. 337.

[81] Teilhard, *The Vision of the Past,* p. 231; cf. *The Future of Man,* p. 277.

[82] Teilhard, *The Future of Man,* p. 121.

[83] *Ibid.,* pp. 205-6.

[84] Teilhard, *The Vision of the Past,* pp. 171-72.

[85] Teilhard, *Christianity and Evolution,* pp. 205-6.

[86] Teilhard, *Human Energy,* p. 139.

[87] Teilhard, *The Phenomenon of Man,* p. 229.

[88] Teilhard, *The Divine Milieu,* pp. 23-24.

[89] Teilhard, *The Phenomenon of Man,* p. 230.

[90] Teilhard, *Science and Christ,* tr. René Hague (New York: Harper & Row, 1968), p. 42.

[91] Teilhard, *The Future of Man,* pp. 207, 296; *Letters from a Traveller,* p. 45.

[92] Teilhard, *The Phenomenon of Man,* pp. 269-70.

[93] *Ibid.,* p. 230; cf. *The Divine Milieu,* p. 24.

[94] Teilhard, *Hymn of the Universe,* p. 139.

[95] Teilhard, *Letters from a Traveller,* p. 45.

[96] Teilhard, *The Making of a Mind;* p. 96.

[97] Bhagavad Gītā 18. 62 (Zaehner).

[98] Teilhard, *Activation of Energy,* p. 148.

[99] Bhagavad Gītā 18, 58.

[100] Teilhard, *Writings in Time of War,* p. 50.

[101] Śrī Aurobindo, *The Life Divine,* Vol. III of the Śrī Aurobindo Center of Education Collection (Pondicherry: Śrī Aurobindo Ashram Press, 1960), p. 1246.

[102] Śrī Aurobindo, *The Ideal of Human Unity* (New York: Dutton, 1950), p. 323.

[103] Teilhard, *The Future of Man,* p. 183.
[104] Aurobindo, *The Life Divine,* p. 1102.
[105] *Ibid.*
[106] Teilhard, *The Future of Man,* p. 152.
[107] Aurobindo, *The Life Divine,* p. 1103.
[108] Teilhard, *The Future of Man,* p. 183.
[109] Maryse Choisy, *Teilhard et l'Inde,* Carnets Teilhard 11 (Paris: Editions Universitaires, 1963), p. 57.
[110] Sen, pp. 13-14.
[111] Teilhard, *Christianity and Evolution,* p. 93.
[112] Bhagavad Gītā 3. 21-24 (Zaehner).
[113] Teilhard, *Writings in Time of War,* p. 67.
[114] Choisy, p. 27.
[115] Teilhard, *Christianity and Evolution,* p. 123.
[116] Cf. Kunhan Raja, p. 249.
[117] Bhagavad Gītā 3. 4 (Zaehner).
[118] Teilhard, *Human Energy,* p. 124. Italics his.
[119] Bhagavad Gītā 3. 5 (Zaehner).
[120] *Ibid.,* 3. 25 (Zaehner).
[121] Cf. Bhagavad Gītā 4. 19-23.
[122] Bhagavad Gītā 5. 20.
[123] *Ibid.,* 3. 13.
[124] *Ibid.,* 3. 9.
[125] Mircea Eliade, *Yoga:* Immortality and Freedom, tr. W. R. Trask (New York: Pantheon, 1958), p. 157.
[126] Teilhard, *Writings in Time of War,* pp. 42-43.
[127] Teilhard, *Science and Christ,* pp. 170-71; translation by Christopher Mooney, in *Teilhard de Chardin and the Mystery of Christ* (London: Collins, 1966), p. 162.
[128] Bhagavad Gītā 9. 24.
[129] *Ibid.,* 3. 30.
[130] *Ibid.,* 9. 26.
[131] *Ibid.,* 4. 11.
[132] Teilhard, *The Divine Milieu,* p. 66.
[133] Bhagavad Gītā 9. 27 (Zaehner).
[134] *Ibid.,* 18. 45-47.
[135] Henri de Lubac, *Teilhard de Chardin, The Man and His Meaning,* tr. René Hague (New York: Hawthorne, 1965), pp. 118-19 n. 7.
[136] Cf. Śrī Aurobindo, *Essays on the Gita* (Pondicherry: Śrī Aurobindo Ashram Press, 1950), p. 100.
[137] Bhagavad Gītā 3.19 (Zaehner).
[138] Cf. Bhagavad Gītā 4. 13, 7. 12, 9. 4-5, 9. 17, 10. 8.
[139] Teilhard, *The Making of a Mind,* p. 264.
[140] Bhagavad Gītā 18. 55-57, 65 (Zaehner).
[141] Teilhard, *The Future of Man,* p. 121.
[142] Teilhard, *The Phenomenon of Man,* p. 269.
[143] Teilhard, *The Divine Milieu,* p. 103.
[144] Cf. Teilhard, *The Future of Man.* pp. 206-7.
[145] Teilhard, *The Phenomenon of Man,* p. 272.
[146] Teilhard, *The Divine Milieu,* p. 56.
[147] *Ibid.,* p. 110.
[148] Teilhard, *Letters from a Traveller,* p. 151.

[149] Cf. Teilhard, *The Divine Milieu,* pp. 145-46; *The Phenomenon of Man,* p. 294.

[150] Cf. Teilhard, *The Divine Milieu,* p. 144; *Building the Earth,* pp. 97-98; *Letters from a Traveller,* p.18; *Hymn of the Universe,* p. 155.

[151] Cf. Teilhard, *The Future of Man,* pp. 122-23, 303.

[152] *Ibid.,* p. 302. Cf. Teilhard, *Man's Place in Nature,* tr. René Hague (New York: Harper & Row, 1960), p. 116.

[153] *Ibid.,* p. 123.

[154] Teilhard, *The Phenomenon of Man,* p. 272.

[155] Teilhard, *The Future of Man,* p. 297.

[156] Teilhard, *The Appearance of Man,* p. 264.

[157] Teilhard, *The Phenomenon of Man,* p. 272.

[158] Teilhard, *The Future of Man,* p. 223 n.1.

[159] *Ibid.,* p. 50.

[160] Cf. Teilhard, *The Making of a Mind,* p. 11.

[161] Śatapatha Brāhmaṇa 6.2.2.27.

[162] Cf. Veronica Ions, *Indian Mythology* (London: Hamlyn, 1967), p. 12; Geoffrey Parrinder, *Avatar and Incarnation* (New York: Barnes & Noble, 1970), p. 225; Heinrich Zimmer, *The Philosophies of India* (New York: Meridian, 1958), p. 184 n. Cf. Organ, pp. 137 ff.

[163] Cf. Teilhard, *Writings in Time of War,* p. 45.

[164] Teilhard, *The Phenomenon of Man,* p. 78.

[165] Erik H. Erikson, *Gandhi's Truth* (New York: Norton, 1969), p. 36.

[166] Cf. Wing-Tsit Chan *et al.,* eds., *The Great Asian Religions* (New York: Macmillan, 1969), pp. 8-9; Organ, p. 171.

[167] Radhakrishnan, pp. 111-12.

[168] Teilhard, *The Future of Man,* p. 44.

[169] Teilhard, *Man's Place in Nature,* p. 116.

[170] *Sāṃkhya Kārikā* 59 (Suryanarayana Sastri).

[171] Rig Veda X. 121. 2.

[172] Yajur Veda 39. 11. 13.

[173] Eliade, pp. 4-5.

[174] Teilhard, *The Future of Man,* p. 297.

[175] *Ibid.,* p. 213.

[176] Teilhard, *Hymn of the Universe,* p. 152.

[177] Teilhard, *Man's Place in Nature,* p. 121.

[178] Teilhard, *The Making of a Mind,* pp. 165-66.

[179] Teilhard, *Letters from a Traveller,* p. 140.

[180] S. S. Suryanarayana Sastri, *Collected Papers of Professor S. S. Suryanarayana Sastri* (University of Madras, 1961), p. 159.

[181] Chāndogya Upanishad 6. 10 1-2; 7. 25. 2.

[182] Brihad-Āraṇyaka Upanishad 4. 4. 22, 23.

[183] Īsā Upanishad 5.

[184] Maitrī Upanishad 6. 32.

[185] Organ, pp. 150, 169, 170.

[186] Teilhard, *The Vision of the Past,* p. 171.

[187] Teilhard, *Building the Earth,* p. 103.

[188] Teilhard, *Christianity and Evolution,* p. 205.

[189] Cf. *ibid.,* pp. 204, 222.

[190] Brihad-Āraṇyaka Upanishad IV. iv. 5-6 (Nikhilananda)

[191] Teilhard, *The Making of a Mind,* p. 164.

[192] Rig Veda X. 129. 4-5 (Bose).

[193] Teilhard, *Building the Earth,* p. 108.
[194] *Mahābhārata* Vol. XII (Shanti Parva). tr. M. N. Dutt (Calcutta: Sircar, 1902), p. 186.
[195] Teilhard, *The Future of Man,* p. 61.
[196] Woodroffe and Mukhyopādhyāya, p. 227.
[197] Teilhard, *The Future of Man,* p. 205.
[198] Teilhard, *Human Energy.* p. 138.
[199] Cf. Teilhard, *The Appearance of Man,* pp. 261, 263, 264.
[200] Cf. Teilhard, *The Vision of the Past,* pp. 70-71.
[201] Cf. Teilhard, *Building the Earth,* p. 36.
[202] Cf. Teilhard, *The Making of a Mind,* p. 172.
[203] Rāmānuja, *Commentary on the Vedānta-Sūtra, Sacred Books of the East,* 48. 70.
[204] Teilhard, *The Phenomenon of Man,* pp. 231, 142.
[205] Cf. Teilhard, *The Appearance of Man,* p. 262; *The Future of Man,* pp. 76-77, 145-46.
[206] Teilhard, *The Making of a Mind,* p. 263.
[207] Rig Veda X. 18 (Griffith).
[208] Cf. Bose, *Hymns,* pp. 10-11.
[209] Atharva Veda XII. 1 (Bose).
[210] Teilhard, *The Phenomenon of Man,* p. 36.
[211] *Ibid.*
[212] Cf. Teilhard, *Christianity and Evolution,* pp. 224-25.
[213] Teilhard, *The Divine Milieu,* p. 41.
[214] Teilhard, *The Making of a Mind,* p. 236.
[215] Atharva Veda XII. 1.
[216] Pandit, *Gems,* p. iii.
[217] Teilhard, *The Appearance of Man,* p. 262.
[218] Teilhard, *Human Energy,* p. 41; *Letters from a Traveller,* p. 357.
[219] Cf. Teilhard, *Writings in Time of War,* p. 148.
[220] Teilhard, *Letters from a Traveller,* p. 206.
[221] Teilhard, *The Divine Milieu,* p. 79.
[222] Teilhard, *The Making of a Mind,* p. 188; *Hymn of the Universe,* p. 36.
[223] Teilhard, *The Making of a Mind,* p. 166.
[224] Teilhard, *The Divine Milieu,* pp. 151-52.
[225] Cf. Teilhard, *The Future of Man,* p. 41; *Letters from a Traveller,* pp. 70-71.
[226] Śrī Aurobindo, *The Synthesis of Yoga* (Pondicherry: Śrī Aurobindo Ashram Press, 1957), p. 4: "All life, when we look behind its appearances, is a past Yoga of Nature attempting to realise her perfection in an ever increasing expression of her potentialities and to unite herself with her own divine reality."
[227] Teilhard, *The Future of Man,* p. 117.
[228] *Ibid.,* pp. 56-57.
[229] *Ibid.,* p. 81.
[230] *Ibid.,* p. 91.
[231] Teilhard, *The Phenomenon of Man,* p. 223.
[232] *Ibid.,* p. 180.
[233] *Ibid.,* p. 189. Cf. the remark of Julian Huxley, p. 13.
[234] Cf. Teilhard, *Hymn of the Universe,* p. 77; *The Appearance of Man,* p. 67.
[235] Teilhard, *The Making of a Mind,* p. 181.
[236] *Ibid.,* p. 116.
[237] Teilhard, *The Divine Milieu,* p. 63.

[238] Teilhard, *Christianity and Evolution,* p. 129.
[239] *Ibid.,* p. 184; Teilhard, *The Appearance of Man,* p. 273.
[240] Teilhard, *Christianity and Evolution,* p. 184; cf. *The Future of Man,* p. 224.
[241] Teilhard, *The Future of Man,* p. 224.
[242] Teilhard, *Writings in Time of War,* p. 60.
[243] Cf. Teilhard, *The Divine Milieu,* p. 62.
[244] Cf. Teilhard, *Hymn of the Universe,* p. 23 and n. 1.
[245] Teilhard, *The Phenomenon of Man,* p. 307 n; *The Divine Milieu,* p. 123.
[246] Cf. Teilhard, *The Divine Milieu,* p. 122.
[247] Cf. Teilhard, *Christianity and Evolution,* p. 181.
[248] Teilhard, *Writings in Time of War,* p. 59.
[249] *Ibid.,* p. 50.
[250] Not Teilhard's word, but cf. *Hymn of the Universe,* pp. 76-77.
[251] Cf. Teilhard, *Writings in Time of War,* p. 59; *Hymn of the Universe,* p. 133.
[252] Teilhard, *Writings in Time of War,* p. 78.
[253] Teilhard, *Christianity and Evolution,* p. 147.
[254] Cf. *ibid.,* pp. 182-83.
[255] Teilhard, *Hymn of the Universe,* p. 119.
[256] Cf. Teilhard, *Activation of Energy,* p. 376; *The Making of a Mind:* Christ is "the world's driving force."
[257] Cf. Teilhard, *Hymn of the Universe,* p. 152; *Christianity and Evolution,* p. 96.
[258] Teilhard, *Vision of the Past,* p. 138 and n.1.
[259] Teilhard, *Hymn of the Universe,* p. 144.
[260] Teilhard, *Writings in Time of War,* p. 17.
[261] Cf. Teilhard, *The Future of Man,* pp. 210 f.
[262] Cf. Teilhard, *The Making of a Mind,* pp. 160, 164.
[263] Cf. Teilhard, *The Phenomenon of Man,* pp. 296-97.
[264] Teilhard, *The Appearance of Man,* p. 269.
[265] Cf. Woodroffe and Mukhyopādhyāya, *Mahāmāyā,* p. 133.
[266] Teilhard, *The Appearance of Man,* pp. 266-67.
[267] Teilhard, *Activation of Energy,* p. 382.
[268] *Ibid.,* pp. 259-60.
[269] Eliade, p. 12.
[270] Teilhard, *Activation of Energy,* p. 248.
[271] Cf. Eliade, pp. 14, 27; Teilhard, *The Appearance of Man,* pp. 256-59.
[272] Woodroffe and Mukhyopādhyāya, *Mahāmāyā,* pp. 139-40.
[273] Teilhard, *The Making of a Mind,* p. 165.
[274] Cf. Eliade, pp. 28, 34-35.
[275] Dasgupta, V. 116.
[276] *Ibid.,* V. 116-17.
[277] Cf. Radhakrishnan, *The Principal Upanishads,* p. 122.
[278] Mysore Hiriyanna, *The Quest after Perfection* (Mysore: Kavyalaya, 1952), p. 35.
[279] Paiṅgala Upanishad II.11; cf. Bhagavad Gītā VII.19: After many births, the one who knows surrenders to the Lord who is the cause of all.
[280] Brihad-Āraṇyaka Upanishad IV. 4. 2-4; cf. Bhagavad Gītā II. 13.
[281] Muṇḍaka Upanishad III. 2. 2, 5-7.
[282] Radhakrishnan, p. 115. He expresses a point of view quite similar to Teilhard's, even to committing the same logical error of speaking of "attaining" life "eternal."

[283] M. P. Pandit, *Studies in the Tantras and the Veda,* p. 28.
[284] M. P. Pandit, *Gems from the Tantras* (Madras: Ganesh, 1969), p. 9.
[285] Teilhard, *Writings in Time of War,* p. 32.
[286] Teilhard, *The Making of a Mind,* pp. 181-82.
[287] Teilhard, *The Future of Man,* p. 23.
[288] Organ, p. 90.
[289] Teilhard, *Building the Earth,* p. 68.
[290] Teilhard, *The Making of a Mind,* p. 181; *Christianity and Evolution,* p. 177.
[291] Teilhard, *Letters from a Traveller,* p. 347.
[292] Pandit, *Studies,* pp. 97-98.
[293] Teilhard, *Writings in Time of War,* p. 37.
[294] Quoted in Prosanto Sumar Sen, *Keshub Chunder Sen* (Calcutta: Art Press, 1938), p. 112.
[295] Rabindranath Tagore, *The Religion of Man* (London: Allen & Unwin, 1931), p. 49.
[296] Yajur Veda 39. 4 (Bose).
[297] Teilhard, *The Divine Milieu,* p. 136.
[298] Teilhard, *Hymn of the Universe,* pp. 48-49.
[299] Teilhard, *The Divine Milieu,* p. 126.
[300] *Ibid.,* p. 125.
[301] Radhakrishnan, p. 123.
[302] B. K. Majumdar, *Introduction,* in Pandit Siva Chandra Vidyarnava, *Principles of Tantra,* or *Tantra-Tattva.* rendered into English by Srī Jnanendralal Majumdar, edited by Sir John Woodroffe, 3rd ed. (Madras: Ganesh).
[303] Teilhard, *Building the Earth,* p. 117.
[304] Teilhard. *Letters from a Traveller,* p. 164.
[305] Cf. *ibid.,* p. 298.
[306] Teilhard, *The Appearance of Man,* pp. 266-67.
[307] Teilhard, *The Phenomenon of Man,* p. 232; cf. *The Future of Man,* p. 122.

EPILOGUE

There is no need now to review Teilhard's failure to appreciate the true history and diversity of the Hindu traditions. But we may draw together some of our conclusions regarding the support and the constructive aid that a Teilhardian system could receive from these traditions.

The first and outstanding theme in Teilhard's synthesis is, of course, that of evolution, and on this score the Hindu mainstream tradition offers an interesting type of support. Evolution has different meanings in the different Hindu schools, different again from the scientific definitions of the West. But the image that emerges in all cases is that of a *plastic* Nature, not a *fixed* Nature. Forms are relative; forms pass into one another; no being can be absolutely identified with its current form. The Ultimate Reality is that which underlies the shifting forms. There is a unity and a continuity undergirding the superficially discrete beings.

It is this element in Hinduism which Teilhard mistook for homogeneity and saw as threatening to suck the differentiated entities back into the chaos of its primeval womb. But the Ultimate is not homogeneous—of the "same kind"—for it is not of any "kind" at all. This is not an image of the material foundations of things, as Teilhard charged, but of *continuity, intelligibility,* and *transcendence.*

The Hindu view of Nature is thus what I have called a "hospitable" matrix for Teilhard's theory of evolution. Evolution is a very special kind of change. It requires a certain type of world to support its possibility. And Teilhard's evolution, which is an evolution toward divinity, puts further conditions on that world. "Change" presupposes *plasticity* of some aspect of the being, supported by a *continuity.* "Evolution," as Teilhard sees it, is a series of changes in living things, not in one single line, but in a generalized "sheaf," or "bundle" of lines, whose overall development is in a given direction. Whatever supports it in continuity is also characterized by *intelligibility*. And this given direction, in Teilhard's view, is toward the divine, i.e. the *transcendent*. This is what the Hindu world-image offers, and whether or not it had already developed a scientific theory of evolution comparable to Teilhard's, it would supply a nutritious culture medium, so to speak, in which such a theory could easily grow.

On the other hand, the world-image derived from Greek and Judaeo-Christian sources, which Teilhard inherited in his own culture, had conflicts with these conditions for an evolutionary theory, although it gave him another element—the sense of history—which was supportive. Teilhard himself put the finger on the conflict when he said that his tradition had difficulty with the idea of change. It conceived the world as composed of fixed natures. This concept is tied to the doctrine of creation and no doubt is related to the notion of personal responsibility in the moral realm. Each person is a discrete entity, with a fully given and fixed nature, who can then be held thoroughly accountable for his behavior. This image gives Teilhard trouble again when he comes to the problem of death, because in the Christian tradition, it is the person, a discrete moral entity, fully formed at all times, who lives and dies and whose destiny must be accounted for apart from the hypothesis of evolution.

The stress on the moral dimension of life, together with the presupposition of fixed natures—notwithstanding the concern for history—made a small world quite sufficient for this tradition. There was no need for huge spaces or vast stretches of time, much less for the complex growth relationships of beings to one another. Consequently, the Christian tradition did not develop these notions, whereas the Hindu did. This is why, as Teilhard expresses it, it was a great discovery for the Europeans to realize how immense the universe is. The Judaeo-Christian imagination is primarily a moral imagination, not a cosmic one, and it found it difficult to assimilate the physical universe, which exists on a scale so different from the human one. The Hindu imagination, on the contrary, had always had a cosmic dimension in it, as well as the human ones, and its view of Nature as constituted of transposing forms, suggested, if not demanded, a large universe to accommodate it.

The Hindu view also suggested something about the nature of this underlying continuous, intelligible, and transcendent support of the changing forms. It is true that it is not of any "kind," but it cannot be incapable of the most generalized and universal qualities which can be observed in its own products. In our experience the only thing we know that is a principle of continuity, intelligibility, and transcendence is our own consciousness. We experience it as an energy and as a self. And this is what the Hindus called it: Chit-Śakti and Ātman. Such conceptions point to just what Teilhard's theory concludes: that what is evolving is an energy; that it is a single energy; and that it is basically psychical in nature. When he finally develops the idea of the total Christ as the one being in course of formation through evolution, it is also clear that this energy is a Self.

What, then, of the various particular forms assumed by this evolving energy? Are they, according to the Hindus, only incidental, of no significance, or somehow unreal? Not at all. With the exception of Śaṅkara's extreme interpretation of the Vedānta, the Hindu schools held the simultaneous reality and value of one transcendent Being and the many forms of its flowing energy. This is the mystery and magic (māyā) of existence, but it is also its delight (ānanda) and its glory (virāj). The relation between the two aspects of reality can only be conceived by us on the analogy of the organic. It is a *living* universe. The world is the *body* of God.

Within this complex vital Being we ourselves live with our particular vocations, our dharmas. These are not trivial. They *are* the life of that divine Being. Human action is a matter of prime importance. Duties are to be performed and effort is to be expended to bring human consciousness to ever higher levels and into full coincidence with the Supreme Transcendent Consciousness. This Supreme One may be variously conceived, but among its Hindu conceptions is the one Teilhard prefers: a Person who is also a World. This Person is loving and is to be loved in return—loved as a Person and loved as the World. Rāmprasād had said that when we walk around the city we are walking around the Blissful Mother. To which Rabindranath Tagore added that the Beloved is "in the pupils of our eyes"; that is why we "see Him everywhere." Life, therefore, despite its heavy load of sorrow, is, in Hindu eyes, fundamentally a joy; it should be assented to as joy and sought as joy.

Here we have, surely, a highly congenial environment for Teilhard's worldview: his vision of Christ-the-Evolver, his reconciliation of the values to be accorded both God and the world, his insistence on the importance of action, his refusal to give in to pessimism, his unconquerable delight in life. The Hindu traditions are compatible with Teilhard's synthesis both structurally and emotionally. They do not raise difficulties when he attempts to bring the Divine into the whole of Nature, or when he suggests that history is a great organic growth, or when he speculates that some degree of consciousness characterizes all beings, or when he proposes that the goal of evolution is the realization in adulthood of the embryonic Christ. If he is inspired to worship his Lord on an altar wide as the Earth, in the energies of an obscure and mysterious natural process, or in the daily secular activities of economic, political, and scientific man, the mainstream Hindu tradition makes no protest. These are thoughts and feelings long familiar to it.

Is everything in Teilhard familiar to Hinduism? No, of course not. The sense of history is a peculiarly Judaic contribution and is strikingly absent from the Hindu mentality. Teilhard's theme of personalization is not developed among the Hindus with the accent he gives it, that of "amorization," the love of one person for another as a process intrinsic and crucial to universal evolution. An important consequence of this—which, like its antecedent, is a characteristically Christian insight—is the central position of the human collective in the destiny of the world. Some late Hindu thinkers have emphasized this point, but it can be easily argued that they received their inspiration from Christian sources. Nevertheless, as the case of Aurobindo demonstrates, the thesis can be readily supported by exclusive reference to Hindu traditions. The point is that the foundations for such development are available there, even if their natural heirs did not exploit them.

Basic to these ideas of Teilhard is his great principle that *union differentiates.* This, he feels, is where he fundamentally differs with what he considers to be genuine Hinduism. The Hindus, he claims, made a mistake in the conception of unity, and it led them to a false metaphysics and ultimately to a false mysticism. It is the difference between an unstructured, or homogeneous, unity and a structured, or differentiated, unity. The Ultimate Reality—for Teilhard, the Trinity—is Itself not a pure unity, but a differentiated unity: It has an internal structure, as all living beings do. Similarly, the perfection of creation is reached when the universe draws all its elements into a supremely cohesive union which differentiates each member into a unique and incomparable being in itself. Teilhard explains his difference with the Hindus by saying that he himself "concentrates the multiple," whereas they "suppress the multiple" into unity with "their dim source," a "reservoir of homogeneous ether and latent life."

What Teilhard is doing here is a good example of how the Western way of thinking is fundamentally geared to the moral imperative of making a decision. The "judgment" is a prime category in Western theories of logic, truth, and knowledge. Situations are either "this" way or "that," propositions are true or false, actions are right or wrong, souls are lost or saved. Western thought has a very low tolerance for ambiguity. Unity is achieved either by concentration or by suppression.

But the interesting thing about the Hindu philosophers is that not only are they not limited to the monism which Teilhard would impose on them, but they have tried all sorts of ways to unify the multiple—including not unifying them at all. And beyond this, they have even sought ways to integrate the various ways of solving the metaphysical question. Logical generalization, allegorical accommodation, combination and synthesis, and admission of contradictions on distinct levels of interpretation are some of their expressions of a basic tolerance which is a concomitant of their root desire to embrace and to appreciate all of the real. The Hindu wants to savor all aspects of the Reality—as well as to liberate himself from ignorance, which is the thralldom of the unreal. But he does not feel the urgency to make a decision about reality and to *do* something about it that the Westerner feels.

This high tolerance for ambiguity, or sense of the mystery of Reality, together with a lack of drive to organize and dominate Nature, is perhaps what produces the reactions of impatience and frustration in the Westerner who, like Teilhard, takes only a sweeping, superficial look at the Hindu mind. He tends to feel, as Teilhard felt, that we are never going to "get on with it" so long as we approach life with such a receptive and flexible (read "passive") attitude. Thus, in his eagerness to make decisions, get things organized, and get some productive action underway, the Westerner in general, and Teilhard in particular, tends to classify the Hindu outlook in terms of some strong contrast with his own worldview and to find that it "reduces everything to matter," "denies multiplicity," "identifies unity with homogeneity," is "passive and fatalistic," has "no conception of a loving personal God," and so on—which justifies his position that *his* set of ideas and *his* culture have a divinely ordained destiny to absorb and dominate the other. Teilhard, for instance, said explicitly that the axis of evolution runs through the West, that the old cultures have no strength to persevere, and that they will simply deposit their small store of wisdom into the overwhelming current of Western civilization, which is the floodtide of advancing evolution.

But, as we have been suggesting all along, a longer look might have led to a different conclusion. Consider two examples of what a little Hindu tolerance, integration, and even ambiguity might have done for Teilhard. The first is the union of the personal and the impersonal in the concept-image of the Pervading Deity; and the second—which is structurally related to it—is the union of the finite and the infinite, with particular application to the problem of time and mortality.

Despite his cautious and deferential language, it seems

clear that Teilhard really wanted to invest Christ with a cosmic nature. That is to say, not to put too fine a point on the technical meaning of "nature" in Christian theology, he had a strong feeling for the cosmic component in his Deity. Why could he not follow out the leadings of this instinct in his tradition? Mainly, I believe, because the Judaic religions are fundamentally religions of the will. They conceive reality in terms of what they perceive to be most radical in the human being, his volition. Their God is a God of Will and their religion is a relation between the will of man and the Will of God. It is personalistic and moralistic. Why is a cosmic component incompatible with this view? Because Nature does not seem to operate on moral principles. What Nature does is experienced by man as both good and evil. To avoid making God personally responsible for the evil, it is necessary to separate Him from Nature. However, it should be noted that this is not a solution to the problem but only a clarification which in effect crystallizes the problem and freezes it in an insoluble dilemma. One portion of the psychic reality, from which the human images of Deity are drawn, has been walled off from the remainder: the deliberative faculty has been elevated to the supreme position from which it has no more interaction with the obscure forces of organic life. It says to them in the beginning "Let them be," but thereafter they pursue their own dark ways and by and by acquire a kind of independent volition of their own. Eventually, a need is felt for a Principle (Prince) of Darkness to radicalize their activities, and from here on the mythology, the theology, and the morality become more and more complex and the dilemmas multiply. Ambiguity is not so easily defeated.

The clearly conscious and the relatively unconscious—as perceived and judged by the deliberative faculty, which makes itself the paradigm of clear consciousness—are set in opposition to one another and reified as Spirit and Matter. Once separated in this way, there is no end of the problems about their relations to one another, the nature of the causal intimacy between them, the respective claims of each and their ultimate destinies. Much of Christian theology and morality has been preoccupied with these considerations, and it was precisely this schism which Teilhard inherited and which was the central emotional and intellectual problem of his life. His attempted answer to it we have traced in his concepts of the Cosmic Christ, the Law of Complexity/Consciousness, and the Single Energy. He came very near to closing the gap, especially in the dyadic character he attributed to Omega, which might have been a fruitful ambiguity instead of an inconsistency. But because he did not cut the root of the problem by suspending all the assumptions of dualistic thinking—which would amount, on our hypothesis, to allowing the impersonal, or relatively unconscious, full union with the personal, or deliberative consciousness—he was obliged in the end to abandon that portion of the Cosmos which he had sought to save, his dearly beloved Matter.

How would the Hindu tradition have relieved this situation? I believe that the Hindu conception of human nature is inclined to be more holistic, to admit the psychic reality in its full range of types and degrees of consciousness. The will does not occupy the single dominating position that it does in the Judaic tradition. The radical principle is called "Self," which is both transcendent and also all-inclusive. The perfection of consciousness is called "realization," which again is a comprehensive image. Historically, Judaism, and its offspring, Christianity and Islam, have carefully separated themselves from all others, stressing differences, while Hinduism has tended to take everything in, accept and absorb all others, finding unity under apparent differences. Fundamental to these two ways of life may be two attitudes toward our consciousness itself: a fear of the nondeliberative contents of consciousness (from which derives the fear of paganism and pantheism), together with ruthless measures of repression of these contents (from which derive not only sin-consciousness and guilt, with all their pathological progeny, but the political activities of proselytizing, censoring, and heresy-hunting), as against an acceptance of the more obscure levels of the psyche and gradual but systematic efforts to harmonize them (which results, as already noted, in a certain lack of organization, aggressiveness, and institutional productivity).

This quality of all-inclusiveness, or comprehensiveness, shows in the Hindu images of Deity, as in Kṛṣṇa or the Divine Mother. No attempt is made to separate them from the dimmer movements in the world, or from its evil. They clearly transcend all finite forms and operations, but since they are also embodied as all finite forms and operations, they manifest themselves as both what men call good and what they call evil. The problem of evil is stopped before it can get started. It may be a cruel answer but it can claim to be an empirically truthful one. The explanation is that Reality is not just a Will, the psychic being is not exhausted by moral consciousness.

Once the breadth of the psychic being is admitted and therefore the ambiguity of moral good and evil is accepted in a position which does not attempt to dominate the whole, it is possible to develop a conception of reality which permits the personal and the impersonal to coexist and even to intermingle intimately. This is, we may suggest, what Teilhard was groping for in his Law of Complexity/Consciousness and his extension of consciousness in diminished degree to all beings. He may also have been feeling after some such conception in his treatment of evil as a statistical necessity—i.e., something relative, even adventitious, not a property of the root of reality (as it would be if that root were a will).

But Teilhard was so emphatic about preferring the personal to the impersonal. How can we suggest that he was secretly eager to retain the impersonal? By "person" Teilhard meant reflexive consciousness, self-possessing consciousness. The crucial question is: Is the essence of self-possessing consciousness deliberative consciousness, consciousness which sees the world as composed of alternatives and which chooses between them? This is perhaps something Teilhard never quite clarified for himself. The notion of the "option" was important to him, but he may not have worked out all the implications of making it the central feature of psychic being. He knew that he did not want consciousness to run down into homogeneity again, but he probably never distinguished between the analytic and the synthetic ways of avoiding this. Since in the West heterogeneity has been protected by the analytic (dividing and separating) method, the opposite method of including and harmonizing would tend to be seen as on the side of homogeneity. This may be why Teilhard judged the Hindu mysticism the way he did. It was only homogeneity and death that he feared from the "impersonal."

But if heterogeneity—a differentiated union—can be protected by the synthetic and comprehensive method, then "personal" being need not be limited to the analytic and deliberative faculty, and what had seemed to be "impersonal" may be gradually assimilated to the reflexive level of consciousness as the process of harmonization is completed.

This is what the Hindu images suggest. The world is a multilevel being, pervaded and transcended by an Infinite Being whose body it is. The Absolute Being is thus both transcendent and incarnate, both personal and impersonal, both infinite and finite. A cosmic nature of the Deity is not only not a problem in this framework, it is a necessity. And by the same token a transcendent nature in the individuals composing the cosmos is a necessity. This is the answer to Teilhard's second problem, that of mortality and the passage from time to eternity.

If the model for Reality is the totality of human psychism, in its fully conscious and deliberative aspect and its dimly conscious or unconscious aspects, in its definitely formed dimensions and in its dimensionless center beyond all specific form, then it is evident that the Divine Being—the transcendent and infinite One—incarnates Itself in the multiple world, the world of individuals. This has two consequences: 1) the Divine Being has a cosmic aspect, and 2) the individuals have a transcendent aspect. But transcendent means escaping all definite and particular characters or forms. One such form is temporality. What is not bound by temporality is eternal. The eternal is not that which goes on existing for time without end, but that which is not characterized by temporality at all. Now, the point to be grasped in the Hindu image is that Reality is conceived as *both* eternal and temporal. This applies to the whole world and to each individual. This is an instance in which the synthetic character of the Hindu imagination shows in distinction from the Western. The Western mentality would say that being is *divided* into the temporal and the eternal; a given being is *either* temporal or eternal.

This is why Teilhard has the problem he has with mortality. He wants his world to be the bearer of divinity—the transcendent, the eternal—and to be joined to that divinity. But the world itself he conceives as finite and temporal, in opposition to eternity. He must therefore contrive a passage from the temporal to the eternal. It is one of the demands of human action, one of the properties of Omega, that the values subserved by human action, grounded in Omega the goal, be immune from destruction, that they cross over from the temporal world to the non-temporal world. This is the image of salvation, of rescue from the destruction that essentially comes with evil and inevitably comes with time. But to escape evil, or imperfection, and time, is to step out of evolution. And this is indeed Teilhard's concept of death and immortality. The end (goal) of evolution is the end (cessation) of evolution. In fact, however, there is no intrinsic connection between these two "ends," and so far as we know, the "cessation" always comes before the "goal" is reached. As with Matter and Spirit, the temporal and the eternal, once separated, give rise to an endless chain of puzzles and paradoxes.

In the Hindu image, since the individual is both temporal as to his embodied form and eternal as to his most intimate selfhood, there is no occasion to bridge a chasm between time and eternity or to provide for a passage from this world to that. Eternal life is not something that comes *after* temporal life. One lives in eternity even now. Evolution characterizes the temporal aspect, but there is no need to step out of evolution to attain immortality. The goal of evolution is not the cessation of evolution but the realization of one's eternal reality in relation to one's temporal reality. Thus there is no reason to abandon Matter, as Teilhard finally (but, we may believe, reluctantly) did.

There are two features of Teilhard's system which suggest that this Hindu image would not be totally alien to it. One is his conception of the reflexive consciousness, the self-possessing person. This reflexivity is itself what makes the person transcendent with respect to the rest of the world. There is an aura about it—though it is not expressly said—that speaks of immortality in its very essence. Teilhard says that once the reflexion has occurred, the being can never fall back under the sway of entropy. It is not a full statement of the intrinsic and natural property of eternal existence in the human person, but it can be construed as a leaning toward it.

The other feature is the doctrine of divine Incarnation. This is, structurally, the very thing the Hindu conception of the world proposes: a Being simultaneously transcendent and eternal, as well as embodied and temporal. It was Aurobindo—working with the same set of problems and the same modern scientific background as Teilhard—who pointed out that the Christian West had not taken full advantage of the concept of Incarnation. By restricting it to a single individual, he argued, and making it a mystery—that is, something alien to the normal structural relations of the universe—Christian theologians had deprived themselves of a valuable metaphysical principle for the interpretation of the world as a whole. But Teilhard, with his cosmic Christ, his Christ-the-Evolver, and his Christ-Omega, comes a long way toward correcting this deprivation.

I said above that the Hindu worldview is holistic, integral, and synthetic, that its mentality is pacific and absorptive, with a high tolerance for ambiguity and a predilection for harmonization of contraries. Far from being unsuited for the modern world, as Teilhard charged the Hindu tradition with being, this attitude is precisely what we require at this moment in history, and indeed what Teilhard's own program requires. Our scientific concepts have had to expand beyond the simplicities of Aristotelian logic and Newtonian mechanics to embrace ambiguity (complementarity) and relativity. Theoretical models of interpretation are more and more built on a systems approach, a holistic grasp of natural phenomena in which intelligibility is seen as a function of the integrity of the system, the synthetic union of its differentiated elements. Socially and politically, ideologically and religiously, tolerance for contrary views and a disposition favoring peace and coexistence in constructive harmony have become, as Teilhard predicted, crucial for our survival. Even our sanity must now, in these days of "future shock," be protected by a wide flexibility and capacity to absorb differences. The myths, metaphysics, and mysticism of the Hindu traditions may well make a most valuable contribution to our imaginations, minds, and spirits as we struggle to adjust ourselves to the world that is here and that is coming.

Finally, the characteristic of the Hindu philosophical and religious tradition which makes it particularly appropriate to sustain the evolution toward divinity of which both it and Teilhard speak, is its elan, its taste for life, its eagerness for the divine, together with its optimism, its staying power, and—the last thing, which Teilhard himself did not investigate—its proficiency in technique. The Hindu traditions have never confined themselves to the ivory tower of intellectual speculation. Having set an ideal before humanity, they have always provided practical means for moving toward it. They recognize that technique is a significant part of life, which belongs to the quest for the divine just as do intellectual clarification, moral conversion, and affective devotion. All are forms of yoga, the union in and through which we seek realization of the Whole. Here we have the joining of the scientific and religious programs which Teilhard set as a condition for successful negotiation of the perilous future. We have the faith in human destiny, in the process of evolution, in the reality of the Transcendent, in the harmony of the God of Ahead and of Above and of Within, which Teilhard himself would recognize as the religion of the future, the religion of evolution.

There are many mysteries in history. We can see now how ironic it is that Teilhard never came to understand and appreciate one of the great spiritual heritages of our world which might have meant much to him in his struggle to put together the pieces of preciousness in his own large life. If we have any advantage in vision—having learned a great deal from Teilhard himself—we may dare to protect and fulfill his beautifully constructed model of a world in process by adjusting one of his tenets: The axis of evolution, in the long perspective, does not run through the West, but is, like the lines of specific descent, a sheaf of axes, running through humanity as a whole, knitting together the rich heritages of all cultures in the mighty convergence which Teilhard glimpsed. We, the people of the future, can no longer think of ourselves as heirs only of this culture or that, belonging to one or another corner of our tiny globe. Each of us is the heir of all that humanity has ever produced in diversity and splendor of life, knowledge, art, and wisdom. Only as we bring all of this, our human wealth, into an intense but differentiated union, will we be able to live beyond, to survive, our present phase of development and continue our evolution toward divinity.

SELECTED BIBLIOGRAPHY

Aurobindo. *Essays on the Gita.* Pondicherry: Sri Aurobindo Ashram Press, 1950.

————. *The Ideal of Human Unity.* New York: Dutton, 1950.

————. *The Life Divine.* Volume III of the Sri Aurobindo Center of Education Collection. Pondicherry: Sri Aurobindo Ashram Press, 1960.

————. *On Yoga* II-I. Pondicherry: Sri Aurodindo Ashram Press, 1958.

————. *The Synthesis of Yoga* (*On Yoga* I). Pondicherry: Sri Aurobindo Ashram Press, 1957.

Avalon, Arthur and Ellen. *Hymns to the Goddess.* 3rd ed. Madras: Ganesh, 1964.

Biardeau, Madeleine. *India.* Tr. F. Carter. New York: Viking, 1965.

Bose, A. C. *The Call of the Vedas.* Bombay: Bharatiya Vidya Bhavan, 1960.

————. *Hymns from the Vedas.* New York: Asia Publishing House, 1966.

Bouquet, A. C. *Comparative Religion.* 5th ed. Baltimore: Penguin, 1956.

Braybrooke, Neville, ed. *Teilhard de Chardin: Pilgrim of the Future.* New York: Seabury, 1964.

Bruteau, Beatrice. "Teilhard de Chardin: The Amorization of the World." *World Union* XI (1972). 2, pp. 18 ff.

————. *Worthy Is the World:* The Hindu Philosophy of Sri Aurobindo. Teaneck, N.J.: Fairleigh Dickinson University, 1972.

Campbell, Joseph, ed. *The Mystic Vision,* papers from the Eranos Yearbook VI. Princeton: Princeton University Press, 1968.

Chakravarti, Chintaharan. *The Tantras: Studies on Their Religion and Literature.* Calcutta: Punthi Pustak, 1963.

Chatterjee, Satischandra, and Datta, Dhirendra Mohan. *Introduction to Indian Philosophy.* Calcutta: University of Calcutta, 1968.

Choisy, Maryse. *Teilhard et l'Inde,* Carnets Teilhards 11. Paris: Editions Universitaires, 1963.

Coomaraswamy, Ananda K. *The Dance of Shiva.* New York: Noonday, 1957.

Corte, Nicolas. *Pierre Teilhard de Chardin: His Life and Spirit.* Tr. Martin Jarrett-Kerr. New York: Macmillan, 1960.

Danielou, Alain. *Hindu Polytheism.* New York: Pantheon, 1964.

Dasgupta, Surentranath. *A History of Indian Philosophy,* 5 vols. Cambridge: The University Press, 1922-55.

de Lubac, Henri. *Teilhard de Chardin: The Man and His Meaning.* Tr. René Hague. New York: Hawthorn, 1965.

Diwakar, R. R. *Mahayogi Sri Aurobindo.* Bombay: Bharatiya Vidya Bhavan, 1962.

Edgerton, Franklin. *The Beginnings of Indian Philosophy.* Cambridge: Harvard University Press, 1965.

————. *The Bhagavad Gita,* translated and interpreted. New York: Harper Torchbook, 1944.

Eiseley, Loren. *The Invisible Pyramid.* New York: Scribner's, 1970.

Eliade, Mircea. *Yoga:* Immortality and Freedom. Tr. W. R. Trask. New York: Pantheon, 1958.

Embree, Ainslie T., ed. *The Hindu Tradition.* New York: Modern Library, 1966.

Faricy, Robert L. *Teilhard 'de Chardin's Theology of the Christian in the World.* New York: Sheed & Ward, 1967.

Ghose, Sisirkumar, ed. *Tagore for You.* Calcutta: Cisva-Bharati, 1966.

Gray, Donald P. *The One and the Many.* New York: Herder, 1969.

Hiriyanna, Mysore. *Outlines of Indian Philosophy.* London: Allen & Unwin, 1932.

————. *The Quest after Perfection.* Mysore: Kavyalaya, 1951.

Hooper, J. S. M. *Hymns of the Alvars.* Calcutta: Association Press, 1929.

Ions, Veronica, *Indian Mythology*. London: Hamlyn, 1967.
Kunhan Raja, Chittenjoor. *Some Fundamental Problems in Indian Philosophy*. Delhi: Motilal Banarsidass, 1960.
Mahābhārata Vol. XII. Tr. M. N. Dutt. Calcutta: Sircar, 1902.
Mitra, Sisirkumar. *The Vision of India*. New York: Jaico, 1949.
Modi, P. M. *A Critique of the Brahma-Sutra*. Bhavnagar: Modi, 1943.
Mooney, Christopher F. *Teilhard de Chardin and the Mystery of Christ*. London: Collins, 1966.
Murray, Michael H. *The Thought of Teilhard de Chardin*. New York: Seabury, 1966.
Organ, Troy Wilson. *The Hindu Quest for the Perfection of Man*. Athens: Ohio University, 1970.
Pandit, M. P. *Gems from the Tantras*. Madras: Ganesh, 1969.
————. *Studies in the Tantras and the Veda*. Madras: Ganesh, 1964.
Parrinder, Geoffrey. *Avatar and Incarnation*. New York: Barnes & Noble, 1970.
Prabhavananda, Swami. *The Wisdom of God* (Śrimad Bhāgavatam). Hollywood: Vedanta Press, 1943.
Radhakrishnan, S. *The Principal Upanishads*. (London: Allen & Unwin, 1953).
Raju, P. T. *Introduction to Comparative Philosophy*. Lincoln: University of Nebraska Press, 1962.
Rāmānuja. *Commentary on the Vedānta-Sūtra*. Sacred Books of the East, vol. 48.
Seal, B. N. *Positive Sciences of the Ancient Hindus*. New York: Longmans Green, 1915.
Sen, K. M. *Hinduism*. Baltimore: Penguin, 1961.
Smulders, Pierre. *La Vision de Teilhard de Chardin*. Paris: Desclee de Brouwer, 1964.
Stephen, Dorothea Jane. *Studies in Early Indian Thought*. Cambridge University Press, 1918.
Tagore, Rabindranath. *The Religion of Man*. London: Allen & Unwin, 1931.
Teilhard de Chardin, Pierre. *Activation of Energy*. New York: Harcourt Brace Jovanovich, 1971.
————. *The Appearance of Man*. New York: Harper & Row. 1956.
————. *Building the Earth*. Wilkes-Barre, Pa.: Dimension Books, 1965.
————. *Christianity and Evolution*. New York: Harcourt Brace Jovanovich, 1971.

————. *The Divine Milieu.* Rev. trans. New York: Harper & Row, 1965.
————. *The Future of Man.* New York: Harper & Row, 1964.
————. *Human Energy.* New York: Harcourt Brace Jovanovich, 1969.
————. *Hymn of the Universe.* New York: Harper & Row, 1965.
————. *Letters from a Traveler.* New York: Harper & Row, 1962.
————. *The Making of a Mind.* New York: Harper & Row, 1965.
————. *Man's Place in Nature.* New York: Harper & Row, 1966.
————. *The Phenomenon of Man.* New York: Harper Torchbooks, 1961.
————. *Science and Christ.* New York: Harper & Row, 1968.
————. *The Vision of the Past.* New York: Harper & Row, 1966.
————. *Writings in Time of War.* New York: Harper & Row, 1968.
Vedanta-Sutras, Sacred Books of the East, vol 48.
Woodroffe, John. *Introduction to Tantra Shastra.* Madras: Ganesh, 1969.
————. *The World as Power.* Madras: Ganesh, 1966.
———— and Mukhyopadhyaya, Pramatha Natha. *Mahāmāyā: The World as Power: Power as Consciousness.* Madras: Ganesh, 1964.
Zaehner, R. C. *Evolution in Religion.* Oxford: Clarendon Press, 1971.
————. *Hinduism.* New York: Oxford University Press, 1962.
Zimmer, Heinrich. *Myths and Symbols in Indian Art and Civilization.* New York: Pantheon. 1946.
————. *The Philosophies of India.* New York: Meridian. 1958.

INDEX

ABSOLUTE, 10, 11, 21, 47, 73, 75, 77, 83, 87-8, 93, 106, 138, 141, 153, 156, 165, 193, 196, 197-8, 204, 213, 263, 252. See Brahman.

ACTION, 6-8, 16, 22, 25, 27, 51-2, 67, 73, 75, 82, 83, 96, 130-2, 135, 140, 141, 143, 149, 152, 164, 166, 168, 170, 181-2, 184, 186, 187-8, 189, 192, 195-201, 202, 204-5, 215, 218, 219, 221-3, 229-30, 231, 233, 245, 246, 248, 253.

ADVAITA, 73, 86, 92, 213.

AHEAD/ABOVE, 12, 20-21, 26, 194, 206, 215-6, 223, 255.

ALPHA, 24, 147.

AMBIGUITY, 247, 248, 249, 251, 254.

AMORIZATION, 6, 23, 163, 225, 246.

ANUGRAHA, 132.

ARYANS, 45, 208.

ASCENT, 143, 155.

ATHARVA VEDA, 46-7, 218.

ĀTMAN, 46, 49, 52, 62, 92, 139, 190, 198, 213-4, 244.

ATTACHMENT, 200, 213.

AUROBINDO GHOSE, 6, 50, 106, 156, 181, 197, 213, 221, 233, 246, 254.

AVATĀRA, 65-6, 74, 76-7, 91, 94, 108, 166, 199.

AXIS, 3, 18, 55, 137, 138, 146, 150, 152, 154-5, 185, 248, 255.

BHAGAVAD GĪTĀ, 6-7, 44, 50, 59, 65-70, 73-4, 88-90, 90-2, 95, 108, 121, 183, 196, 198, 200-203.

BHAGAVAN, 66.

BHĀGAVATA PURĀNA, 67, 74, 87-8.

BHAKTI-YOGA, 3, 74, 87-8, 92.

BIARDEAU, MADELEINE, 45, 50.

BINDU, 132, 139-40, 147-8.

BODY, 24-5, 27, 33, 52-3, 55, 56, 60, 62-66, 69, 70, 75-6, 81, 83, 131, 152-3, 157-8, 166, 185-6, 187, 190, 206, 208-9, 211, 229, 230, 253; body of *Christ,* 40 n.141, 42, n.205, 81, 83, 93, 119, 206, 231, 233; body of *God,* 94, 151, 224, 245, 251-2; *human* body, 209, *mystical* body, 81, 206.

BOSE, A.C., 136.

BOUQUET, A. C., 44.

BRAHMA-SUTRA, 88.

BRAHMAN, 47, 48, 50, 51, 62, 71, 73, 75, 86-8, 106, 131, 147, 198, 214, 234.

BRĀHMANAS, 63.

BRAIN, 18, 119, 154, 206, 212, 220.

BRIHAD-ĀRAṆYAKA UPANISHAD, 61, 208, 209, 213, 215, 234.

BUDDHISM, 74, 85, 86, 107, 108.

CAITANYA, 75, 86.

CAUSE, 29, 34, 64, 68, 76, 87, 90, 120, 130, 131, 132, 149, 191, 193.

CENTER, 16, 23-4, 25, 29, 32, 55, 57, 58, 65, 72, 76, 81, 82, 84, 137-40, 141, 143-6, 147, 148-50, 153, 155, 158, 161, 163, 165-6, 188-9, 193, 201, 205, 212, 216, 224, 226, 231, 233, 252; *Supreme* Center (Center of centers), 138, 147, 166, 205.

CENTREITY (centration), 84, 126, 136-9, 141, 146, 149, 150, 193, 204, 205, 207, 210, 212, 214, 225, 228, 234.

CEPHALIZATION (cerebralization), 18, 20, 25. See Brain.

CHAKRAS, 150, 151, 153.

CHANCE, 20, 116, 126, 146, 188-90.

CHĀNDOGYA UPANISHAD, 67, 70, 143, 213.

CHANGE, 13, 20, 243-4; change of *state*, 23, 113, 137, 142, 144, 148, 151, 157, 161, 194, 206.

CHATTERJEE, SATISCHANDRA, 47.

CHIT (Chit-Śakti), 127-8, 131-3, 138-9, 145-6, 189, 245.

CHOICE, 145, 152, 168, 170, 189, 192.

CHOISY, MARYSE, 2, 3, 37 n.10, 86, 198, 199.

CHRIST, 11-12, 16, 23-6, 32-3, 36, 53-4, 56-8, 60-1, 69-71, 75-7, 81-4, 96, 119-20, 135, 149, 165, 167, 199, 201, 205, 210-11, 221-2, 224, 226, 229, 231, 233-4, 245-6, 254; Christ-the-*Evolver*, 225, 246, 254. See COSMIC CHRIST. Compare 130.

CHRISTIANITY, 1, 3, 9 n.11, 11, 12-13, 16, 17, 24, 27, 38 n.41, 58-9, 68, 77, 81, 82, 84-5, 87, 89, 93, 94-5, 106, 107, 154, 196, 202, 221-2, 223, 226, 244, 246, 249-50, 254.

CHRISTOGENESIS (Christification), 7, 33, 145, 221, 224, 226.

COLLECTIVE, 6, 23, 55, 57, 79, 96, 112, 129, 156-8, 160-4, 166, 168, 170, 193-5, 197, 206, 218, 227, 232-3, 246. See COMMUNITY; also, SOCIETY; TOTALIZATION.

COMMUNICATION, 23.

COMMUNITY, 35, 182, 197.

COMPLEXITY, 7, 8, 13, 14, 17, 19, 20, 29, 34, 35, 79-81, 83-4, 110-11, 114-16, 123, 125-6, 136, 138, 146, 149, 154, 188, 204, 215, 222, 244; Complexity/*consciousness*, 6, 19, 23, 82, 116-7, 121, 123, 130, 137, 157, 188, 193, 206, 209, 246, 249, 251.

CONE,, TEILHARD'S IMAGE OF THE, 30-1, 80, 146, 169.

CONSCIOUSNESS, 19, 23, 32, 34, 54, 64, 77, 78, 80, 83, 111, 116, 118-19, 127, 129, 134, 137, 150, 154, 156-7, 161, 163, 181, 191, 204, 206, 220, 230, 245, 249; *centers* of consciousness, 137; *degrees* of consciousness, 147, 197, 250; consciousness as *Energy*, 128-30, 145-6, 151, 165-6; *evolution* of consciousness, 2, 142, 144, 153; *mental* consciousness, 170; consciousness as *power*, 133, 140, 163-4; *pure* consciousness, 131, 151, 190; *self*-consciousness, 83-4, 186, 188, 215. See REFLEXIVE CONSCIOUSNESS; *supreme* consciousness, 93, 124, 136, 139, 143, 165. See SUPERCONSCIOUSNESS; consciousness as a *world*, 22, 24.

CONTEMPLATION, 183.

CONTINUITY (discontinuity), 19, 22, 34, 58, 109, 115, 119, 142-6, 162, 209, 212, 216, 243-5.

CONTROL, 145-7, 151, 155, 192.

CONVERGENCE, 1, 4, 8, 13, 55, 57, 81, 146, 148, 149, 167-8, 170, 206, 226, 232, 256.

CORPUSCULIZATION, 109, 112, 115, 116-7, 137-8, 139, 157.

COSMIC CHRIST, 5, 7, 24-5, 52, 53, 54-5, 58, 88, 96, 228, 249-50, 252, 254.

COSMIC DIVINITY, 77-8, 93, 96.

COSMIC SENSE, 26.

COSMOGENESIS, 7, 18, 21, 22, 24, 33, 80, 145-6, 155, 167, 205, 206, 208, 210, 224.

CREATION, 16, 21, 25, 28, 33-5, 48, 53-4, 58, 60, 64, 69, 71, 87, 93, 131, 145, 154, 187, 190, 192, 203, 224, 244, 247.

CREATIVE UNION, 29, 35-6, 42 n.205, 82, 110, 115, 126, 225.

CRITICAL POINT (Crisis), 19, 113, 116, 162, 168, 181, 188, 206.

DANIELOU, ALAIN, 64, 67, 118, 133, 218.

DASGUPTA, SURENDRANATH, 65, 67, 68, 73, 76, 86, 87, 88, 95, 113, 114, 155, 229.

DATTA, DHIRENDRA MOHAN, 47.

DEATH, (destruction), 7, 11, 47, 61, 62, 64, 67, 69, 123, 124, 182, 195, 203-4, 213, 220, 221, 228, 244, 248, 252-3. See REINCARNATION.

DEISM, 95.

DELIGHT (bliss), 7, 15, 127, 131, 145, 151, 189, 220, 231, 233, 245, 246.

DE LUBAC, HENRI, 53, 54, 202.

DEMATERIALIZE, 211.

DESIRE, 20, 21, 131, 160, 164, 190, 194, 196, 202, 213, 215-8, 220-1, 222, 230, 248.

DESPAIR, 203, 204, 214, 217, 221, 227.

DESTINY, 136, 162, 163, 201, 208-9, 244, 246, 248, 255.

DETACHMENT, 202, 228.

DETERMINISM, 3, 120, 128, 137, 143, 152-3, 162, 188-91, 214-5; determinism/*freedom,* 188, 192, 194, 197-8.

DEVAS, 46, 61, 63, 124, 132, 135-6, 185.

DEVĪ, 151, 153. See GODDESS.

DEVOLUTION, 108.

DHARMA, 43, 61, 63, 92, 182, 187, 245.

DIAPHANY, 27.

DIFFERENTIATION, 3, 80, 82-4, 88, 90, 93, 109, 112, 114, 126, 128, 131, 133, 146, 161, 223-4, 243, 247, 252, 254-6.

DIRECTIONALITY, 123, 125, 129, 144, 146, 152, 154-5, 159, 163, 186, 203, 223, 244.

DIWAKAR, R. R., 49.

DOMINATION, 248, 250.

DUALISM, 73.

EARTH, 12, 19, 23, 25-6, 33, 46, 47, 55, 81, 142, 144, 151, 152, 153, 159, 162, 170, 181, 185, 187, 204, 206, 211, 218, 219, 220, 221, 223, 234, 246.

EAST, 3-4, 80, 85, 86, 93, 96.

ECKHART, MEISTER, 95.

EGO, 36, 160, 166-7, 183-4, 210, 225, 228.

EISELEY, LOREN, 40 n.128.

ELEMENT, 23-4, 31, 36, 48, 57, 76, 78, 81, 82, 83, 84, 88, 93, 110, 114, 116, 123, 126, 133, 136, 138, 139, 141, 143, 146, 151, 158, 188, 194, 205, 224, 225, 226, 230, 233, 247.

ELIADE, MIRCEA, 115, 117, 118, 133, 151, 201, 227.

EMBREE, AINSLEE, 107, 135.

ENERGY, 22-3, 24, 33, 53, 57-8, 61, 63, 78, 96, 109, 111, 112, 114, 116, 118, 124-5, 127-8, 140, 153, 155, 163, 165, 166, 184-5, 187-8, 205, 215, 219, 221, 223, 229, 232, 234, 245-6, 250; energy *centers,* 150-1; *Christic* energy, 33; *cosmic* energy, 147, 152; *creative* energy, 131-2, 190; *Divine* energy, 139, 149; energy of *evolution,* 136; see TANGENTIAL/RADIAL ENERGY; *human* energy, 163, 168, 190; *psychic* energy, 122; see CONSCIOUSNESS, as energy, PSYCHIC ENERGY; *spiritual* energy, 156, 196-7; energy-*system,* 82; *transformation* of energy, 147, *unicity* of energy, 6, 129-36.

ENTROPY, 120, 122-3, 145-5, 127, 128, 205-6, 222, 228-9, 254.

ERIKSON, ERIK, 210.

EUCHARIST, 27, 50, 60, 71, 233.

EVIL, (sin, suffering), 7, 35, 56, 60, 63, 65, 75, 87, 90, 133, 201, 227-9, 234, 249, 251, 253.

EVOLUTION, *Aurobindo's* theory of evolution, 157, 160-1; evolution of *consciousness,* 6, 20, 119, 127-9, 134, 150-1, 152, 153-4, 157, 161, 167, 186; *critical* points in evolution, 113-4, 142; see CRITICAL POINT; evilution and *death,* 207; see DEATH; *demands* of evolution, 204; see IRREVERSIBILITY; *directed* evolution, 3, 18-9, 32, 34-5, 57, 84, 120, 125, 185, 193, 203, 206, 253; see DIRECTIONALITY; evolution of *energy,* 134, 137, 146; see ENERGY; evolution and *entropy,* 122-3; see ENTROPY; evolution and *evil,* 227-8; see EVIL, evolution of *freedom,* 19, 20, 188; evolution and *God,* 1, 14, 16-7, 21, 25-6, 33-4, 56-7, 81-2, 96, 130, 167, 196, 222; evolution in the *Hindu* traditions, 118, 121, 127-8, 131-2, 139, 147, 150, 226-7, 229, 243, 255; evolution as *improbable,* 188; see IMPROBABILITY; evolution as *necessary,* 76, 215, 234; *our cooperation* with evolution 4, 7, 9, 19-20, 38 n.41; 187-8, 200, 220; evolution and *pantheism,* 78, 84; *pattern* of evoluion, 14, 83, 110, 114, 118-9, 138, 142, 161, 188; see GROPING PATTERN; *religion* of evolution, 80, 255; *Teilhard's* conception of evolution, 17-8, 20-1, 23, 30, 84, 116, 126, 188, 203, 222; evolution *toward divinity,* 1, 6, 7, 33, 125-6, 154, 163, 170, 223-6, 230, 233-4, 244, 255-6; *value* of evolution, 13, 195.

FAITH, 14, 16, 26, 65, 80, 85, 92, 162, 168-70, 182, 195, 214, 216, 220, 221, 234, 255.

FARICY, ROBERT L., 38 n.38.

FATALISM, 193, 248.

FEAR, 16, 22, 78, 91, 162, 223, 250.

FIRE, 63, 134-6, 219.

FREEDOM, 6, 7, 8, 17, 19, 20, 62, 75, 94-5, 115, 120, 126-8, 143, 151, 154, 156, 160, 170, 181, 183, 186, 188-94, 197, 203, 214, 225, 229.

FUSION (absorption) 36, 84, 88, 93, 94, 109, 150, 167. See TEILHARD, errors; also, UNITY, according to Hindus.

FUTURE, 1, 14-5, 22, 31-2, 35, 47, 111, 135, 141, 146, 149, 158-9, 162, 164, 166, 167, 169-70, 194-6, 204, 214, 216, 217, 255-6.

GANDHI, MOHANDAS, 62, 156.

GOAL, 1, 11, 16, 18, 20, 24, 28, 32, 36, 45, 48, 51, 64, 69, 76, 81-2, 84, 89-92, 93, 119, 125, 128, 133, 152, 160, 165, 185, 187, 190, 203, 205, 214, 221-2, 228, 231, 246, 253.

GOD, *Cosmic* aspect of God, 72, 78, 80-2, 83, 93-6, 131, 249, 252; the *Divine*, 7, 27, 29, 32-3, 46, 50, 52, 56, 69, 121, 127, 130, 134, 152, 165, 169, 186, 197, 202, 207, 220, 225, 232, 244, 252; God and *evolution*, 16, 20-1, 33, 38 n.45, 170, 222, 234; *Hindu* views of God, 44, 46, 48, 50, 52, 61-2, 63-6, 68, 72-3, 74-5, 76-7, 87-8, 89-90, 92-4, 95, 121, 131-2, 229, 234, 251; God *incarnate*, 24, 26, 56-7, 72, 74, 76-8, 94, 221, 223; God of *iron*, 10-11; *Love* of God, 1, 3, 26, 89, 90-1, 92-3, 167, 201-2; God and *man*, 88, 96, 186, 193, 249; *need* for God, 237; *personal* God, 12, 26, 83-4, 87-8, 90, 93, 96, 121; *Teilhard's* feeling for God, 11, 14, 27, 56, 57, 220-1; *union* with God, 81-2, 87, 90, 93-4, 95, 201, 221, 228-9, 234; God *within*, 21, 26-7, 217-8; God and the *world*, 12, 14-16, 23, 26-9, 34, 35, 37, 55, 58-9, 63, 69, 75, 82, 90, 93-6, 126, 130-1, 134, 165, 184, 199, 203, 222-5, 231, 234, 246, 249, 252, 254.

GODDESS, 124, 130, 132-3, 151, 183, 190-1, 218. See Śakti.

GOSWAMI, BIJAY KRISHNA, 233.

GRACE, 16, 72-4, 77, 87, 91-2, 94, 132, 196-7, 203.

GRAY, DONALD P., 41 n.167.

GROPING, 9 n.11, 119, 125-6, 155, 158, 161, 230.

GROUSSET, RENÉ, 2.

GUNAS, 46, 111-3, 117, 200.

HEAVEN, 11, 46, 47, 67, 74, 81.

HENOTHEISM, 47.

HEREDITY, 19-20.

HINDU TRADITIONS, on *action*, 182-4, 198; *avatara*, 76-7; *collective*, 232, 246-7; *death*, 208, 210-2, 214. See LIBERATION; *Diversity*, 2, 44, 85; *energy*, 124, 129, 135, 227-8; *evolution*, 106-7, 108, 121, 127, 143, 151-2, 156, 227, 229-30; *fatalism*, 193; *freedom*, 189-90, 192; *God*, 27, 46-7, 60, 61-3, 64-5, 86, 88-91, 93, 96, 130, 134; *humanity*, 185-7; *individual*, 253; *practicality*, 9, 255; *reality* of the world, 139, 245; space-time, 107-8, 121, 212, 244; *synthesis* (integrality), 44-5, 46-7, 49, 96, 150, 231-2, 247-7, 250-3, 254; *taste* for life, 255; *Teilhard's differences* with, 86, 246; in *Teilhard's view*, 2-4. See TEILHARD, errors; *ultimate Reality*, 48, 50-1, 190-1, 243, 245, *unity*, 44; *universe*, 109-10, 117, 118.

HIRIYANNA, MYSORE, 230.

HISTORY, 23, 25, 49, 77-8, 120, 152, 167, 192, 232, 244, 246, 255.

HOMINIZATION, 188, 206, 215, 223, 224; *superhominization*, 57.

HOMOGENEITY, 122, 125, 146, 222, 243, 247-8, 251.

HOPE, 14, 167, 195-6, 208, 216.

HUMANITY (man), 44, 213; *creative* power of, 37, 127, 128, 155, 159, 184, 186-8, 192, 194, 204, 232, 233-4; *death* of, 210, 212, 214, 220; peak of *evolution*, 19-20, 22, 23, 33, 136, 143, 145, 152-5, 157-8, 167, 215, 222-

3, 234, 255; man and *God,* 184, 249; *research* on, 8, 184-5; *responsibility* of 181. See ACTION; WORK; as *spirit,* 16, 57; *value* of, 45, 52, 184-6, 195; *vocation* of, 23, 156, 157-9, 162, 164, 166, 167, 169, 196-7, 205, 216-7, 223, 225, 230, 231-2.
HUXLEY, JULIAN, 15, 24, 27.

IGNORANCE, 161, 169, 186, 213, 227-8, 230, 248.
ILLUSION, 75, 88, 139, 193, 234. See WORLD, reality of.
IMAGE, (symbol), 12, 29, 49, 53, 87, 124, 132, 134-5, 138, 140, 146-7, 149-51, 155, 157, 185, 194, 201, 210, 225, 229-30, 243-4, 248-53. See CONE.
IMMANENCE, 29, 33, 48, 58, 61-2, 65, 69, 75, 76, 87, 93, 126-7, 146, 170, 213.
IMMORTALITY, 12, 47, 58, 59, 60-2, 69, 120, 135, 167, 195, 204, 206, 210-11, 213, 217, 253.
IMPROBABILITY, 119, 123, 170, 188-9, 194, 198.
INCARNATION, 25-6, 28, 33, 54, 56-7, 58, 67, 74, 76-8, 81-2, 120, 164, 185, 211, 221, 223-4, 252, 254.
INDIA, 2, 4, 44, 49-50, 85-6, 87, 91, 92, 107, 118, 121, 182, 193; Indian *thought,* 51, 87, 95, 118, 121, 232.
INDIVIDUAL, 60, 116, 128, 189, 233, 252, 253; *death* of, 204, 206-7, 208, 210, 211; and *evolution,* 150, 151, 226; *freedom* of, 95, 193, 197; and *God,* 50, 75, 133, 139, 191, 213, 229, 252; *preservation* of, 35, 83, 85, 87, 93, 181; *separate* (egotistic, selfish), 160-1, 167, 170, 186, 228; and *totality,* 55, 79, 80, 159-60, 162, 163-4, 168, 193-4, 203; *vocation* of, 43, 153, 167, 230-1, 232.
INFINITE, 27, 46, 48-9, 70-1, 76, 87, 93, 109, 130, 187, 213, 248, 252.
INTELLIGIBILITY, 31-2, 114, 243-5, 254.
INVENTION, 119.
INVOLUTION, 227.
IRREVERSIBILITY, 123, 129, 137, 146, 155, 188, 194, 204, 211-2.
ĪŚĀ UPANISHAD, 62, 213-4.
ISOSPHERES, 138, 140-1, 146, 148.
IŚVARA, 66, 121, 131, 149.

JAINISM, 74, 107.
JESUITS, 54, 219.
JESUS, 10, 24, 33, 56-7, 59, 71-2, 199, 201, 224.
JÑĀNA, 87.
JUDAIC TRADITION, 58, 184, 244, 246, 249, 250.
JURIDICAL, 81, 82, 94.

KALPA, 108.
KARMA, 4, 192-3, 201.
KAṬHA UPANISHAD, 51, 87, 92.
KINGDOM OF GOD (heaven), 25, 221, 233.
KNOX, RONALD, 54.
KṚṢṆA, 6, 44, 56, 64, 65-70, 72-3, 74, 77, 88-9, 92, 108, 199-201, 202, 251.
KULĀRNAVA TANTRA, 183.
KUṆḌALINĪ, 132, 150, 153.
KUNHAN RAJA, CHITTENJOOR, 118, 184.

LARGE NUMBERS, 125, 191.
LAW, 18, 20, 61, 82, 90, 115, 118, 125, 135, 137, 140, 145, 160, 162, 166, 169, 188; law of *Complexity/Consciousness,* 19, 109, 116; law of increasing *entropy,* 137; *Eternal* law, 48; *physical* law, 123; law of *recurrence,* 137: See PATTERN, *recurrence* of.
LEROY, PIERRE, 3.
LEVELS OF ORGANIZATION (grades, orders, phases, planes, stages, steps, types), 14, 23, 26, 29, 30-2, 50, 82-3, 84, 113-4, 122-4, 128, 131, 132, 134, 137-42, 143, 145, 146-8, 151-2, 153, 155, 156-8, 160, 164-66, 168, 188, 189, 191, 203-4, 207-9, 227, 230, 252; levels of *consciousness,* 150; *higher* levels, 161, 189, 192-4, 245; *human* level, 194; *last* level, 206; *next* level, 166, 170, 197, 203, 227.
LIBERATION, 63, 74, 89, 121, 132, 160,

166, 169, 185, 196, 199, 206, 211, 213-4, 224-5, 227-8, 229-30, 232, 234, 248.

LIFE, 26, 30, 35, 46, 52, 68, 73, 85, 106, 115, 116, 119, 123, 124-6, 128-9, 131, 135, 141-2, 143, 145-6, 151, 152-4, 160, 189-90, 193, 206, 208-9, 215, 220, 223, 226, 245; *eternal* life, 64, life-*force,* 61, 216; *limits* of life, 145; life of the *second* degree, 144; *vitalization,* 126-7.

LĪLĀ (play), 131, 189, 191, 192, 227, 231.

LOGOS, 136.

LOKAS, 151.

LOVE, 8, 24-6, 33, 35, 36, 40 n.141, 67, 72, 74-5, 77, 84, 88-9, 90, 135, 145, 163, 164-7, 170, 194, 196, 201, 205, 216, 224-5, 228, 246; love-*energy,* 6, 23, 226; *evolution* of love, 203-4; love of *God,* 3, 84, 89-91, 93, 131, 167, 201-2, 248; *personal* love, 163.

MACROCOSM/MICROCISM, 150-2.

MADHAVA, 86.

MAHĀBHĀRATA, 64-6, 68, 72, 91-2, 216.

MAHĀNIRVĀNA TANTRA, 133.

MAITRĪ UPANISHAD, 214.

MAJUMDAR, BARADA KANTA, 234.

MANIFESTATION, 47, 50-1, 62, 65, 67, 124, 131, 134-5, 155, 162, 166, 170, 191, 192, 216, 225, 227, 231, 234, 251.

MARKANDEYA PURĀNA, 132.

MARTINDALE, C. C., 54.

MARY, 57.

MATTER, matter and *Christ,* 25, 33, 58, 223, 233; matter and *consciousness,* 22, 80, 139, 153; matter as *corpuscular,* 109, 116, 138; matter and *determinism,* 137, 152, 188, 191, 192; *evolving* matter, 18, 20, 29, 33, 56, 115, 116, 119, 129-30, 142-3, 151, 187, 205; matter and *God,* 65, 75, 131, matter and *life,* 127, 135, 141; matter in *Prakriti,* 111-2; *Teilhard's* love of matter, 10, 15, 250.

MATTER/SPIRIT, 35, 40 n.121, 81, 134, 189, 209, 210-2, 249, 253; according to *Aurobindo,* 50; in the *Bhagavad-Gita,* 73; *Hindu* errors regarding, according to Teilhard, 4, 85, 87, 96.

MĀYĀ, 4, 63, 68, 73, 131-2, 191, 193, 245; Mahāmāyā, 132, 191; Māyavādā, 181, 184.

MEDIATOR, 55, 57, 63, 79, 95, 135.

MEDITATION, 147.

METHODOLOGY, 123, 222, 247, 251-2.

MIND, 141.

MIRACLES, 28, 58.

MOKŚA, 214, 232.

MONISM, 2, 50, 51, 61, 73-4, 79, 81, 86-7, 88-9, 247.

MONOTHEISM, 47, 50, 74.

MOONEY, CHRISTOPHER, 54.

MORALITY, 14, 19, 22, 25, 34, 46, 156, 226, 231, 244, 247, 249, 251, 255.

MOTHER GODDESS, 6, 78, 184, 218, 220, 231, 234, 246, 251. See ŚAKTI.

MOTIVATION, 14, 20.

MUKHYOPĀDHYĀYA, 228.

MÜLLER, MAX, 46.

MUṆḌAKA UPANISHAD, 230.

MUTATION, 125, 144, 157-8, 167, 189.

MYSTICISM, 5, 11, 13, 14, 16, 26, 55, 81, 85-6, 90, 94, 109, 150, 234, 247, 252, 255.

NĀRĀYAṆA, 64, 91.

NATURE, 17, 18-9, 21, 26, 37, 46, 50, 63, 70, 119-20, 125, 129, 145, 150, 157-8, 161-2, 164-5, 168-70, 184, 188, 192-3, 195, 197, 200, 219, 224-7, 243, 245, 248-9.

NERVOUS SYSTEM, 18, 119, 154. See CEPHALIZATION.

NIMBARKA, 86.

NIRVĀNA, 3, 78, 181.

NOOGENESIS, 123.

NOOSPHERE, 2, 8, 135, 138, 144, 146, 148, 158, 207, 210, 212.

NOVELTY, 20, 30, 82, 145, 169, 195 .

OLD TESTAMENT, 77.

OMEGA, 10, 24, 26, 32, 33, 38 n.45, 118, 119-20, 137-8, 146-7, 152, 165-6, 170, 205-7, 211-2, 217, 224, 230, 234, 250, 253, 254.

ONE/MANY, 2-3, 28, 48, 57, 85, 86, 110, 130, 148, 151, 154, 165, 186, 190, 198, 205-6, 221, 245, 247-8, 252.
ORGAN, TROY WILSON, 44, 46, 68, 118, 120, 153, 185-7, 193, 214, 231.
ORGANIZATION, 17, 18, 19, 23, 24, 29-31, 57, 80, 82-3, 96, 109-10, 112, 114, 119, 123, 125, 126, 128, 138-9, 141, 146, 150, 153, 157-8, 161, 162-3, 168, 188, 205, 212, 222, 224-5, 231; *superorganization,* 203.
ONTOGENESIS, 22.

PAIṄGALA UPANISHAD, 230.
PANDIT, M. P., 186.
PANTHEISM, 2, 6, 59, 61, 78-9, 80, 82, 83-4, 95-6, 224, 250.
PAN-CHRISTISM, 81, 83-4, 88.
PARAMĀNUS, 110, 117-8.
PAROUSIA, 221, 225.
PARRINDER, GEOFFREY, 76-7, 88.
PATAÑJALI, 66, 229.
PATTERN, 17-8, 20, 30, 35-6, 76, 114, 138, 147, 148, 158, 161, 194; *recurrence* of 23, 30, 110, 138, 145, 165, 188.
PEDUNCLE, 40 n.128.
PERFECTION, 44, 56, 116, 124, 149-50, 165, 170, 187-8, 193, 197, 199, 202, 210-11, 221, 223, 230-1, 232, 247, 250.
PERSON, personality, 59, 160; personalization, 23-4, 81, 84, 93, 96, 211-12, 246; person, *Absolute,* and Cosmos, 78, 95, 208-9, 213; person as *center,* 24, 148, 205, *Christ* as person, 54, 56; personal *consciousness,* 134; *cosmic* Person, 47, 60-1, 96; person in *evolution,* 19, 22, 57, 83, 123, 164, 229, person's *goal,* 210; personal *God,* 48, 59, 62-3, 65-6, 72, 74, 75, 76-7, 78, 87, 89-90, 93, 96, 130-1, 165, 167, 196, 198, 234, 248; personal *immortality,* 204-5, 206-7, 253; personal/*impersonal,* 251-2; *juridical* person, 244; *reincarnated* person, 209, personal *relationships,* 81, 165-6; person in *Sāmkhya,* 111, 120; See PURUSA; *supreme* person, 14, 15, 66, 69, 73-4, 88, 90, 95, 165-7, 196, 199, 205, 234, 245-6; See PURUŚOTTAMA; *union* of persons, 14, 15, 38 n.44, 83-4, 158, 160, 163, 166, 205, 222; *value* of person, 90; *world* of persons, 6.
PERVADER, 46, 59, 61-3, 64-5, 67, 68, 71, 75, 130-1, 133, 165, 199, 229, 248, 252.
PESSIMISM, 5, 51.
PHILOSOPHY, 38 n.39, n.40.
PHYLOGENESIS, 22.
POLYTHEISM, 50, 58.
POPULATION, 23, 168.
POWER, 124, 128, 131-3, 135, 139, 145, 147-9, 152-3, 163-4, 166-8, 170, 191-2, 215.
PRABHAVANANDA, SWAMI, 68.
PRAJĀPATI, 61, 64.
PRAKṚTI, 111-2, 117-8, 120-1, 200, 229.
PRE-LIFE, 146.
PRESERVER, 63, 64.
PROCESS, 17-8, 20, 53, 110, 115, 120, 127, 142, 151, 155, 169, 187, 193, 205, 221, 223, 227, 229-30, 232, 255.
PROGRESS, 3, 19, 25-6, 44, 80, 93, 110, 120, 128, 129, 143, 152, 154, 155-6, 162, 169-70, 182, 186, 193, 196, 201, 203-4, 207, 208, 213, 216, 218, 223, 227, 229-31, 234.
PROVIDENCE, 28, 218.
PSYCHIC ATTRACTION, 146.
PSYCHIC BEING, 251.
PSYCHIC ENERGY, 127, 128, 129, 134, 137, 153, 203, 215, 245.
PSYCHIC ENTITY, 160.
PSYCHIC LIFE, 223.
PSYCHIC SPACES, 234.
PSYCHIC TENDENCY, 192.
PSYCHISM, 252.
PURĀNAS, 87, 88, 107, 185.
PURPOSE, 21, 22, 76, 88, 90, 115, 120, 131, 161.
PURUṢA, 49, 59-61, 64, 111, 118, 120-1, 229.
PURUṢA-SUKTA, 47, 60, 64, 70.
PURUṢOTTAMA, 73, 75, 88, 167, 199.

RADHAKRISHNAN, S., 62, 210, 230, 234.
RADIOACTIVITY, 32.
RAJU, P. T., 153.
RĀMA, 91, 92, 108.
RAMĀNUJA, 75-6, 86, 89, 91-2, 93, 217.

RĀMAYĀNA, 91.
RAMPRASAD, 246.
RECONCILIATION, 16, 25, 35-6, 45-6, 47, 49, 65, 73, 145, 188, 194, 196, 198, 246.
REFLEXIVE CONSCIOUSNESS (reflection), 19-20, 35, 114, 127-8, 143-4, 146, 154, 157, 161, 186, 188, 206, 209-210, 215, 223, 225-6, 228, 251, 253.
REINCARNAAION, 208-9, 215, 230.
RELIGION, 1, 12, 14, 25, 38 n.40, 43, 49-50, 79, 80-1, 84, 88, 92, 93, 181; *ancient* religions, 3; religious *consciousness,* 13; religion of *evolution,* 255; religion of the *future,* 13, religion in *India,* 2; *Judaic* religions, 249; religion/science, 13-4.
RENUNCIATION, 199-200, 202.
RESEARCH, 8, 13, 96.
RESPONSIBILITY, 22, 79, 182, 186, 244.
REVELATION, 11, 13, 33, 80, 87, 92, 95.
RIG VEDA, 5, 7, 47, 51, 59-60, 61, 70, 108, 133, 135, 183, 190, 208, 211, 215, 218.
RISHIS, 46.
ṚITA (order), 49, 61, 135, 201, 215, 219.
ROMAN CATHOLIC CHURCH, 1, 11, 13, 25, 54, 86, 89, 207, 223.

SACRAMENT, 27, 60.
SACRIFICE, 27, 45, 50, 60-1, 63, 69, 74, 135-6, 164, 201-2.
SĀDHANA, 7, 231-2.
SAINT PAUL, 24, 53, 54, 96.
ŚAIVA SIDDĀNTA, 87, 90, 130, 131, 229.
ŚAKTI, 6, 122, 124, 128, 130-3, 139, 147, 150, 151, 230, 232.
ŚAKTISM (Śakti-Vada), 6, 87, 128-9, 133-4, 138-41, 142-3, 145-6, 148, 150, 153, 155, 183, 189, 190-2, 231.
SALVATION, 11-12, 25, 51, 74, 81, 92, 95, 187-8, 200, 204, 210, 223, 226, 229, 233, 253; *Savior,* 61, 72, 226.
SĀṂKHYA, 6, 44, 111-5, 117-8, 120-1, 133, 153, 210, 229.
SAMNYĀSA, 184.
SAMSARA, 91.
SANCTITY, 201, 225-6, 233.
ŚAṆKARA, 86, 89, 181-2, 217, 245.
SASTRI, S. S. SURANARAYANA, 213.
ŚATAPATHA-BRAHMĀNA, 63.
SAT-CHIT-ANANDA, 131, 139, 216-7.
SCIENCE, 1, 3, 13-4, 18-9, 21-3, 29, 36, 38 n.39, 38 n.44, 38 n.45, 80, 82, 109, 118, 123, 134, 184, 191, 205, 209, 231; *scientists,* 137, 154; science and *religion,* 8-9, 15, 18-9, 29, 41 n.161. 55, 222, 226, 231, 255.
SEAL, B. N., 112.
SELF, 51, 62, 69, 115, 130, 139, 147, 149, 150, 164, 166, 185, 191, 215, 229, 245, 250, 253; Self*hood,* 138-9, 146; Self-*realization,* 193; *Supreme* Self, 149.
SEN, K. M., 45, 183, 199.
SEN, NESHUB CHENDER, 232.
SIN, 62, 67, 90, 161, 228, 250.
ŚĪVA, 62-3, 87, 90, 124, 131-3. 229; *Śīva-mahāpurāna,* 131, 190.
SMULDERS, PIERRE, 54.
SOCIETY, 14, 19, 24, 32, 79, 108, 154, 159, 164, 166-7, 232.
SOUL, 21, 25, 28, 32, 57, 62, 64-5, 66, 69, 74-5, 81, 84, 87, 88, 90, 94, 111, 121, 132, 134, 136, 151, 154, 160, 163-4, 165-7, 186, 187, 202, 205-9, 212, 213-4, 224, 229-30; *Christ* as soul, 119; Soul of the *universe,* 234.
SPACE-TIME, 3, 108, 121, 124, 147, 150, 169, 186, 206, 207, 211-12, 227, 244.
SPECIES, 119, 142, 144, 164, 168, 170, 223.
SPINOZA, 79, 95.
SPIRIT, 4, 10, 19, 20, 21, 34, 35, 37 n.11, 40 n.121, 46, 50, 56-7, 61, 63, 71, 73-4, 76, 85-6, 116, 120, 127, 132, 153, 158, 162, 167, 169, 182, 191, 197, 204-5, 206, 210-1, 228; spirituality, 168; spiritualization, 152, 223, 234; spiritual *energy,* 134; spiritual *life,* 120-1, 231; spirit/*matter,* 81; spiritual *substance,* 163.
SPONTANEITY, 119, 126, 128, 131, 140, 146, 153, 187-90, 191, 193-4.
ŚRIMAD BHĀGAVATAM, 88.
STATISTICS, 191, 198, 227, 251.
STEPHEN, DOROTHEA JANE, 46.
SUDARŚANĀCĀRYA, 76.
SUPERCONSCIOUSNESS, 35, 128, 163, 222, 225.
SUPERMIND, 165, 168.

SUPERNATURAL, 162, 182.
SUPREME PERSON, See PERSON, *Supreme*.
SUPPORT (Skambha), 47, 49, 51.
SURVIVAL, 23, 129, 145, 158, 168, 181, 196, 205, 209, 212, 256.
ŚVETĀŚVATARA UPANISHAD, 62, 74, 87, 92, 130.
SYNTHESIS, 31-3, 36, 49, 51, 55, 75, 82, 83, 94, 96, 109, 116, 121, 123-4, 126, 138, 143, 145, 163, 166, 189, 226, 243, 246, 252, 254.

TAGORE, RABINDRANATH, 49, 213, 233, 246.
TAITTIRĪYA UPANISHAD, 153.
TANGENTIAL/RADIAL ENERGY, 42 n.204, 136-7, 140-2, 161, 165, 166, 168, 192, 230.
TANMĀTRAS, 117.
TANTRISM, 7, 150, 153, 208, 216-7, 220, 227, 232, 234. See ŚAKTISM.
TAPAS, 190.
TASTE FOR LIFE, 7, 51, 79, 203, 214-21, 246, 255. See DELIGHT.
TECHNOLOGY, 11-12, 159, 255.
TEILHARD DE CHARDIN, *achievement*, 1, 8; Aphorisms: "All energy is physical in nature," 130, 136, 137; "Fuller being consists of closer union," 30, 109; "God makes us make ourselves," 21, 36, 187, 208; "To create is to unite," 42 n.205; "Union differentiates," 30, 109, 247; "We are evolution," 159, 188; as a *child*, 10; his *concern*, 181; his *errors* with respect to Hinduism, 2, 51, 73, 78-9, 84-6, 88-9, 93, 96, 107, 109, 121, 127, 129, 139, 141, 143, 150, 181, 184, 186, 190, 193-4, 199-201, 247-8, 254, 255-6; his conception of *evolution*, see EVOLUTION; as *mystic*, 11, 15, 57; see GOD, *Teilhard's* feeling for; his *problem*, 1, 55, 78, 79, 93, 95, 249.
THEISM, 61-2, 65, 86-7, 89, 90-1, 94, 95.
THOUGHT, 19, 130, 139, 142, 143, 145-6, 152, 169, 185, 206, 212.
THRESHOLD, 6. See LEVELS also CRITICAL POINT.
TIME, 12, 19, 35, 44, 63, 65, 74, 75, 82, 107-8, 115, 121, 123, 124, 129, 131, 141, 146, 149, 153, 159, 169, 183, 188, 195, 204, 206-7, 211-2, 227, 232, 248, 252-3.
TOTALIZATION (totalitarian), 159-161, 166, 188, 226.
TRANSCENDENCE, 36, 40 n.128, 59, 147-8, 151, 160, 182, 243-5, 255; in the *avatara*, 76; of *becoming*, 213; in *Brahman*, 51, 87, 88, 147, 213; in *Christ*, 81, 119-20; of *cosmogenesis*, 224; of *death*, 208, in *freedom*, 191, 198, 214; as the *goal*, 28, 165; in *God*, 26, 28, 48, 51, 63, 65, 93, 130, 152, 165, 197-8, 251, 252; in the *Hindu* traditions, 245, 251-2; in *Omega*, 149; in *ourselves*, 22, 250, 254; in *Puruṣa*, 59, 61; in *Śiva*, 87, 90, 131, 132; in *Tantrism*, 151-2.
TRANSCENDENCE/IMMANENCE, 46, 47, 61-2, 74, 95; in the *Cosmic Person*, 96; in *God*, 69, 70, 73; in the *Hindu* traditions, 254.
TRANSFORMATION, 20, 24, 27, 33, 56, 71, 82, 131, 133, 135-6, 142, 144, 146, 147, 150, 152, 155, 156, 158, 169, 185, 207, 221, 224, 226, 228, 229, 233.
TRINITY, 42 n.205, 291.
TUKARĀMĀ, 92.
TULSIDASA, 91-2.

UNION, 3, 23-4, 30, 93, 109, 247 See CREATIVE UNION; also DIFFERENTIATION; GOD, *union* with; PERSONS, *union* of.
UNITY, in *Christ*, 83, 222, 224-6; and *complexity*, 14, 29, 31, 33-4, 42 n.204, 82, 110, 112, 115, 146, 147, 161, 222, 224, 247; with the *cosmos*, 12, 27; as the *goal*, 31, 35, 84, 87, 125-6, 146, 147-8, 165, 207, 221; of *God* and world, 16, 33, 62, 69, 82, 88, 165, 225; *Hindu* concept of, 2-3, 45, 46, 47, 50-1, 62, 69, 75, 85, 86-8, 93, 95-6, 147, 243, 247, 250; as *homogeneity*, 112 (see HOMOGENEITY); as *intelligibility*, 31-2, 80; of *matter* and consciousness,

80; among *men*, 38 n.44, 160, 197; in *Omega*, 146-7; of *purpose*, 82; of the *world*, 13, 17, 38 n.45, 55, 80, 112, 119, 126, 142, 145, 243.

UNIVERSE, 49, 118, 142, 152, 164, 185, 198, 208, 210-1, 244; *Christ* in the universe, 25, 32, 33, 53, 56-8, 60, 83, 149, 210, 222, 224-5, 233; as *consciousness*, 22, 54, 124, 137-8, 223-4; *destruction* of, 23, 132, 205, 229; of *energy*, 132, 137, 146, 150, 152, 234; expression of *God*, 16, 26-7, 53, 60-1, 63, 64-5, 68, 71, 82, 132, 224, 225, 234; *personalizing*, 81, 96, 152, 185, 205-6; *religious* attitude toward, 12-13, 164, 169, 201, 219, 226, 245; *Unity* of, 17-18, 35, 55, 129, 133, 164, 247.

UPANISHADS, 47-8, 49, 59, 61, 65, 73-4, 75, 87, 88, 92, 118, 199, 213.

UPANISHAD BRAHMAYOGIN, 67.

VAIŚEṢIKA, 110.

VAIṢṆAVISM, 44, 74-5, 87, 89-90.

VALLABHA, 86.

VALUE, 1, 33, 43, 49, 57, 73, 80, 83, 85, 119, 122-3, 170, 186, 187, 195, 210, 219, 223, 227, 230, 245-6, 253.

VĀSUDEVA, 64, 66-7, 69, 91.

VEDIC VIEW OF LIFE, 44-7, 48-50, 52, 60-1, 63, 72-4, 87-8, 108, 182-3, 201, 215, 218, 220.

VEDĀNTA, 2-3, 75, 86-7, 88, 140, 142, 153, 184, 213, 245.

VIDYĀBHŪṢAṆA, BALADEVA, 75.

VIJÑĀNA BHIKṢU, 133.

VĪRA-ŚAIVISM, 131.

VIŚIṢṬĀDVAITA, 75, 94.

VIṢṆU, 6, 63-6, 68, 74, 88, 108, 124, 132-3.

VITALISM, 189.

WAR, 160, 217.

WEST, 3-4, 7, 28, 78, 86-9, 90, 106-7, 111, 115, 117, 127, 129, 139, 145, 150, 199, 231, 243, 244, 247-8, 251-3, 254-5.

WHOLE (ALL), 31, 57, 79-82, 83, 85-6, 95, 110, 112, 114, 119, 139, 148, 150, 162, 163-5, 185, 206, 212, 217, 219, 223-4, 226, 228, 232-3, 250-1, 254-6.

WILDERS, N.M. 116.

WILL, 38 n.40, 76, 88, 90, 131, 132, 162, 190, 194, 197-8, 202-4, 216, 221-2, 249-51.

WITHIN (interiority), 20-1, 26, 32, 39 n.107, 76, 115-7, 118, 123, 126-7, 129, 134, 136-8, 146, 152, 161, 164-5, 192, 197, 211, 216, 255.

WOODROFFE, JOHN, 139-40, 143, 148, 150, 155, 189, 191, 193, 228.

WORK, 7, 25-6, 36, 49, 51, 68, 122, 187-8, 195, 196, 199, 200-3, 205, 209, 215-6, 223, 225, 232.

WORLD, 147, 246; *another* world, 1, 11-12; and *Christ*, 12, 25, 33, 36, 56-7, 71, 76, 233; *evolving*, 6, 7, 22, 27, 82, 115, 118, 120, 127, 134, 141, 155, 159, 170, 188, 191, 194, 207, 208, 211-2, 216, 233, 243. See COSMOGENESIS; and *God*, 6, 21-2, 27, 47-9, 51, 60, 61-2, 64-5, 67-8, 70, 75-6, 78, 79, 82, 87, 96, 131, 134-5, 212, 231; *love* for, 11, 45, 79, 216, 224, 231; as *organized*, 17, 19, 112, 128, 141, 146, 162, 218-9; and *person*, 209; *reality* of, 2-3, 73, 88, 90, 106, 213-4, 230-1; *renunciation* of, 12, 182, 202; *temptations* of, 55; *value* of, 1, 25-6, 49-50, 52, 166-7, 170, 223, 231; *variety* of worlds, 108, 150-1.

WORSHIP (adoration, devotion), 44, 95, 167, 196, 200-3, 220, 222, 228, 246, 255.

YAJUR VEDA, 211, 233.

YANTRA, 138, 146-8, 150, 151.

YOGA, 7, 8, 44, 51, 74, 87, 108, 121, 143, 156, 160, 201, 210, 221, 226, 227-9, 255.

YUGA, 108.

ZAEHNER, R. C., 61, 68, 73, 86, 87, 89, 90.

ZIMMER, HEINRICH, 151.